A HISTORY OF THE
MEXICAN-AMERICAN PEOPLE

A
the Mexican-

History of American People

Julian Samora and
Patricia Vandel Simon

Revised by Julian Samora, with the assistance of
Cordelia Chávez Candelaria and
Alberto L. Pulido

UNIVERSITY OF NOTRE DAME PRESS
NOTRE DAME - LONDON

JULIAN SAMORA, Professor Emeritus of Sociology of the University of Notre Dame. He is the editor of *La Raza: Forgotten Americans* and the author of *Los Mojados: The Wetback Story.*

PATRICIA VANDEL SIMON holds a Master of Arts degree from Stanford University in Hispanic American and Lusa-Brazilian Studies.

Library of Congress Cataloging-in-Publication Data

Samora, Julian, 1920–
    A history of the Mexican-American people / Julian Samora and Patricia Vandel Simon. — Rev. / by Julian Samora, with the assistance of Cordelia Chávez and Alberto L. Pulido.
        p.   :   cm.
    Includes bibliographical references and index.
    ISBN 0-268-01097-8
    1. Mexican Americans—History. I. Simon, Patricia Vandel, 1939–.   II. Candelaria, Cordelia.   III. Pulido, Alberto L.   IV. Title.
E184.M5S25 1993
973′.046872–dc20   92-33492
                                                                          CIP

Manufactured in the United States of America

*To the memory
of
Julian Robert Samora*

Contents

PART TWO

The Foreign Intrusion

PART THREE

The Mexican Heritage

PART FOUR

The New Awareness

Acknowledgments

We wish to thank the following persons and institutions for their help in the writing of this book:

Juan Garcia and Kenneth Barber researched and drafted the preliminary versions of the chapters on Mexican-American organizations.

The students in a seminar on The Chicano Movement read and criticized the total manuscript.

Dr. Cordelia Candelaria, Professor of English at Stanford University, wrote the chapter on literature and the arts, "A Rich Tradition Continues."

Prof. Alberto Pulido of Arizona State University wrote the new chapter on Mexican American religion.

Irene Hinojosa typed innumerable versions of the manuscript.

Mr. Raul Ruiz gave us permission to use the article on Rueben Salazar from *La Raza Magazine*.

Stanford University Libraries and the Libraries of the University of California at Berkley gave access to resources which made much of the historical research possible.

Multi-Media Productions, Inc., Palo Alto, California, provided access to photographic files accumulated in the production of audio-visual materials in Mexican American history.

The editors at the University of Notre Dame Press, in particular John Ehmann and Ann Rice, were most helpful throughout the preparation of the book.

We alone are responsible for the flaws in the final product.

Julian Samora
Patricia Vandel Simon

Sources of Illustrations

The Bettmann Archives, New York: pages 15, 17, 31, 45, 53, 75, 81, 84, 111, 123, 125, 128

California State Library, Sacramento: page 114

El Centro Campesino Cultural: page 206

El Grito del Norte: page 192

George Ballis, Images, Fresno, California: pages 137, 148, 150, 152, 153, 154, 155, 158, 163, 166, 167, 168, 169, 171, 175, 181, 185, 191, 195, 197, 201, 208, 212, 214, 215, 216, 236, 237, 239

James Newkirk, *Notre Dame Magazine,* page 243

Library of Congress: page 70

Los Angeles Times, Patrick Downs and José Galvez, pages 207, 229, 233

Maryknoll Fathers and Brothers, M. Sandoval, page 225

New York Public Library: page 23

Jaime Rasura, page 224

San Antonio Light: page 199

Stanford University Library: pages 55, 72, 73, 96, 108, 116

United Press International: page 141

U.S. Border Patrol: page 145

PART ONE

The Indian-Spanish Heritage

CHAPTER 1 | Introduction

Our study of Mexican-American history stems from an interest in the subject which spans many years. During this time, the authors have been deeply concerned over the inadequacies of American history as it is taught in schools throughout the United States, whether at the elementary, secondary, or college level. Invariably, this history is biased because it begins with the Pilgrim fathers and English colonists, and emphasizes the westward movement of English culture. It neglects almost entirely events which occurred on the North American continent prior to 1600.

Furthermore, American textbooks, whether of history, political science, sociology, or social studies, tend to neglect present-day minority groups that make up a significant proportion of the population of the United States. Some groups are scarcely mentioned. If they are mentioned, their contributions to the development of American society are not treated adequately.

What does an American Indian think when told that Columbus discovered America, yet his own ancestors inhabited the continent long before Columbus arrived? What does a black American think when being portrayed as a person whose enslavement was justified by the belief that Africa had no viable cultures? How does a Chinese American feel when being described as inscrutable, a "coolie," and part of a yellow peril? Similar questions can be raised about other minorities—Japanese, Puerto Rican, Filipino, Korean, and so forth.

Mexican Americans are such a minority group. They have long been given minor roles in history books. More often than not, Mexican Americans do not appear in U.S. history textbooks, except for a brief mention of "Spanish" history and possibly in texts dealing with the Mexican-American War.

It is our belief that any history of the United States—and specifically the southwestern United States—is incomplete and fails to provide a basis for understanding contemporary society unless the Mexican-American contribution is fully covered. Present-day American society is a consequence of fusions of various cultures which have occurred over a period of several hundred years. In order to understand the present, it is necessary to understand the factors contributing to its development.

The Mexican American is an important element of modern American society. And he, too, is a product of cultural fusions which have occurred over the centuries. His culture, a significant aspect of southwestern American society, has developed from the fusion, first, of Spanish and Mexican Indian cultures and the subsequent introduction of northern Indian, European, Anglo-American, and modern Mexican cultures. Thus, to understand the Mexican American, we must look back in history and trace the various influences that have created his unique, present-day culture.

Our purpose in writing this book is to place in proper perspective the Mexican-American contribution to the history of the United States and to fill the gap which exists in that history. Any book must have certain limitations imposed on it by the authors and the subject matter. Obviously, a comprehensive history of the geographical area that now comprises the United States should begin with the American Indian. It should then take up the sixteenth century explorations, settlements, and colonization efforts of Spain. Only later would the Pilgrim fathers and other English colonists appear on the scene.

However, we are not writing a comprehensive history of the United States—an effort which would require many volumes—but rather of Mexican Americans. We must limit our discussion, then, to this population. We will not consider Indian history in its entirety, nor the history of the United States as such. But we will discuss those influences as they are related to the development of Mexican Americans.

The text will follow an orderly progression of Mexican-American cultural development. In the second chapter, we will state as clearly as possible what we mean by the term "Mexican American." We will also present demographic characteristics and the current status of Mexican Americans in the United States in terms of numbers and concentration in geographical areas.

Since a history of Mexican Americans must invariably begin with the Indian heritage and the Spanish heritage, we will review why Spain came to the New World and how the Spaniards met and conquered the native Americans. We will concentrate on the area that is now Mexico rather than on the total Western Hemisphere. We will briefly discuss the general culture and social organization of native Americans in Mexico at the time of the Spanish conquest of that area.

The territory that comprises present-day Mexico was conquered by the Spanish very quickly; this is the subject of chapter 3. In chapters 4 through 7, we shall see how the Spanish explorers moved north into the land that we now call the United States and we will show what their motivations were. We will also indicate the groups of people they encountered, how they treated or mistreated them, what kinds of settlements and colonies they established, and what this meant to the native Americans as well as to the Spaniards. This period of approximately three hundred years, from the early 1500s to the early 1800s, constitutes Part I of the book, "The Indian-Spanish Heritage."

Part II is entitled "The Foreign Intrusion." These six chapters (chapter 8 through chapter 13) discuss what happened in the United States from the early

The Melting Pot

The symbol of the melting pot originated in Israel Zangwill's play of the same name published in 1909. At that time Americans were beginning to question the effect of the stream of immigrants which had poured into the country during the nineteenth century. They wondered if alien ideas and customs threatened American institutions and unity.

Zangwill coined the "melting pot" phrase in answer to these criticisms. It symbolized his belief that representatives of the world's people, after arriving in America, were uniformly transformed and fused into a new and finer nation—the United States. This picturesque expression calmed the misgivings of the time; as a result, immigration quotas which had been contemplated were not imposed until after World War I.

In the 1970s ethnic Americans are becoming more aware of the culture they brought with them, and how they still express this in the United States. The melting-pot concept is being questioned. Have the immigrants to America really been absorbed in a melting pot? Is this desirable?

Many immigrant Americans still live in ethnic neighborhoods in our cities, although their children have often moved to the suburbs. Old customs, ways of worship and celebration, are still observed by these groups in their community. We may be familiar with fairs and other events where ethnic foods are sold, crafts and art work are displayed, and dances are demonstrated.

These expressions of their culture show how the ideas and ideals of a nation of origin have formed a people's customs and their own ways of doing things through a long history and tradition. Such expressions give visibility to the roots of ways of family and community life. They keep people together and give them the necessary stability and strength to go out to work and live with the other communities of a city.

We can appreciate why it is not necessary for the United States to be a melting pot. People can still preserve their own unique ways of expressing family and community traditions and values while cooperating with others in the civic and political affairs of a city toward the good of all.

1800s to the beginning of the twentieth century. At the beginning of that period, Spain was fairly well entrenched in what is now the southwestern and western parts of the United States, having colonized areas that are now the states of California, Arizona, New Mexico, and Texas.

Events in other areas proved to be of great importance to the Southwest. During the late eighteenth and nineteenth centuries, European nations such as France, England, along with Russia, demonstrated a growing interest in the southwestern regions of North America. The thirteen original colonies, after rebelling against England and establishing a nation, began to show considerable interest in the territory beyond the first mountain frontiers.

The United States eventually did acquire the territory between the Atlantic and the Pacific Oceans, aided in the quest, to some extent, by the series of events which began with the revolt against England. After the American Revolution, other European colonies in the Western Hemisphere began to follow the American example, revolting against the mother country. During the early years of the nineteenth century, Portugal lost Brazil. And one after another of Spain's many colonies declared independence and began the battle for national sovereignty. The nineteen Spanish-speaking nations of Mexico and Central and South America resulted from these rebellions.

Chapter 9 discusses in some detail the formation of the nation of Mexico. After Mexico won independence from Spain, the new republic included all of present-day Mexico as well as all of the territory that today constitutes the five south-western states of the United States and more territory farther north.

Chapter 10 examines the first American influx, describing how settlers from the United States came to Texas with the approval of the Mexican government. Within a few years, these settlers revolted against Mexico and formed their own republic. Then and in the years that followed, the United States pushed farther and father westward, as described in chapter 11. Under the banner of Manifest Destiny—the belief that God had destined the nation to be a territory bordered on the east and west by the Atlantic and the Pacific—the United States encroached upon Mexican territories and finally provoked a war in 1846 that enabled her to take more than half of Mexico's national territory.

Chapter 12 examines the treaty which ended the Mexican-American War and the violations of this treaty by the United States. The consequences of these violations are still with us today and discussions of such topics as land claims and bilingual education are of continuing concern.

The third section of the book, called "The Mexican Heritage," attempts to explain the modern-day Mexican influence on the history of the Mexican American. In chapter 14, we discuss the Mexican Revolution and its impact on both Mexicans and Mexican Americans. The first of the larger migrations from Mexico is presented. During the second decade of this century, events in Europe also had a considerable effect on the history of Mexican Americans. When the United States entered World War I and the defense industries began to develop, and as the industrial and agricultural development of the Southwest continued, improved job opportunities attracted increasing numbers of Mexicans to the United States.

Mexicans and Mexican Americans became the main source of cheap labor in the southwestern part of the United States particularly, and in other parts of the country as well. It is primarily their labor that built the farms, the railroads, and the industries in the southwestern states. It is Mexicans who, in large proportion, continue to be the sowers and harvesters of the fields today.

During the Great Depression of the 1930s, Mexicans were repatriated to Mexico in large numbers. World War II brought them back to the United States in even greater numbers as contract laborers and as illegal aliens. The consequences of this large movement of people are discussed in chapter 15.

The last part of this book, Part IV, we call "The New Awareness." We attempt to show, in these chapters, the progression of events from the middle 1950s to the present time. Chapter 16 examines the Mexican American in an industrial and urban age. We see how two world wars and a great depression have changed the character of the Mexican American in terms of his status and situation. Often his entire way of life has been changed from that of a rural person to that of a person living in a large urban society. We show, too, how difficult this change has been for the Mexican American. In chapter 17, we discuss the question of discrimination and prejudice and the Mexican American's struggle for civil rights, justice, and an important place in the scheme of American society.

Chapters 18 and 19 trace the beginnings and development of organizations within the Mexican-American community which are working for political, economic, and social betterment. Chapter 20 presents the Mexican American's contribution to art and literature. A critique is made of the various art forms: poetry, drama (in particular the *teatros*), and the novel.

In conclusion, we provide a summary of the history of Mexican Americans. More important, perhaps, we have attempted to look into the future, to speculate on what the years ahead may hold for the Mexican-American population.

It is our hope that all who read this book will gain an appreciation and understanding of the forces which have molded this frequently neglected segment of our population. We hope, too, that Mexican Americans may find themselves throughout this history and that, having read it, will have a greater appreciation of themselves, develop positive identity as a group, and gain pride in the tremendous heritage and the great contributions Mexican Americans and their ancestors have made to our society.

CHAPTER 2 | The Mexican Americans

There are no "pure" races in the world. In tracing the heredity of any group we soon discover that a great diversity of physical, social, and cultural traits are represented within a people. Mexican Americans are no exception.

First among their ancestors, the Mexican Americans can count a great variety of native Americans—that is, the many Indian groups who once lived in Mexico and the American Southwest. Another major component is European, for Mexican Americans are also descended from the Spaniards who came to this hemisphere during the early periods of exploration, conquest, and settlement. But we must remember that the Indians themselves are a mixture of many groupings and the Spaniards are the product of the "melting pot" of Caucasian European peoples and Arabic and black admixtures from Africa. Some blacks were involved also in the early history of exploration and colonization of the Spanish territories in the New World. Finally, during the 1800s, another element was added to the ancestry and hence the physical makeup of Mexican Americans: namely, "Americans," who themselves are a mix-

ture of all peoples of the world, even though they are predominantly of Caucasian, European background.

Who then are the Mexican Americans? They are a mixture of diverse peoples. In many, the Indian racial types predominate. Most are dark of complexion with black hair, traits inherited in large part from their Indian ancestors. But many are blond, blue-eyed, and "white," while others have red hair and hazel eyes. This population is so varied physically that the stereotype of the Mexican who is short and stout, with dark brown complexion and black hair, does not really hold true. Thus the Mexican Americans are obviously not a distinct race. This fact is reflected in the names they bear. Most have Spanish surnames. But many Mexican Americans have surnames which are obviously not Spanish, such as Weaver, Gold, Taylor, McCormick, Glass, Von Robineau, Baptiste, Davis.

The mixing of peoples which has created the Mexican American continues today. Although we do not have accurate statistics regarding intermarriages, isolated studies suggest that in some areas, perhaps 25 percent of Mexican Americans have married non-Mexican Americans. The United States census of 1970, which enumerated people of Spanish origin (including Mexican Americans), indicated that 25 percent of those people of Spanish origin were married to people of non-Spanish origin.

In numerical terms, it is difficult to follow the history of Mexican Americans in the United States because the U.S. Census Bureau has been inconsistent in its reporting. Beginning in the 1970s, the Census Bureau became aware of the Mexican-American population as an ethnic population and began to deal with it. To date, most other federal agencies have not performed as well.

Before the 1930s, about the only estimate available concerning the numbers of Mexican Americans in the United States came from rather inaccurate statistics of the Immigration and Naturalization Service, which recorded Mexican immigrants. This, of course, tells us nothing about the population that was already here when Mexico was conquered in 1846.

Census Bureau Count 1930–1960

In 1930 the United States Census Bureau attempted to enumerate this population under the heading of "Mexican." Census takers were instructed to record all persons born in Mexico or having parents born in Mexico, if these persons were not definitely white, Negro, Indian, Chinese, or Japanese. This definition, of course, confused racial and cultural concepts and it excluded all persons who were not born in Mexico or who did not have parents born there.

Further complicating the issue, the standards changed each time the census was taken. The Bureau of the Census dropped the classification of "Mexican" in 1940 and attempted to enumerate this and other foreign-language groups by using the criterion of language spoken in the home. This enumeration was again inadequate because for some persons of Mexican or Spanish descent the principal language was English while for others it was Spanish.

Ten years later the Bureau of the Census again changed its criterion for enumerating the "Mexican" population.

A list of several thousand Spanish surnames was compiled, to be used as the means of identification. But as we have seen, many people who would call themselves Mexican American do not have a Spanish surname. Moreover, the 1950 census survey was limited to the five southwestern states and the Mexican-American population living outside of that geographical area was not enumerated. Further, many Native Americans in the Southwest have a Spanish surname. Thus it is impossible to compare the numbers of Mexican Americans before 1930 with those enumerated in the census of 1930 or 1940 or 1950. In none of those years was the same criterion for identification used, and in 1950 the enumeration was limited to the five southwestern states.

In 1960 the Census Bureau used the same criterion as in 1950. For the first time it was possible to compare one enumeration with another. But this held true only for the five southwestern states. Although we do have some indication as to the number of Mexican Americans in

What's in a Name?

Mexican American—an American of Mexican descent

Mexicano—strictly speaking a Mexican; it is also often used for a Mexican American

Chicano—a Spanish-speaking person of the southwestern United States; this term is derived from *Mexicano* and stresses historical and cultural ties with Mexico ethnic nationalism and activism

Hispano—a Spanish-speaking person; in the Southwest it often refers to the descendant of the 17th- and 18th-century colonizers

Latino—a person of Latin-American ancestry in general, including Mexicanos and Chicanos, among others

Mexicano, Chicano, Hispano, Mexican American, Spanish American, and *Latino* are often used interchangeably in the Southwest.

La Raza—all Spanish-speaking people of the New World collectively, with overtones of a common spirit and destiny

Anglo—an American of Anglo-Saxon ancestry; a non-Mexican American

gringo—a derogatory term for whites or Anglos

rinche—a derogatory term for a Texas Ranger

migra—a derogatory term for officials of the Immigration and Naturalization Service, generally members of the Border Patrol

---

the Southwest in 1950 and 1960, we have no indication of the population count for the rest of the United States.

Before the next census was taken in 1970, the Bureau was persuaded, under pressure, to change its categories for the enumeration of the Mexican-American population. The results have given us a much clearer, although not ideal, demographic picture of Mexican Americans in the United States.

It should be noted here that this particular population has been known by a variety of names. The descendants of those who explored and colonized the Southwest before the nineteenth century and who, in fact, lived under the flag of Spain, have often been called or have called themselves Spanish Americans. The name *Spanish American* described them well since the original settlers did come from Spain. But the name failed to take into consideration the admixtures with the native population.

After the revolutions against the mother country, this area became Mexico and its inhabitants became Mexican. But as Anglo-Americans settled in this area, the term *Mexican* gradually took on disparaging connotations. Therefore, *Spanish American*—particularly for some areas of northern New Mexico, southern Colorado, parts of Arizona and parts of California—became the preferred term. When the term *Mexican* was used in English it was considered to be quite derogatory, yet when the term *Mexicano* was used in Spanish by the Spanish-speaking, it was quite acceptable. In Texas the term *Mexican* acquired such bad connotations that for years Mexican Americans have been known as *Latins* or *Latin Americans*.

Other terms have been used to describe this population. In California, *Californios* has been used; in New Mexico *Manitos* (coming from the word *hermano*, meaning "brother") or *Hispano;* in Texas, *Tejano*. The term *Spanish surname* as used by the Bureau of the Census has not been popular and *Spanish-speaking* includes so many other people that it does not describe the Mexican-American population well. The term *La Raza*, which literally means "the race," but popularly means "the group" or "the people," seems to be acceptable to all, but it is as encompassing as *Latino* or *Hispano*. In recent years a new term has evolved and that is *Chicano*. It appears that even though some object to it, this term will become most popular and will be used in the future to describe the Mexican-American population. In recent years the term *Hispanic* has been widely used to include Mexican-American, Puerto Rican, Cuban, Central American, and South American people.

1970 Census Count

Before 1970, the United States Census Bureau had become aware that the criteria it was using for enumerating the population was less than adequate. In preparation for the 1970 census, a group of consultants was called in to give advice concerning the categories and the criteria to be used. The consultants suggested that Mexican Americans should be counted throughout the country, not just in the five southwestern states, and that a self-identification process be used whereby people would be asked if they considered themselves to be Mexican American. It was also suggested that the term *Mexican American* be broken down in such a way to include *Chicano, Mexicano,* and *Spanish American* and that other populations be enumerated on the principle of self-identification.

When the question was finally worded on the forms, it asked: "Are you of Mexican descent?" This of course, would tend to confuse those who were not of Mexican descent but considered themselves Mexican American, namely those who were Spanish American. The question was placed under the category of persons of Spanish origin and this category included people of Mexican descent, Puerto Ricans, Central and South Americans, Cubans, and other Spanish and it was asked in all states. The enumeration of white persons with Spanish surnames, which was begun in 1950 and continued in 1960, was also made in 1970 for the five southwestern states. Thus, the five southwestern states will have comparable data for the decades of the 1950s, 1960s, and 1970s.

Since the self-identification question was asked for the first time in 1970 throughout the United States on a sample basis, we now have new data for the

TABLE 1
NUMBER OF PERSONS OF SPANISH ORIGIN:
1970 CENSUS AND MARCH 1973 CPS

		1973 Census Publication Series	
Type of Spanish Origin	*1970 Census*	*Number*	*Percent Change*
Total, Spanish origin	9,072,602	10,577,000	16.6
Mexican origin	4,532,435	6,293,000	38.8
Puerto Rican origin	1,429,396	1,548,000	8.3
Cuban origin	544,600	733,000	34.6
Central or South American origin	1,508,866	597,000	−60.4
Other Spanish origin	1,057,305	1,406,000	33.0

Source: Persons of Spanish Origin in the United States, March, 1973 (Advance report), p. 3.

TABLE II
PERSONS OF HISPANIC ORIGIN, BY TYPE OF ORIGIN

Type of Spanish Origin	*1970*	*1973*	*1980 census*[2]	*March 1982 CPS*[1]	*March 1987 CPS*[1]
Total					
Hispanic Origin	9,072,602	10,577,000	14,609,000	15,364,000	18,790,000
Mexican	4,532,435	6,293,000	8,740,000	9,642,000	11,762,000
Puerto Rican	1,429,396	1,548,000	2,014,000	2,051,000	2,284,000
Cuban	544,600	733,000	803,000	950,000	1,017,000
Central or South					
American	1,508,866	597,000		1,523,000	2,139,000
Other Hispanic	1,057,305	1,406,000	3,051,000[3]	1,198,000	1,588,000

Source: For 1970 and 1973 data: Persons of Spanish origin in the United States, March 1973 (Advance Report), p. 3. For 1980, 1982 and 1987 data: The Hispanic population in the United States: March 1986 and 1987 (Advance Report), p. 5.

[1] Estimates from the March 1987 and 1982 CPS's reflect the civilian non-institutional population of the United States and members of the Armed Forces in the United States living off post or with their families on post, but excludes all other members of the Armed Forces.

[2] Data from the 1980 census are based on 100 percent tabulations of the resident population in the United States on April 1, 1980.

[3] In the 1980 census, the "other Spanish" category included persons from Spain, the Spanish-speaking countries of Central and South America, and Hispanic persons who identified themselves generally as Latins, Spanish-American, Spanish, etc. In the CPS, the category "Central or South American" is listed as a separate origin.

entire country. A second question concerning the use of Spanish in the home was also included in the 1970 census for the total United States. Researchers will now have comparable data on Spanish surnames for the five southwestern states from 1950–1970. And regarding the entire United States, there will be data based on self-identification and language usage.

The 1970 census estimated 9.07 million persons of Spanish origin, of whom 4.53 million were of Mexican origin. In March of 1973, the Census Bureau did a count but changed a few categories and methods of gathering data; the results showed a considerable increase in the population of Spanish origin (see Table 1).

In April 1974, the United States Commission on Civil Rights published a report *(Counting the Forgotten)* in which the Census Bureau was charged with using procedures insensitive to this population. The commission further charged that uniform measures were not used, that adequate assistance was not provided, that bilingual census takers were insufficient in number, that the educational program was too small and that its failure to employ a sufficient number of persons of Spanish background contributed to the inability to enumerate this population effectively, leading to an undercount greater than that of the black population, which the Census Bureau placed at 7.7 percent for the 1970 census.

Location

Mexican Americans were a rural population before and during the 1940s. Today they have become a predominately urban population. The large concentrations of Mexican Americans are found in Los Angeles, the Bay area of San Francisco, San Antonio and other cities in Texas such as El Paso, Corpus Christi, Dallas, Fort Worth, and Houston. The cities of Texas along the United States-Mexico border also have considerable Mexican-American populations. In New Mexico the urban population of Mexican Americans is primarily in Albuquerque, Las Cruces, Santa Fe; in Arizona the urban Mexican-American population is centered in Phoenix and Tucson, and in Colorado the urban

population is centered in Denver and Pueblo. In other parts of the United States, Mexican Americans have concentrated in Chicago and East Chicago Heights, Illinois; Gary and East Chicago, Indiana; Lansing, Saginaw, Flint, and Detroit, Michigan; Toledo, Ohio.; and Kansas City, Kansas. There are substantial numbers of Mexican Americans in some cities of Minnesota, Washington, Iowa, and in Washington, D.C. As to states, the majority of the population is in the five southwestern states with over 80 percent of those in the states of California and Texas. New Mexico and Illinois have the next largest concentrations, and Arizona and Colorado follow.

CHAPTER 3 | Conquest of Mexico

Mexican Americans come from roots put down centuries ago. Understanding the modern Mexican American depends, to some degree, on understanding these roots. Although much may be written of the Indian cultures of pre-Columbian Mexico, any history of Mexican Americans must begin with the arrival of the Spaniards in the Western Hemisphere. This event provided a catalyst for the development of modern Mexican Americans.

The story began when Christopher Columbus, sailing under the auspices of Queen Isabella of Castille, sought a westward route across the Atlantic Ocean to the Far East—a route intended to open up for Spain a share of the lucrative trade monopolized by the merchants of Venice. When, after long weeks at sea, he first sighted the islands of the Caribbean, Columbus thought he had indeed come upon the East Indies. He called the people of the islands "Indians" and claimed the land for Spain. On his first voyage, Columbus established a colony on the island of Hispañola (now shared by Haiti and the Dominican Republic).

Thus began the Spanish experience in the New World.

By the early years of the sixteenth century, thriving Spanish colonies were to be found on Hispañola and on Cuba, with lesser colonies throughout the Caribbean. People of various backgrounds left Spain to seek their fortunes in the New World. Many of them were adventurers who sought danger and the pleasure of discovery in any unknown world. This was the fabric of which the *conquistadores*—the conquerors—were made.

Among those who settled in Cuba was a young man named Hernán Cortés. He had come to America in a lowly position with the Spanish colonial administration. But Cortés dreamed of greater things for himself. This was an age of exploration and the romance of discovery pushed men beyond the boundaries of the world they knew. Such an era would not occur again until man began to feel his way into outer space five centuries later. Rumors—usually false—of fantastic riches in distant unconquered and unexplored regions ran like wildfire among the populations of established colonies.

Hernán Cortés

Hernán Cortés (1485–1547), when only 16 years of age, decided to give up the study of law in Spain and seek adventure in the New World. In Santo Domingo in the West Indies he fought the native Indians as Spain conquered new territories. He then helped Diego Velazquez in the conquest of Cuba, and Velazquez commissioned Cortés to conquer Mexico.

Cortés sailed from Cuba with a fleet of 11 vessels, with 700 Spaniards, 18 horses, and a few artillery pieces. After he built a fort at Veracruz on the east coast of Mexico, Cortés scuttled his fleet. He wanted his men to know they had to be successful in their conquest of the Aztec empire. There was no way to turn back!

Cortés' Expedition

Hernán Cortés heard such a rumor in Cuba. It was said that a land of unbelievable riches, called Mexico, lay across the sea to the west of Cuba. Cortés decided that Mexico must be conquered. At first he won the support of the Spanish governor, who set about organizing an expedition to sail to Mexico. But the governor—probably with reason—soon began to fear Cortés would steal the glory of discovery and he recalled the aggressive and enthusiastic young man from the expedition. Cortés, not about to be thwarted, persuaded the sailors and soldiers who had signed on with the expedition to join him in defying the governor. One day in 1519 he stole away from port with the governor's fleet. Thus began an adventure that would end in the conquest of Mexico.

When Hernán Cortés set sail he knew virtually nothing about the land ahead. He could only hope that the rumors of fortune were true. His first encounters on the new continent were hardly encouraging. The fleet landed at Yucatan, where the expedition saw little more than tropical overgrowth. Cortés then ordered his ships to sail north, following the outline of the new continent. A few weeks later he landed near the site of modern Tabasco.

All this time the local grapevine had been working, and the Indians of Mexico followed the progress of the Spaniards up their coastline. To understand the fright they felt, we must look at the Mexico of 1519 and at the beliefs of its inhabitants.

This area was one of the culturally advanced regions of pre-Columbian America. Its peoples had achieved a high degree of civilization centuries before the Spaniards reached the New World. Many different tribes, speaking many different languages, populated the land. But in the final years of the fifteenth century, most of the tribes had been subjugated by one group of empire builders—the Aztecs. The Aztecs had built their society on the institutions and cultures of older Mexican civilizations. They were a militaristic people and had expanded their control first over the valley of central Mexico and then over more distant lands. They conquered and they demanded that the subjugated tribes pay them tribute. Most of the other tribes hated the Aztecs but lacked the strength to overcome them.

Like other peoples of the Americas (and the Europeans of that era, too) the Aztecs were superstitious. And the omens that had come to them before the Spaniards arrived told of impending disaster. Legend tells us that the Emperor Montezuma II was brought a bird with a mirror in its head. When Montezuma looked into the mirror he saw a strange army. Then a rival chieftain bet Montezuma that the land of the Aztecs would be invaded by strangers, and Montezuma lost the game planned to decide who was right.

Most important was an old legend, predating the Aztecs by centuries, which had been passed down from generation to generation. It told of the god Quetzalcoatl, the feathered serpent god, who was fair-skinned and bearded. Quetzalcoatl lost a fight with the warrior god and was banished from Mexico. He disappeared into the sky, but before he left he promised the people he would return and told them when to expect him. The

First visit of Cortés to Montezuma

year on the Indian calendar was the equivalent of the European year 1519. Thus when fair-skinned and bearded Spaniards arrived, the Indians of Mexico were convinced that Quetzalcoatl was returning from the sun.

The Emperor Montezuma II sent emissaries, bearing gifts of gold, to meet the Spaniards at Tabasco. His purpose was twofold. On the one hand, the gifts were designed to appease Quetzalcoatl, should he actually be among the strangers. On the other hand, Montezuma reasoned, if the Spaniards were enemies, they would be satisfied with the gold and would leave his land. Little did he know that the gold served as an invitation to adventurers in search of fabulous riches. The Spaniards became more determined than ever to claim the territory where such wealth existed.

An Easy Victory

The military conquest of Mexico was surprisingly simple. Hernán Cortés led only a handful of soldiers against thousands of Aztec warriors. But in less than two years he succeeded in subduing the armies of Indian Mexico. He accomplished this even though he was defeated in some crucial battles and many of his men were killed. But the accomplishment seems less marvelous when we look closely at the factors that aided the Spaniards.

We have seen that superstition played an important role in the life of the Indians. They believed that they would be conquered and thus were emotionally prepared for defeat. The belief that Quetzalcoatl might be among the invaders acted as a powerful deterrent: the Indians hesitated to attack and incur the wrath of their god. They also considered the possibility that all the Spaniards might be gods. This was reinforced when they first saw the Spaniards mounted on their horses—animals as foreign to Mexico as the fair-skinned men they carried. At first, the Indians thought man and beast were one, a fierce new god that must be appeased. Their fear was further reinforced by the fact that the Spaniards proved resistant to Indian witchcraft. The spells the Aztec sorcerers cast upon the invaders had no effect at all.

A second factor that contributed to the Indians' defeat was the differing concept of war between the two peoples. To the Aztecs, war was a ceremony. Its primary purposes were to capture prisoners for sacrifice to the gods—in itself a great honor for the victim—and to win the tribute of conquered enemies. Furthermore, war was secondary to such vital activities as planting and harvesting. Crops could be grown only with difficulty in much of Mexico. Famines, common enough in ordinary times, had become even more of a threat in the early years of the sixteenth century as population pressure on the arable land increased. When the Indians put down their arms to tend the crops, the cease-fire was mutually respected by belligerent tribes.

But the Spaniards refused to recognize such a cease-fire. Spanish warfare was not a ceremony but a battle to the death. If victory could be achieved by destroying the crops of the enemy, then so much the better. To the amazement of the Indians, the Spaniards killed their enemies on the battlefield, rather than taking them prisoner. And they did so with weapons far superior to the swords and spears of Indian armies; Spanish guns could kill or wound a man at distances that seemed incredible to Indian warriors.

Arms superiority certainly provided the Spaniards with a great advantage in their campaign against the Aztecs. But a further advantage must not be overlooked: the all-important alliances between Cortés and tribes hostile to the Aztecs.

When Cortés arrived in Mexico, an Indian girl called Malinche (or, as the Spaniards named her, Marina) joined the expedition. She learned Spanish quickly and was invaluable as interpreter, guide, and spy. Malinche told Cortés of the hatred many Indians felt for the Aztecs and urged him to form alliances with these people. This was a difficult task, for most Indians feared the Spaniards as much as the Aztecs did. A few joined the strangers immediately. Most had to be cajoled or forced into an alliance. Some had to be defeated in battle before they would join the Spaniards. But once they had allied themselves with Cortés, these Indians represented the difference between victory and defeat. They added to the numerical strength of the Spanish army. More important, perhaps, they supplied the Spaniards with food and acted as messengers and carriers, keeping the lines of communication open between the front and rear.

A final factor aided the Spanish cause. The Europeans brought new diseases with them to America—diseases like smallpox, typhoid, measles. The native Americans had no natural immunity as the Europeans had, and the diseases decimated Indian populations all over the New World during the sixteenth and seventeenth centuries. In 1520, shortly after Cortés landed in Mexico, the first epidemic of smallpox struck the Indians. The effects of this epidemic (and of all other European diseases) were disastrous. Thousands died and Indian armies and Indian morale were severely weakened.

La Malinche

When the Spaniards landed in Mexico in 1519 Cortés was unable to communicate well with the natives. One of his soldiers knew the dialect spoken along the coast, but was ignorant of the Aztec language. An Indian chief gave the Spaniards a young female slave named Malinche who was familiar with both native tongues and proved to be an excellent interpreter for Cortés. The conquistadores called her Doña Marina.

Malinche was the daughter of a powerful cacique or chief, but after her father's death she had been sold into slavery by her mother and stepfather. She was attractive and intelligent and quickly learned Spanish. On many occasions her knowledge of Mexican dialects and customs and her ability to judge the designs of the natives saved the lives of the Spaniards as Cortés played the dangerous game of trying to turn the Indian tribes against one another.

Malinche remained with Cortés all through the conquest and early settlement of Mexico and bore him a son, Don Martin Cortés. In 1525 Cortés married her off to a Spanish knight, giving her a large estate in her native province as a dowry.

Converting the Indian

By summer 1521, after much difficulty and bloodshed, the military conquest of Mexico was complete. Hernán Cortés claimed the land for the Spanish crown and called it New Spain. But military conquest alone was not enough to consolidate the Spanish position on mainland America. The culture and institutions of Spain would have to be imposed upon Mexico and the Indians made an integral part of the empire that was emerging in the New World.

Spanish conquerors and colonists sought to create a utopia in the new land:

Hernán Cortés dreamed of a new world that would bring together the best of both Indian and Spanish societies. But most of the conquerors were greedy opportunists, intent upon finding fortune and fame for themselves—at the expense of the Indians if necessary. They could best achieve their goals within a familiar system, and so the next century was one of superimposing the language, laws, and institutions of Spain on Indian Mexico. It was a century of conflict between Indian and Spanish ways of life. But it was also a century of some fusion, in which Indian and Spanish cultures blended to create a society uniquely American, uniquely Mexican.

The first step in the hispanization of Mexico would be the conversion of the Indians to Roman Catholicism. The conquerors came from a country where religion was deeply ingrained in daily life. Spanish armies had only recently driven the last Moslems from the Iberian Peninsula after more than seven hundred years of occupation. In the course of that long conflict, Spanish Roman Catholicism had become extremely powerful, and explorers and conquerors transported this religiosity to America. In their view, the Indians were heathens, in spite of the highly organized religious systems that existed in America. The Spaniards came duty-bound to convert the Indians—not only in service to God but in service to their monarch, whose political strength would increase as the number of Catholic subjects under control increased.

The conversion process began immediately, and was simplified by the fact that the Indians of Mexico, throughout their long history, had accepted new gods with ease. Conquered tribes traditionally incorporated the deities of their conquerors into their pantheon of gods. Thus when the Spaniards forced a new religion on them, few of the Indians questioned the change (although many continued to worship the old gods in secret). Then too, the old gods failed to rise up in anger when the foreigners destroyed the temples and smashed the idols, and many of the Indians lost faith in the powers of their traditional religion; fatalistically, they accepted the new.

Conversion was further simplified by some basic similarities between Catholicism and the religions of Mexico. Both

Spaniards and Indians believed in an ordered, supernatural world. Both believed in life after death. Both accepted a Supreme Being. And the Indians, used to worshipping many gods, accepted as supreme the God the Spaniards worshipped and equated the saints with their own lesser gods. The new religion offered hope when a whole world had been destroyed; it served as a bridge between the old system and the new.

The builders of that bridge were the priests and monks who began arriving in Mexico almost as soon as the military conquest was complete. The Franciscans arrived in 1522, the Dominicans in 1526. They worked hard, not only to convert the Indians, but also to teach them and to care for their health and well-being. They established schools and hospitals. And under their tutelage the Indians learned better farming methods, along with new and easier ways of weaving and making pottery. There was some question in the minds of the priests—indeed, in the minds of all Spaniards—as to whether or not the Indians were really men, deserving of baptism and, thus, salvation. A few were baptized, but the early priests held back from wholesale baptisms; they waited for some higher authority to decide whether or not the Indians had souls. Finally, in 1537, Pope Paul III declared that "the Indians are truly men." From that time on, the conversion effort gained momentum; the priests' main goal was to convert all the Indians of Spain's New World territories.

Most of the early priests were good, hardworking men. They accomplished their goal with incredible speed and, within a few years, considered the task of conversion complete. Lesley Bird Simpson (p. 77) tells us that "the missionaries did their work so thoroughly they soon found themselves with time on their hands. A spirit of emulation and even of rivalry developed between the [Franciscan and Dominican] orders. . . . It was not long before they were competing in building convents and churches on a scale beyond reasonable necessity."

Creating a Labor Force

The colonial effort of the Spaniards had two main goals. The first, the idealistic goal, was to save the souls of the Indians. The second, the materialistic goal, was to create a labor force to build a colony. The priests—sometimes willingly, sometimes unconsciously—contributed to the achievement of the second goal as well as the first. They did so by changing the life style of the Indians of Mexico.

Before the Spaniards arrived, most Indians had lived in tiny villages or hamlets. The cities of pre-Columbian Mexico were, for the most part, ceremonial centers, inhabited by priests and nobles. The common people lived outside the cities, close to the land they farmed. Distance made communication with the city, and even with other hamlets, difficult.

Congregaciones

The Spanish priests quickly saw that it would be difficult to work among these scattered peoples, that the conversion effort would be slowed down if not halted completely by lack of communication and the inaccessibility of many Indians. And so they decided that the Indians should be gathered together in villages call *congregaciones.* Each *congregación* would have its own church and priest to look after the instruction and welfare of the inhabitants. The Indians would farm the surrounding fields, raising food for themselves and crops for sale in Europe. The system was advantageous to some

purposes. It enabled the priests to work closely with the Indians, a captive audience, and so speeded up the conversion process. It gave the priests the laborers they needed to build the churches (and the Indians performed this task, just as they had worked building the temples in the old days). But the system also had disadvantages. The congregación robbed the Indian of his pride and independence; it made him a child of the priests, who forced him to adopt European dress, to plant the crops the priests wanted grown and to accept a religion he did not really understand. A few Indians fled to the hills and rebuilt their lives in the old manner. But most remained in the Spanish villages, drained of their self-sufficiency, accepting their new role with a strange fatalism. And in the villages they were further exposed to the diseases of the Spaniards. The diseases that had killed them during the military conquest became even more of a threat when the Indians were gathered together in the close quarters of the congregación. Epidemics often decimated entire villages. The Spaniards were little concerned, for death by disease was common in sixteenth-century Europe and they accepted the epidemics without attempting to understand their cause. Between 1519 and 1650, probably more than two-thirds of the Indians died of European diseases (Wolfe, 1959: p. 30).

The congregación put the Indians to work for the benefit of the priests. The conquerors and colonists also needed Indian labor. If the Spaniards were to reap the profits of the colony, the Indians would have to be put to work in the mines and fields. The Spanish gentleman of that era abhorred manual labor of any kind and his attitude was adopted by even the poorest Spaniard who settled in the New World. The colony, to succeed, would have to be built by the conquered Indians.

Slavery was one way of creating an Indian labor force. In the early years, some Indians were enslaved, denied their freedom and made the property of their conquerors. But Indian slavery won the immediate disapproval of the priests and was soon forbidden.

Encomienda

The *encomienda* provided an easier way of accomplishing the same thing. An encomienda was a grant from the crown to those conquerors and settlers who served Spain well. The settler (or *encomendero*) was granted the right to the services of stipulated Indian villages and tribute payments from the Indians of those villages. In return the encomendero was expected to care for the health and physical needs of his Indians, and to assure their religious instruction. It was not a land grant but a trusteeship. However, the encomenderos became so deeply entrenched, and their control over the Indians so complete, that it might as well have been a land grant. The encomienda differed from slavery only in that the Indians were legally free men and not property. But the grant of an encomienda could be passed on from father to son, and there were no restrictions on what the early encomenderos could demand of their Indians.

The abuses of the system were appalling. Many of the encomenderos, lusting for gold and riches, forced the Indians to work beyond the capacity of human endurance, cared little for their physical needs, and, of course, paid them nothing. The system soon came under attack by priests who feared for the welfare, even for the survival, of the Indians. Led by men like Father Bartolomé de las Casas, who later earned the title "Protector of the Indians," the priests brought the abuses of the encomienda to the attention of the crown. It soon became apparent that if the Spanish monarchs failed to act, the incensed priests would take their complaint to the pope. To a large degree, the Spanish crown owed its position in the New World to the papacy. It was through the good offices of Pope Alexander VI that Spain and Portugal had, in 1493, agreed to the Treaty of Tordesillas, dividing the unknown world between them, with Spain getting the lion's share of the land and Portugal getting mostly ocean. Furthermore, the Spanish crown was in debt to the papacy for its support during the long struggle to oust the Moslems from Spain and for concessions the popes had made to Spanish rulers.

The crown, therefore, issued the "New Laws" of 1542. The New Laws, among other things, abolished the encomiendas and severely restricted the colonists' control over the Indians. A wave of protest spread throughout the American colonies. It was so strong in Mexico that a break with Spain was threatened. The crown was forced to modify the laws, allowing each encomienda to remain in force until the death of the original trustee. The protest graphically demonstrated that the growing power and wealth of the encomenderos constituted a threat to the supremacy of the crown; it

Bartolomé de las Casas

Bartolomé de las Casas (1474–1566) gave up his law career in Spain to travel to the Spanish Antilles. Here he was an advisor to the colonial governors, but became a priest a few years later.

Father Las Casas became convinced that the encomienda system was wrong. Under it the native Indians were enslaved and cruelly treated. Through their encomiendas the conquerors forced the Indians to labor long hours in the fields and mines and perform many other tasks in violation of the king's laws. The native population of the Caribbean islands was reduced drastically in a few decades.

In 1514 Father Las Casas gave up his own encomienda and started a long fight to improve the lives of the Indians under Spanish rule. After failing at first to better their lot, Father Las Casas wrote *The History of the Indies.* This work tells of the cruelty of the Spanish settlers toward the Indians. It is a very important source of information about the early Spanish colonies in America.

But Father Las Casas also found a chance to put into practice his belief that the Indians must be converted to Christianity by word and good example. This he did in Guatemala in 1537, when he went there to bring about peace among some warlike Indians. He won the trust of the Indians by his kind and fair treatment of them.

Later, after Las Casas succeeded in pacifying some of the warlike Indians of Guatemala he returned to Spain to help write the New Laws. Although objections to this reform of the Indian code were many and its enforcement was lax, the New Laws eventually led to more humane treatment of the natives and changed a thin disguise for slavery into a form of social system.

Many have criticized Father Las Casas for not understanding the problems of the Indians and for exaggerating the evils of the Spanish rule in New Spain. Yet he has won the title "Apostle of the Indies" from those who appreciate his work.

---

would have to be checked if the monarchy, hindered by distance and poor communication, was to remain in control of the colony.

The encomienda did remain, but a series of laws restricted it, and the crown slowly undermined and destroyed the system. After 1549 the encomienda no longer included the the right to Indian labor, and the amount of the tribute which Indians owed to their trustees was set by royal officials. Finally, the monarch made the Indians vassals of the crown and claimed the right to their tribute payments. The encomienda was offically dead.

Repartimiento

But the colony still needed a labor force. The Spaniards had to find a means of forcing the Indians to work for them. And so a new system, called the *repartimiento*, replaced the encomienda. Under the repartimiento, Indians were to work a specified number of days a year on projects judged essential by the crown; they were to be paid wages, fed, and

housed during this period by the colonists using their services, and any person wanting the services of Indians had to apply to the royal officials.

The abuses of the repartimiento surpassed even the worst aspects of the encomienda. In the first place, no one was any longer responsible for the well-being of the Indians; the men who used them had no concern for them other than in getting the most work possible for their money. Royal officials succumbed to bribery and assigned Indians to jobs that should not have been considered "essential." Indian laborers were transported far from their homes in defiance of the law and most Spaniards ignored the time limit on their use of specific Indian groups. If wages were actually paid (and many colonists ignored this requirement) they were usually meagre. If the employer provided housing and food (again, frequently ignored), it was of the poorest quality.

The Indians of Mexico certainly suffered under Spanish rule, as conquered people have always suffered. Their institutions were effectively destroyed, and

Spanish religion, government, and society imposed upon them. In the face of conquest the Indian changed. But the Spaniard changed as well. At the time he was imposing his own institutions and way of life on Mexico, he also came under the influence of Indian customs. The result was a blending of Indian and Spanish culture, the creation of a new and unique society. It was aided, in part, by the mixing of the races. Children were born of Spanish fathers and Indian mothers. At first these *mestizos* were accepted by neither group. But as time passed their numbers increased to the point where today most Mexicans are of mixed Indian and Spanish heritage. The mestizos were the new race of the Americas. They represent the blending of blood and of culture that has produced the modern Mexican and Mexican American.

REFERENCES

Las Casas, Bartolomé de. *Historia de las Indias.* Mexico City: Fonda de Cultura Economica, c. 1951.

Simpson, Lesley Bird. *Many Mexicos.* Berkeley: University of California Press, 1959.

Wolfe, Eric. *Sons of the Shaking Earth.* Chicago: University of Chicago Press, 1959.

CHAPTER **4** | # Dreamers and Schemers

As soon as Hernán Cortés had conquered the land he called New Spain, the large-scale colonization effort began. In the years that followed the Spanish and Spanish-Indian culture spread throughout much of the Americas. This colonization process formed a base for the origin of today's Mexican-American culture.

The early colonization effort in New Spain was concentrated in the central valley of Mexico, the heartland of the Indian civilization. The Spaniards built their capital, Mexico City, atop the ruins of the old Aztec ceremonial city of Tenochtitlán. Droves of colonists flocked to the new city. But even before the Spaniards arrived in Mexico, the population pressure on the valley's arable land had reached such proportions that not enough food could be grown to feed the people. The conquest meant still more mouths to feed in an already overpopulated region. In addition, the Spaniards brought with them animals previously unknown to Mexico—sheep, cattle, and horses. This livestock, while adding new meats to the diet, used land for pasture that might otherwise have produced crops. The only solution was to move out-

ward from the valley of Mexico into less populated, and frequently unexplored, regions of the colony.

Overpopulation and lack of food were not the only reasons for the exodus from the population centers. More important, the valley of Mexico failed to live up to the expectations of Spaniards who came in search of God, glory, and gold. True, there were thousands of Indians to be converted, but as we have seen, the conversion task was a fairly simple one. Within a few years, the Indians had embraced the Roman Catholic faith to the satisfaction of the priests who worked among them. The zealous missionaries needed new fields to conquer, fresh souls to save.

Nor did Mexico City offer opportunities for fame and glory to more than a few colonists. The conquerors, and some of the early arrivals among the colonists, had cornered the market on glory. They controlled the new colonial society and government during the first few years. Later, they and their heirs were displaced by officials appointed by the crown and sent from Spain. The average colonist had little chance of breaking into this closed and very elite society; if he wanted to make a name for himself, he would have to do so in the hinterland of some new colony, in territory not yet controlled by Spaniards.

Finally, the valley of Mexico failed to offer the fabulous riches in gold the Spaniards expected. The Indians had brought Cortés gold when he landed at Tabasco and thus fed the greed of the conquerors. But it soon became apparent that most of this gold, in the form of jewelry, came from small placer mines which could never yield enough to make every Spanish soldier the wealthy man he dreamed of being. The colonists were unwilling to give up their dream of El Dorado—the land of riches and gold that surpassed anything the mind could imagine. If the gold was not available in the valley of Mexico, they would continue the search in more distant regions of the New World.

Outward Expansion

Within months of the conquest, Spanish colonists began to move away from the populated valley of Mexico, into the unexplored regions of the new continent. They were the adventurers, willing to face danger and even death for a chance to fulfill the dream of fortune and fame. Their story, generally speaking, is one of disillusionment, for they found nothing that lived up to their preposterous expectations. The first expeditions traveled south. But in Central America they found unattractive jungle. Soon they gave up and turned their attention to the arid desert lands north and west of Mexico City. The movement toward what is now the southwestern United States had begun.

The priests were among the first to move north. They sought out the nomadic Indians of the sparsely populated desert and set about converting them to Christianity. The tribes of northern Mexico proved less cooperative than the Indians of the valley. They were constantly on the move, difficult to gather together for instruction in the new faith. Many of them were hostile and attacked the priests. And so the priests turned to new tactics—tactics that, a few years later, they would carry into the settlements of New Mexico, Texas, Arizona, and California. They began to build a new kind of mission settlement, an outgrowth perhaps of the early congregaciones, but with a character entirely its own.

The Franciscans and Jesuits led the mission effort in New Spain. At outposts in the wilderness they built their communities. Their purpose was to convert the Indians and to protect them from slave-hunting Spaniards. They began to gather the Indians about them in the new settlements; if necessary, and it often was, they would use force to capture the Indians and bring them to the safety of the missions.

The missions were self-contained communities. The priests and their charges grew crops and raised livestock to meet their requirements for food. They made all their own clothing and whatever household articles they needed. The priests taught religion, of course, but they also taught agriculture and crafts. Early in the colonial period, the missions were self-sufficient, but little more. Later (see chapter 7) they would become thriving commercial enterprises and would act as military bastions protecting the perimeters of the empire.

Thus the priests served God and the crown. But few of these dedicated men are remembered in history. Most of those who are remembered are the ones who sought, above all, glory.

The Struggle for Power

From the advantage of nearly five hundred years hindsight, it would appear that Hernán Cortés achieved the fame he coveted. Once the conquest was complete, Cortés established himself as governor of New Spain and developed a power base which no one in the colony could challenge. Cortés was a little king in his colony. As such, he was destined to become part of a struggle for power which nearly destroyed the colony in the sixteenth century and which would continue throughout the colonial period.

Cortés and the Crown

The first conflict developed between Cortés and the crown. The conqueror believed that it was his right to control Mexico since he had subdued it and claimed it for Spain. He grabbed power without waiting for it to be granted by higher authorities. The crown saw this as a threat. The Spanish monarchs, believing in the divine right of kings, demanded total control over their subjects. To curb the power of the conquerors, and to prevent the threat of strong men gaining power, Spain created an immense bureaucracy to govern the American colonies. In the end, Cortés, angry and disillusioned, returned to Spain to spend his last years of life.

The bureaucracy was generally a tool of the *peninsulares* (Spaniards born in Spain). The peninsulares held all the best jobs and formed the elite of colonial soci-ety. But as time passed, a new breed of men developed—the *creoles*, or Spaniards born in America. The creoles wanted power, but Spain gave them little chance of displacing the peninsulares; in nearly three hundred years of colonial rule, only four creoles were appointed to the top position in the government of all the American colonies. The conflict was worsened by the fact that many (though not all) of the peninsularies appointed to high positions were corrupt and inefficient.

The Audiencia and Nuño de Guzmán

One of the worst was Beltrán Nuño de Guzmán, a schemer of the first order. He is remembered as the·cruelest Spaniard to come to America.

Nuño de Guzmán's rise to fame began in 1527, when the Spanish crown established the *audiencia* in New Spain. The audiencia was a court which traveled throughout the colony listening to cases. It consisted of four judges and a president, who represented the crown in the colony. In theory it answered to the Council of the Indies, that body created to oversee the administration of all the American possessions. But the Council of the Indies was far away and little involved in the day-to-day life of the colonies.

The decisions of the audiencia were subject only to the king's veto. Thus it became, in effect, a legislative and administrative as well as a judicial body. It was an elite organization, since only peninsulares could be members. The president was the highest authority in the colony. And the president of the first audiencia in Mexico was Beltrán Nuño de Guzmán.

The policy followed by the first audiencia's president and its two judges who survived the trip from Spain to the New World was one of vengeance. Guzmán wanted, above all, to destroy Hernán Cortés. He was insanely jealous of the conqueror, who had carved out a place for himself that no man could challenge and who, apparently, had the wholehearted support of colonists and Indians alike. Nuño de Guzmán pressed charges, some well founded and some ridiculous, against Cortés and his followers, and he used his power to seize their encomiendas, their property, and even their jobs.

But the audiencia, under Guzmán's leadership, proved inadequate as a tool of royal authority. It was incapable of handling the powerful conquerors and their heirs. It was corrupt and inefficient. Furthermore, Nuño de Guzmán came under attack by priests and bishops for his infamous treatment of the Indians: he enslaved Indians, ruthlessly slaughtering

those who fought him, and depopulated entire regions. Eventually, the bishops won a partial victory. Nuño de Guzmán was removed from office. The scandal led the king to reduce the power of the audiencia and appoint a viceroy (vice-king) as the highest authority in each colony.

However, before Guzmán was removed from office, he had undertaken to conquer a territory known as New Galicia. He was allowed to complete the conquest and to become governor of the territory—in other words, to create a kingdom for himself just as Cortés had done. Guzmán's government of New Galicia was vicious. His brutal treatment drove the Indians to rebellion. He committed senseless atrocities. For these crimes he and his two underlings were tried by the second audiencia. The underlings were convicted and shipped off to prison in Spain. Somehow Nuño de Guzmán escaped imprisonment, on the grounds that he was still needed to complete the pacification of New Galicia, and it was not until 1536 that he returned to Spain.

The Search for Gold

Most Spaniards in America sought glory only as a consequence of fortune. Their chief aim was to find gold, and the wealth would make them famous. The search for gold—both for personal aggrandizement and for the enrichment of the crown—was a constant feature of life in the century after the conquest of Mexico. Every man dreamed of finding a fortune. And the stories of the quest for riches often border on the bizarre.

The Indians had mined gold and silver

long before the conquest. But the metal they acquired generally came from streambeds or from veins of ore that were close to the surface. These small amounts of metal were not enough to satisfy gold-hungry conquerors who dreamed of enormous riches. The Spaniards, their imaginations running wild, undertook the search for the fabled wealth of El Dorado. Before long, they turned their attention to the north.

In a way, the story begins with Pánfilo

de Narváez, who, along with Hernán Cortés, had served as an aide to the governor of Cuba. When Cortés stole the governor's fleet and set out to conquer Mexico, Narváez was sent to supplant him. Cortés outwitted Narváez, took him prisoner, and recruited his eight hundred soldiers for the army of the conquest. For Narváez it was an inauspicious beginning.

A few years later, Pánfilo de Narváez undertook another expedition, with even less success. In 1528, he landed in Florida with four hundred men. Most of them soon died of fever or at the hands of hostile Indians. Narváez was one of the victims. Only four men survived.

Cabeza de Vaca

The four survivors led by Álvar Nuñez Cabeza de Vaca, began an epic journey that was to take eight years. They traveled overland across the North American continent. They survived by living as the Indians lived, and eating whatever food the land provided. They were the first white men to travel across the South and Southwest of what is now the United States.

Nuñez Cabeza de Vaca arrived at Mexico City in 1536. He told a colorful tale of fantastic riches in the northern lands, which soon reached the ears of Viceroy Antonio de Mendoza. The viceroy, normally a wise and prudent man, realized that he would win the favor of the crown—as well as enriching himself—if he could locate new sources of wealth. He met with Cabeza de Vaca, who reported that the Indians of New Mexico had told him of the Seven Cities of Cíbola, built of gold and precious gems. gems.

The viceroy was realistic enough to

doubt the story and, at first, to proceed with caution. He ordered a friar, Marcos de Niza, to travel north and verify the story. The friar departed, accompanied only by a black slave named Estevanico. In the weeks that followed, gold fever and the lust for wealth began to undermine Mendoza's natural prudence. He decided to prepare an expedition that could leave immediately should the friar verify Nuñez Cabeza de Vaca's story. The expedition was to be headed by Francisco Vásquez de Coronado.

Marcos de Niza returned alone, claiming that Estevanico had been killed by Indians. He told Mendoza that the Seven Cities of Cíbola did exist and that, in fact, he had seen one of them. There is no reasonable explanation for why the friar told this colossal lie. It has been suggested (Simpson, 1959: pp. 49–50) that he may have made a previous agreement with Mendoza to verify the tale whether it was true or not. The search for wealth aside, it was important for Mendoza to send an expedition north as part of a plan for surrounding the territories held by those great arch-rivals, Cortés and Nuño de Guzmán. Even after Guzmán had been relieved of his power, the viceroy still had to deal with Cortés.

The Coronado Expedition

The Coronado expedition—six hundred men strong—headed north in February, 1540. Of course, Coronado found no cities of gold. The "fabulous" Seven Cities of Cíbola turned out to be villages of adobe huts, quite barren of riches. But the Indians of New Mexico told of a legendary city of gold further to the north called Quivira. Coronado continued his wild-goose chase into what is now Oklahoma and Kansas, but he found

Francisco Coronado in search of Quivira

no treasure. The expedition suffered severe hardships. Extremes in the weather, shortage of food, and disease killed many of the men. Francisco Vásquez de Coronado claimed the barren and apparently worthless lands for Spain and then returned to Mexico empty-handed and disillusioned.

The legend of El Dorado had been effectively destroyed by Coronado's failure.

Exploration of the North continued, but it was no longer guided by a frenzied search for nonexistent riches. This is not to say that the explorers made no effort to find gold and silver; that effort would continue, but the Spaniards now turned their attention to the hard work of mining rather than aspiring to acquire wealth by conquest.

The Silver Rush

The heroes of the era were prospectors who traveled north and west of Mexico City and located mines deep within the earth. They found some gold, but more often they found silver, and silver turned out to be the real mineral wealth of the New World. Soon, a "silver rush" began, comparable to the later gold rushes in California and Alaska. In Spain and in the cities of Spanish America, men left their families and their jobs to seek a fortune in distant mines.

New Wealth for Spain

At first, mining was a chore and profits were hard to come by. Only high-grade ores were of any value—metals that were

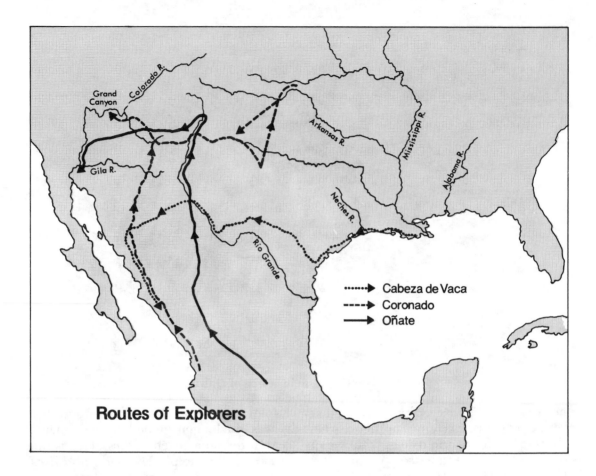

Routes of Explorers

········▶ Cabeza de Vaca

----▶ Coronado

——▶ Oñate

almost pure. But in 1557 Bartolomé de Medina, a Mexican miner, invented the patio process. Mercury was used to extract silver from the ore, which not only made refining less expensive but also made possible the use of low-grade ores. The great mining boom which resulted made Spain, for a time, the wealthiest nation in the world.

Spain, like other European countries, followed a policy of mercantilism. That is, colonies should exist for the benefit of the mother country. They existed solely to provide the mother country with the raw materials and wealth they produced. In turn, they were expected to buy from the mother country, at high prices, any finished goods they needed. (This was the reasoning behind a royal ban on most manufacturing in Spanish America.) Mercantilism meant taking the most you could and giving as little as possible in return.

Mining fit the mercantilistic scheme perfectly. It provided a raw material and was a source of instant wealth. The silver of the New World, and what gold was found, enriched the royal coffers, especially after the patio process reduced the cost of converting ore to a useful product. (The patio process was so important to the whole scheme that Spain created a royal monopoly on mercury. This served to control the refinement of silver and to ensure that the government knew exactly how much silver was being produced.)

The government was willing to make a supreme effort to promote mining.

Most of the yield from the mines went to Spain. Legally, all mines were owned by the crown, which took one-fifth—called the *quinto*—of all precious metals for its personal use. The quinto made the Spanish monarchy extremely wealthy. There were royal rewards for engaging in mining. Miners had the protection of the crown. They were exempt from foreclosures, and they were granted special leniency in the courts. This meant that the miners, no matter what their previous position in society, became privileged creatures in the new society.

The character of that society changed drastically under the influence of the mining boom. The population shifted from the traditional centers to the new mining areas. In New Spain, this meant a shift from fertile valleys to arid plains. New towns began to appear around the mines. At first they were little more than rough gathering places for wild and boisterous men, but they soon settled down to become prosperous centers, with shops and markets, surrounded by farms. By the end of the sixteenth century the mining community of Zacatecas had grown from an unknown village to a full-fledged rival of Mexico City in importance among the cities of New Spain.

Silver Barons

The tone of the society changed as well. A new class of silver barons emerged, replacing, to some extent, the traditional aristocracy. These miners were seldom accepted by the aristocracy. But they could and did buy their way to power. The signs of their new wealth were evident everywhere. They spent vast sums of money for lavish decoration of the churches of New Spain; altars were gilded with gold and silver, studded with gems. They reveled in personal ostentation—spending their money to adorn themselves and their homes. The magnificence the mines engendered bordered on the vulgar.

It was a rich society. But while the prosperity of the mines brought wealth and happiness to some, it created more misery for many. The gulf between rich and poor had always been wide in the colony. Now, as the silver barons flaunted their wealth, it became even wider. The poor—mostly Indians and mestizos, but also a few Spanish colonists—were pushed further down the social ladder. Many of them became hangers-on in the mining towns, beggars and drunks idly dreaming of fortune for themselves while living off the crumbs they could gather from the more fortunate. All suffered at the hands of the miners, but none more than the Indian. In New Spain, as throughout Spanish America, Indians were forced to work the mines. In some cases, especially in the more isolated regions, they were subjected to outright slavery. Generally, however, the repartimiento (see chapter 3) was applied to the mines, which were considered essential projects by the crown. Still thousands of Indians died of overwork and mistreatment in the mines of New Spain.

Expensive Consequences

In the long run, the mining boom also brought sorrow to the mother country that sponsored it. The wealth of the mines was supposed to enrich Spain and end her financial worries forever. But even before the great mines were discovered, the wealth of the New World had begun to create inflation in Spain. As the treasures in silver began to reach Europe, costs in Spain spiraled. Even the most common of items—food and clothing, for instance—commanded exorbitant prices. This combined with the tremendous cost of maintaining and administering distant colonies (which according to the tenets of mercantilism should cost nothing) brought about the decline and eventual collapse of the Spanish empire.

The mines yielded great wealth, but Spain and her colonies paid dearly for the silver treasure. Mining created an aura of success. But it was not a solid and lasting base on which to build a colony, and men soon discovered that the real wealth of America was not gold or silver, but land—land on which to build a new life and a new society.

REFERENCE

Simpson, Lesley Bird. *Many Mexicos.* Berkeley: University of California Press, 1959.

CHAPTER 5 | Farms and Forts— The Expanding Settlement

The Europeans who migrated to America during a period extending from the fifteenth through the eighteenth centuries had one thing in common: an overwhelming desire to own land. This was equally true in Spanish America. The Spanish settlers came from a country where good land was scarce and the average man had no chance of owning his own farm. Spain is a harsh land, arid or semi-arid almost in its entirety. It has little timber and few fertile valleys; for generations, the choice land has been owned by a privileged few.

Many of the settlers in Spanish America had been poor in Spain; they came from among the huge peasant populations. Having had little to make their lives easy or enjoyable, they came to America in search of opportunity. Their dream of gold and wealth collapsed and land supplanted gold as the key to happiness for the vast majority of settlers in New Spain—land where a man could be his own boss.

Yet even here there was to be disillusionment. Title to land proved to be almost as elusive as gold so far as most settlers were concerned. Nevertheless land and agriculture became the key to the future of the colony.

Commercial agriculture, like mining, was in keeping with Spain's mercantilistic policy. If crops could be grown on a large scale in America, the crown would benefit. This theory was reinforced when early settlers discovered that certain crops native to the New World were greatly in demand on the European market. Those that could be grown without any great outlay of capital were, of course, especially profitable. Cacao, for example, had long been grown by the Indians of Mexico. The bean had been used as a beverage (chocolate) and as a medium of exchange. The Spaniards soon discovered that chocolate, an exotic taste for Europeans, was much in demand, and they vigorously encouraged the cultivation of cacao. It cost them little, for they acted only as distributors, leaving cultivation in the hands of the Indians.

Other crops required more in the way of machinery and facilities. When a large capital outlay was needed to convert crops into saleable products, the Spaniards themselves took control of the cultivation and refining processes, often with aid from the crown. Indigo—a blue dye greatly in demand in Europe—and sugarcane were such crops. Great indigo and sugar plantations were established in the lowlands of Mexico to raise the crops and produce the finished product.

Migration Northward

Commercial agriculture was profitable, but as we have seen, mining had turned the attention of the colony northward. The North was not an attractive region for farming, and at first only a few farmers settled there. The soil was poor. It could yield crops only with extensive irrigation, and this was often difficult because of the lack of water. Moreover, labor was in short supply. The Spaniards depended on Indian labor to tend fields and harvest the crops. But the population had always been sparse in the North. The small population that did exist was further decreased during the early years of settlement when the encomiendas were plundered for Indian slaves and many died from European diseases. Even today the region is sparsely populated; only 19 percent of Mexico's people live in the North, which constitutes 40 percent of the nation's territory (Preston, p. 611).

Despite the problems, Spanish colonists made a success of agriculture in the North. They did so because the climate and environment of the area were similar to the climate and environment of the mother country. Spain was arid; so was northern New Spain. In their homeland, the Spaniards had had to rely on irrigation to make their crops grow; in the colony they applied the same techniques that their families had used for generations. And not being accustomed to having timber in Spain, they built their homes of adobe and bricks. However, few farmers were attracted to the North at first, for agriculture in this arid land offered a man little opportunity to make a fortune. Yet in the final years of the sixteenth century, a steady flow of migrants moved northward.

The migration was spurred, at least in part, by conditions in the mother country. Spain, for a short time the wealthiest and most powerful nation in the world, went into steady decline after the middle of the sixteenth century. And the deterioration of the mother country adversely affected the colonies.

The influx of precious metals from the New World had created rampant inflation in Spain. As prices skyrocketed there, the colonists also found their purchasing power reduced. Few could afford to buy finished goods shipped from Spain. The colonies, prohibited by Spain from either manufacturing their own goods or buying from foreign countries, suffered a decline. Of course, smuggling and illicit manufacturing provided some goods, but the prices were almost as high as they would have been through legal channels. The quality of colonial life deteriorated noticeably as Spain's fortunes changed for the worse.

Spain began to lose control over her distant colonies. Communication across the Atlantic had always been difficult. Many months might pass before a message from the crown or the Council of the Indies reached Mexico City; it might never arrive if a ship went down in a storm or was attacked by pirates. Also,

England's defeat of the Armada in 1588 disastrously weakened Spanish sea power and, consequently, the ties between mother country and colonies. Colonial administrators, lacking continuous direction from the crown, had to use their own discretion in governing; they were, more often than not, the sole authority over the colonies.

All this resulted in a certain confusion in government. Decisions made by viceroys or their subordinates might be rescinded many months later; laws passed by colonial governors might be at variance with the wishes of the crown. No one knew at any given time what the laws of the land were. To add to this, the crown subjected its colonial administrators to rigorous inspections by royal representatives, and it frequently recalled or transferred viceroys on the basis of these checks. Each new viceroy, to make his presence and power felt, had to overhaul the system completely; he went through the work of his predecessor with a fine-toothed comb and rejected much of it. Thus there was no continuity in colonial government and a great sense of insecurity among colonial peoples.

The Haciendas

As the mines became less profitable and commercial crops like indigo and cacao commanded lower prices on the European market, economic depression was added to the political and social insecurity the colonists felt. Many sought to escape these conditions and dreamed of creating a new and better life. Out of the chaos of the sixteenth century, a new way of life did emerge. Its basis was the *hacienda*—the privately owned estate.

During the early years of colonization, the crown considered all the land in America as its own personal possession. The kings awarded a few grants of land to those men who served them especially well; these grants were rarely given and jealously guarded, and private ownership of land was the exception rather than the rule. As we have seen (chapter 3), the crown more often granted encomiendas, or trusteeships over Indian villages. The encomiendas did not involve ownership of the land, but merely the right to the tribute payments and personal services of the Indians. However, this was not enough to satisfy land-hungry colonists.

The conditions that had led to the confusion and insecurity among the colonists forced the crown to change its policy. As Spain's financial situation became more desperate, it sold its lands in an attempt to replenish the royal treasury. In New Spain, as in other parts of Spanish America, the wealthy colonists bought up vast tracts of land. The enormous size of these tracts served two purposes. In the first place, the immensity of his holding satisfied the ego of the purchaser and gave him independence and personal security; he could retreat from the confusion of society to the isolation of his own little kingdom. In the second place, a large tract of land was essential for the changed use to which the land would be put. The hacienda was to be based not on crops but on livestock—livestock which needed vast tracts for pasture. This change in orientation further served to turn the attention of the colony northward. For although the North was poorly suited to the cultivation of commercial crops, it was suited to the needs of livestock. Cattle and sheep thrived in the semi-arid North and thus provided the impetus for the northward movement of the *hacendados* (landowners) during the sixteenth century.

The hacienda, in order to function, needed labor—as did every endeavor the Spaniards undertook in America. To fill this need, the new hacendados invited workers to settle on or near the estates. Most of the workers did so willingly. Generally they were Indians; however, some were poor Spaniards who had failed to make satisfactory lives for themselves. The hacienda offered them protection in a disrupted society. If too few workers came voluntarily, the hacendados found other means of filling their labor needs. It was increasingly common in the sixteenth and seventeenth centuries for them to attach neighboring Indian lands to their tracts and thus bring entire communities under their control.

A strange alliance, basically feudal in nature, evolved between workers and hacendados. The workers who came to the hacienda were rarely paid straight wages—a salary for their services. Even if they did receive wages, the money was never enough for survival. They were forced to turn to the landowner, who provided for them and demanded com-

plete loyalty in return for his paternalism. Occasionally, the hacendado paid workers in kind for their services; that is, he provided for their basic needs—food, clothing, housing, recreation—as payment for their labor. Most commonly, however, the hacendado assigned each worker (and his family) a plot of land on the hacienda. The worker became combination laborer and tenant farmer. He worked the lands of the hacendado and, when time permitted, his own.

These tenant farmers rarely produced more than enough for bare subsistence. Whatever extra they did produce, they could sell—usually to the hacendado at prices well below the market value. Moreover, the hacendado extended credit to his tenants throughout the year—to buy food, tools, livestock, fodder, and seed. By the time the workers were ready to sell the goods they produced, they did not receive enough to cover the debt to the hacendado. The debt grew with each passing year and served to tie the worker permanently to the land and the landowner. More important, a son inherited his father's debt. In this manner, generations of hacienda workers were made dependent on the landowner, their master and provider.

New World Aristocrats

The history of Spain's colonial experience demonstrates that control of the labor force meant power and position in colonial society. This was true because the Spaniards, with their traditional aversion to manual labor, depended on Indians, mestizos, poor settlers, and later, black slaves to keep the colony operating.

As the hacendados gathered more and more workers into their fold, they replaced conquerors and silver barons as the elite of the highly stratified social structure. Certainly by the end of the seventeenth century, but probably earlier, the hacendados dominated the society of New Spain as surely as they controlled the land. And by the time Mexico proclaimed her independence from Spain in 1821, most of the nation's land was in the hands of only ten thousand private owners (Preston, 1959: p. 591).

The hacendados formed a body of self-made noblemen and the display of their wealth and position in society exceeded even the most vulgar ostentation of the silver barons. The landowners decked themselves in the most splendid clothing they could acquire—in sharp contrast to the frequently ragged dress of the workers. They built great mansions on their haciendas—again, in contrast to the hovels and shacks of the hacienda laborers. Some of them maintained private armies, thus demonstrating their supremacy over the crown in their own territories. They were independent, yet they represented the epitome of tight control and power in the colonial world.

The hacienda created generations of New World aristocrats. Yet it was completely at odds with all the prevalent views of what constituted success. The hacienda was self-sufficient. It provided all that was necessary for its own survival. The goal, ostensibly, was profit. But it always produced below capacity. And much of the money it did make was spent on an unproductive display of wealth—the dress, house, and fabulous parties of the hacendado. It became an isolated bastion in the wilderness, intent not on the world that surrounded it, but on maintaining itself.

Indian Raids–Spanish Garrisons

The hacienda moved the colony northward, as the mines had done. In its own way, it represented the permanence of the Spanish presence in New Spain. But as the colony moved into the North, new forces threatened its existence. Hostile Indians began to attack the farthest frontier settlements, the isolated haciendas. Soon the Indians began to send raiding parties farther and farther south into the populated areas of New Spain. Often, the raiding parties came out of the territory of Arizona and New Mexico. Among the most ferocious of these Indians were the Apaches. They had apparently been a peaceful people in preceding generations. But the northward movement of the Spaniards made them fearful for the sovereignty of their own territory, and horses left behind by the Coronado expedition made them mobile. Their raids into New Spain frequently devastated small mining communities and haciendas. Soon, the roads throughout the northern reaches of the colony were unsafe for travel. The North was being effectively cut off from the administrative center of the colony, Mexico City, and continuing operation of the mines was threatened.

Spain's economy depended on keeping the mines open, expecially since New Spain was one of the most important silver producers among the American colonies. The Spanish treasury depended heavily on silver to keep the country solvent, and protecting the mines became an issue of the greatest importance. Spain, therefore, took steps to protect the road north and, in so doing, added yet another element to the diversity of northern society. Forts and garrisons were built along the main routes and at the mines. And the soldiers who manned them joined the throngs of Spaniards moving northward. They often took their families with them and new communities sprang up around the forts.

Each garrison was staffed by about sixty Spanish soldiers. They were equipped with horses and firearms. However, their duties were far more diverse than mere soldiering. These men acted as policemen in rowdy mining and military communities; they served as guards and escorts for important persons traveling the dangerous road between Mexico City and the mines, and they were the mail carriers and messengers who kept open the lines of communication with colonial administrators.

The Indian raids continued, becoming more and more destructive as northern communities grew in size. It soon became apparent, even to the distant crown, that the soldiers could not provide sufficient protection. There were simply too many Indians, too many raids to be effectively stopped by a few widely scattered troops. But at the end of the sixteenth century, Spain—her sea power at low ebb, her treasury depleted, her ties with the New World growing weaker—could scarcely afford the cost of more soldiers and stronger fortifications. A new solution had to be found.

The most effective solution, it seemed, would be to create a buffer state. The crown reasoned that a colony north of the mining area would absorb the Indian attacks. It would act as a buffer, or cushion, between hostile Indians and the crucial mining communities.

Thus in 1595 the king authorized the settlement of a Spanish colony in the far North, to be called the Kingdom of New Mexico. Its purpose would be to bear the full burden of Indian hostility. A new chapter in the history of Spanish-speaking people in America was about to begin.

REFERENCE

Preston, James. *Latin America*. New York: The Odyssey Press, 1959.

CHAPTER 6 | The Buffer State

The decision of the Spanish crown to create a buffer state on the northern frontier of its possessions in the New World had far-reaching effects. By this act, Spain placed her indelible stamp on yet another vast area of the Americas. Spain transferred her own character and that of the Hispanic-Mexican culture that had evolved in seventy-five years of colonization to a territory that is now part of the United States, and so set the stage for a unique fusion of Anglo- and Hispanic-American cultures.

The crown, in announcing its intention to establish the Kingdom of New Mexico, offered the right to lead the colonization effort to the highest bidder. One who answered the challenge was Juan de Oñate, a silver baron from Zacatecas. Oñate not only had wealth behind him, as one of the four or five richest men in New Spain, but social prestige as well: his mother was a descendant of Hernán Cortés and, according to legend, of the Emperor Montezuma. He was enough of an adventurer to see a great opportunity in the colonization of New Mexico. And he was greedy enough to dream of finding new fortunes in precious metals; should this

fail, Oñate envisioned a thriving trade in wool and buffalo hides. He expected also to find ocean harbors, rich in pearls, which demonstrates how little the people of the colony knew of their new world.

Thus Juan de Oñate bid for the opportunity to form the new colony. He offered to recruit colonists and soldiers, reasoning that a sufficient number of fortune hunters would be willing to settle in the unknown land. He would take, at his own cost, all the provisions necessary to start and maintain a colony. In return, Oñate asked for the title of captain-general and governor of the Kingdom of New Mexico, the right to make all government appointments in the colony and an annual salary. He asked that the crown provide only the friars and church bells that the colony would need. The viceroy of New Spain, Luis de Velasco, accepted the bid in the name of the crown, although he reduced by one-fourth the salary Oñate had asked. The mining millionaire began to recruit his colonists and collect his provisions. Viceroy de Velasco, true to the ideals of his king, advised Oñate: "Your main purpose shall be in the service of God our

Lord, the spreading of His holy Catholic faith, and the [missionizing] of the natives of the said provinces'' (Horgan, 1954: p. 176). In other words, Oñate was charged with the duty of pacifying the colony, preferably by peaceful means, and thus ending the Indian threat to New Spain.

While Juan de Oñate was preparing for the journey north, recruiting his colonists and collecting his supplies, a new viceroy arrived from Spain, replacing Velasco. The new official, typical of his breed, found it necessary to reexamine all the business of his predecessor, including the Oñate colonization contract. The colonists, already gathering at the departure point, waited many long months while the viceroy considered. In the end,

Oñate's expedition was authorized, but his privileges were sharply curtailed. For instance, he was denied the right to appoint government officials in his colony—this was to be left to higher authorities in Mexico City and Spain. Oñate had no choice but to submit or completely lose his right to lead the colony. Under these new conditions, the northward march got under way on January 26, 1598. It consisted of eighty-three wagonloads of supplies, seven thousand head of stock, four hundred soldiers, and one hundred and three families (Horgan, 1954: p. 179). Traveling an average of five or six miles a day, the settlers made their way north.

Building the New Colony

In September, exhausted and covered with the dust of long months on the trail, the party finally arrived at a choice spot for settlement at the edge of the Rio Grande in northern New Mexico near present-day Española. They called the place San Juan de los Caballeros and began the difficult task of building a colony. The land was parcelled out among the settlers. They immediately set about to create a means of irrigating the farmlands. They used their knowledge of Spanish irrigation and they borrowed from the techniques of the Pueblo Indians, who had been irrigating their own crops for many centuries. The only water system that could possibly work in such an arid land was a communal one; the settlers would have to share the available water equally, regardless of their wealth or social position, if the colony was to survive. To this end, the colonists elected a council to regulate the water rights.

Under the direction of the council, they dug a ditch—the *acequia madre*, or mother ditch—to carry water from the river, and smaller secondary canals leading off it to irrigate each man's plot of land. These farmlands, intended for cultivation, were owned outright by the settler. But the pasture lands were communally owned, shared by all as was the water. Fences were unheard of and each colonist was responsible for keeping his grazing livestock out of the crops. This system of open range and shared water rights was so ideally suited to the environment that it is still, nearly four hundred years later, a common feature of ranching in many parts of the Southwest.

Once the first colonists finished digging the acequia madre and the secondary canals, they turned to the task of building a settlement. The first building erected was a church, large enough to serve all the settlers and soldiers. While it was under construction, the people continued to live as they had lived on the trail—in wagons or perhaps tents. By this time it was well into September, and the brisk cold of early autumn nights must have made them uncomfortable indeed. We can imagine that the builders finished the church as quickly as possible and threw themselves wholeheartedly into the construction of their homes. Anxious to have cover over their heads before winter set in, they built the village of San Juan in short order. This village, and those settled later in New Mexico, was designed for protection. Its houses and public buildings, adjoining one another, formed a square. All opened onto a central plaza. The village was a fortress against possible Indian attacks.

At first, the settlers at San Juan, insecure in alien territory, all lived in the village. They left its protection to tend the fields only by day. Later, as the settlement expanded and more towns were established, people began to move away from the safety of the village. There was a very good reason for this: land grants were often located at some distance from the village and it was more convenient to live on the land than to travel to it each day. The hacienda system (chapter 5) was transported to New Mexico, too. On these vast estates, often at great distance from the settlements, colonists built homes that were villages in minature. The houses formed a great square around a central courtyard, a fortress in the wilderness.

Pueblo Resistance

The pacification of the local Indians was of the greatest concern, both from a moral and an economic standpoint. To Juan de Oñate and his little band of settlers, this meant converting the Indians to Christianity and putting them to work for the benefit of the colony. But the two peoples got off on the wrong foot from the very start. The arriving Spaniards demanded supplies and met with strong resistance. The Pueblos were not fierce warriors like the Apaches; but they were not about to bow to the mastery of invaders in their homeland. For nearly a year, an uneasy peace was maintained between settlers and Indians.

War broke out in 1599. The Spaniards were determined to defeat the Indians and permanently subdue them. Juan de Oñate told his officers, "inasmuch as we have declared war on them without quar-

ter, you will punish all those of fighting age as you deem best, as a warning to everyone in this kingdom. All of those you execute, you will expose to the public view.... If you should want to show lenience...make the Indians believe that you are doing so at the request of the friar with your forces" (Forbes, 1964: p. 36). The war was short; the Pueblos were not a fighting tribe and the Spaniards, with the advantage of superior weapons, killed eight hundred Indians and wounded many more. Oñate decreed the punishment for the defeated Indians. Men over the age of twenty-five were to have one foot cut off and be sentenced to twenty years of personal servitude; those twelve to twenty-four years old received the sentence of twenty years of servitude. Thus the colonists subdued the Indians and secured a labor supply for the immediate future. However, trouble with the Indians did not cease. Pueblo resistance surfaced from time to time during the next few years, and Apache raids on both Spanish and Pueblo communities grew in intensity during the seventeenth century. From that standpoint, New Mexico served its purpose well: it did act as a buffer colony, absorbing much of the Indian hostility and thus protecting New Spain.

The friars who had come north with Oñate pursued their calling among the Pueblos and worked hard to convert them. They built missions near Indian villages (by 1630 there were twenty-five such missions in New Mexico) but, unlike their counterparts in Mexico, they did not gather the Indians into the mission community. The Pueblos were allowed to remain in their own villages and the friars went there to work among them. The missionaries believed they were making great progress, instilling in the Indians the true faith. However, they failed to see that, in many instances, the Indians accepted the externals of Roman Catholicism but reverted to their old religious ways in the privacy of their homes, or combined the most attractive aspects of both religions. As any rate, the friars considered their task essentially finished within a few years. And the colonists believed the pacification of the Pueblo Indians complete—a false assumption for which they would pay dearly toward the end of the seventeenth century.

Frontier Hardships

Life was hard in New Mexico, even after villages and water supplies had been established and the Indians "pacified." The main characteristic of the colony was its extreme isolation. The colonists of New Mexico were almost completely cut off from the centers of their civilization. Mexico City was many months away. Communication was slow and sporadic at best. The problems created by lack of communication between Spain and Mexico City were compounded in the case of New Mexico. A directive from the crown was not just months late, but sometimes a year or more in reaching the northern colony. New Mexico was a forgotten, frequently ignored part of the colonial system and its colonists, in turn, frequently ignored the workings of government and society in Spain and Mexico. They had to be independent since they rarely had any contact with the outside world.

The settlers were isolated from one another, too. People in the small colonial villages which were established along the river lived an insular existence. They had little if any contact with other villages. Their society became very ingrown, almost stagnant, because it lacked any stimuli other than the routine of daily living. On haciendas away from the villages the isolation was still more severe. Social contacts were few; a visit even to a neighboring hacienda was a strenuous undertaking, involving a long journey and the danger of Indian attacks. "Society" to most of these people meant family and servants and was confined to the courtyard of the house. The sons of wealthy hacendados married the daughters of nearby landowners and these families formed a closed circle almost totally independent of the larger society.

Life in the Kingdom of New Mexico was a struggle even for the very rich.

The Hopi Indians

The Hopi Indians call themselves *Hopituh,* which in their language means "Peaceful Ones." They live in twelve villages on or below three remote mesas in northern Arizona, where the surrounding desert helps to isolate them and protect their peaceful ways. One of their villages has been inhabited continuously since 1150 A.D.

The Hopi belong to a group of tribes the early *conquistadores* called Pueblo Indians. *Pueblo* is the Spanish word meaning "village." When Coronado was looking for the fabled cities of Cibola in 1540 he made contact with these Indians. He called them Pueblo Indians because, unlike many of the nomadic tribes, the Pueblo Indians lived in permanent villages of adobe houses.

Because of their isolation, the Hopis were better able to withstand the inroads of the Spanish than the other Pueblo people. In 1680 they killed the early missionaries and then, to avoid further trouble, moved their villages from the springs at the foot of the mesas up the steep sides to the flat tops. Bands of Navajo, Ute, Apache, and Comanche, who used the white man's horses to penetrate the desert, raided their cornfields below the mesas, but the Hopi held out. For a while the land of the Hopi was part of Mexico, and then it became part of the United States.

Today the Hopi share a reservation with the Navajo, though they live in separate villages. Hopi women make beautiful pottery and wicker baskets, while the men weave cloth and grow their crops in the low valleys near their mesas. Their main crop is still the special strain of corn their ancestors grew; ordinary corn would not survive in the dry soil of the desert. Water for everyday use must still be carried up to the villages by hand or on burros.

The Hopi have been quick to adopt the conveniences, tools, and techniques of modern civilization, but they retain many of their ancient values, customs, and ceremonies. Although the children learn the ways of the white man in school, they also learn the traditions and rituals of their clan in their houses high on the cliffs.

Food was a basic problem, for the soil of the colony produced crops unwillingly. At times, the water was so scarce that the fields could not be irrigated properly. As a result, the diet of the colonists was routine. The rich ate mostly lamb, rice, raisins, and tamales, and used spices to add flavor to their foods; the poor lived on dried beef and tortillas along with beans and chili (Horgan, 1954: p. 796).

A nineteenth-century traveler to New Mexico, Josiah Gregg, reported in amazement that the people took their meals not at a table but while holding their dishes on their knees. Homes were so sparsely furnished that few families had dining tables (Gregg, 1967: p. 147). The settlements boasted no craftsmen and few tools. Whatever the people needed in the way of furniture, clothing, or kitchen wares, they had to make themselves. Clothing was perhaps the least of their worries; the Spaniards brought with them

a skill for weaving and also taught the Indians to weave fine woolen cloth. But other items were often primitive. Homemade furniture served its purpose, but the carpentry—done without the tools of the trade—was crude and represented long hours of painstaking labor. Thus most homes had little furniture—hard wooden beds, a few chests, a few wooden chairs.

New Mexico lacked other services, too. There were no doctors in the colony. The women learned to tend to most of the medical needs of their familes. They could care for wounds and used common herbs to treat illnesses. Nor was education available. Illiteracy was common, but it mattered little in a colony that had no newspapers and few books. However, there was evidently some early effort to teach the colonial children, and what education did exist was under the control of the priests and theological in nature.

Few parents sent their children to school. Sons were needed to help with the farming, to assure a family's survival. Daughters were trained in the art of homemaking by their mothers and aunts; education for women was not considered necessary or even desirable.

The product of isolation was a new and unique culture. It was modified Hispanic-Mexican culture, but it was further changed by contacts with the Pueblo Indians, whose knowledge of the land was added to the experience and institutions of the settlers. Life in New Mexico was a struggle for survival. Out of that struggle grew a society far stronger, far more viable than the one the colonists had left behind.

Internal Strife and Oñate's Downfall

Political problems compounded the struggle for survival. From its earliest days, the Kingdom of New Mexico was torn by internal conflict. Under the charter for colonization, the governor was the most powerful official, the absolute authority in all colonial affairs. Juan de Oñate, as captain-general and governor, headed a discontented settlement. A revolt, led by forty-five officers and soldiers, threatened the new territory almost at once (Horgan, 1954: p. 186). Oñate arrested the men and condemned them to death. Outraged citizens threatened to desert the infant colony and return to Mexico. Rather than face the failure of his colonial experiment, the governor responded to popular pressure and granted the rebels clemency. But his problems were not over.

The crown, not yet ready to give up the elusive dream of El Dorado, had directed Oñate to search for riches. In 1601, the governor, accompanied by a small force of men, led the first of several expeditions to seek gold and silver and pearls. In his absence, the settlement divided into opposing camps. Few settlers were satisfied. Many felt that the promise of the colony had been broken; they saw a life of hardship ahead of them rather than opportunity and fortune. Leaders of the discontented element prepared a letter of complaint and sent it off, via messenger, to the viceroy in Mexico City. But many were unwilling to wait for an answer. They loaded up their wagons, gave up on the colony, and headed south for home. When Oñate returned he found that only a skeleton colony remained. With few people left, the colony's struggle for survival—and Juan de Oñate's personal struggle for success—intensified.

After due consideration, the crown recalled Oñate in 1606. Because of the slowness of communication, he did not leave New Mexico until three years later. Like so many Spanish colonists with a dream, Oñate returned to New Spain a disillusioned man. His personal fortune was depleted, his enthusiasm spent. As a final blow, his only son was killed by Indians on the journey home.

After Oñate left, New Mexico floundered. New governors were appointed, new villages built (Santa Fe was founded in 1610), and a few new settlers made their way north to the colony. But Spain had second thoughts about the wisdom of founding the Kingdom of New Mexico. True, it served as a buffer state. But the first settlers found no precious metals, and the land offered no promise of profit from commercial agriculture for the crown. According to Spain's mercantilistic policy, a colony that did not enrich the mother country was worthless. New Mexico offered the crown nothing in the way of profit, yet it had to be maintained and administered at considerable cost. It was, in short, a financial disaster. As early as 1601, Spain was considering whether or not to abandon the effort. At the time Oñate was recalled and a new governor appointed, the crown had decided to continue the colony, but to ignore it as much as possible. New Mexico, if it was to survive, would have to do so without support, either financial or moral.

Conditions in the colony deteriorated steadily throughout the seventeenth century. Ignored by Spain, New Mexico found isolation an ever more prominent feature of life. Long periods of time passed without any communication between Mexico City and the colony. The crown even failed to send priests north to care for the religious needs of the settlers and carry on the work among the Indians. Years of drought, when the water supply dried up completely, further complicated the situation. During the famines, hungry Apaches raided Pueblo communities and Spanish settlements alike, stealing livestock and spreading devastation wherever they went.

Indian Rebellion

The Pueblo Indians became increasingly resentful of the Spanish intrusion as the years passed. The crisis finally came to a head in 1680. Agitated by a violently anti-Spanish medicine man, the Acoma pueblo revolted against the Spaniards. They were soon joined by other pueblos. They attacked Spanish villages, farms, and haciendas with even more ferocity than the Apaches had shown. They killed colonists by the scores and burned the homes and crops. The devastation of the colony was total. The Indian rebellion resulted in the complete expulsion of Europeans from the Kingdom of New Mexico. The few terrified Spanish survivors, carrying what belongings they could salvage and accompanied by the small number of Indians who remained loyal to them, fled south. They stopped at the mission of Our Lady of Guadalupe at El Paso on the Rio Grande. There they remained for the next twelve years.

Sporadic efforts to reconquer the colony began immediately. In 1681, an expedition tried to subdue the Indians and retake New Mexico. It was turned back by the still active Pueblos. Other expeditions met the same fate. Meanwhile, Spain had decided that the New Mexico colony should, after all, be maintained. The crown continued to treat the colonists, in exile, as part of the empire, to recognize the officials of the colony and to encourage the reconquest. Finally, a new governor was appointed and charged with the task of reestablishing Spanish settlements in New Mexico. His name was Diego de Vargas.

The Kingdom Rebuilt

In 1692, Vargas, after carefully planning his military strategy, led a small army up the banks of the Rio Grande and ruthlessly attacked the Pueblo forces. Once he had defeated the Indians, he returned to El Paso and led some eight hundred people (including a throng of Indian allies) back to New Mexico (Hollon, 1968: p. 63). It was like starting all over again. The colony had to be rebuilt from scratch; the settlers had to go through much of the same agony their ancestors had experienced nearly a hundred years before. Indian uprisings continued. The Pueblos were not permanently subdued until 1696, and Apaches continued to harass the settlements for the next two centuries. Moreover, the isolation of the colony from the outside world increased. In succeeding years Spain ignored New Mexico more completely than it had ever done before.

Still the colony grew, slowly and steadily. By 1750, the Spanish citizens (only adult men were counted) in the Kingdom of New Mexico numbered 3,779; ten years later the number had increased to 7,666. During that same period the Indian population decreased from 12,142 to 9,104. And by the end of the eighteenth century, 18,826 Spanish citizens resided in New Mexico—almost double the Indian population which had grown only to 9,732 (Jones, 1966: p. 153).

These settlers laid the foundations for the modern society of the southwestern United States. The economic structure of the region is the child of their invention—ranching based on the open range, where livestock roam at will; communal water rights, still regulated by council and recognized in many communities. The settlers left an indelible mark on the culture of the Southwest. Many of its institutions are of Spanish origin. Most important, thousands of the region's people are of Indian-Spanish descent. The heritage of the first settlers is still very much alive in New Mexico and throughout the Southwest.

REFERENCES

Forbes, Jack D. *The Indians in America's Past.* Englewood Cliffs: Prentice-Hall, 1964.

Gregg, Josiah. *The Commerce of the Prairies.* Lincoln: University of Nebraska Press, 1967.

Hollon, W. Eugene. *The Southwest: Old and New.* Lincoln: University of Nebraska Press, 1968.

Horgan, Paul. *Great River: The Rio Grande in North American History.* 2 vols. New York: Holt, Rinehart and Winston, 1954.

Jones, Oakah L., Jr., *Pueblo Warriors and Spanish Conquest.* Norman: University of Oklahoma Press, 1966.

CHAPTER 7 | Mission Settlements

During the colonization of New Spain, the Roman Catholic faith was an integral part of Spanish life. Spanish colonists came to America fired with religious fervor; they came with an enthusiasm—even a compulsion—to convert the non-Christians of the New World. But the Christianization of Indian America cannot be explained by religious fervor alone.

The sixteenth-century Spanish Church was an arm of the crown, as much a political as a religious institution. The experience in America magnified the political aspects of the Church. In 1508 Pope Julius II conferred on the king of Spain a *patronato*, or patronage, over the Church in America. Under the protection of the patronato, the crown exerted absolute authority over all ecclesiastical matters in the colonies. Nowhere was the political role of the Church more evident than in Spain's dealings with the Indians.

True, many of the more devout missionaries were oblivious to politics. They worked hard to convert the Indians, whom they considered childlike and innocent, and strove to protect them from exploitation by the conquerors. Although it was often a futile effort, the crown

applauded the achievement of the missionaries. The kings of Spain, however, considered the salvation of souls to be of secondary importance. They directed a Church designed, first and foremost, to control Indian populations and turn the Indians of the Americas into loyal, tax-paying subjects of the crown. This provided the rationale behind the mission settlements of colonial America.

The mission became the primary medium for settling the northern frontiers—the so-called "borderlands"—of New Spain. The crown reasoned that if the hostile Indians of the far north were converted to Christianity—"civilized," in other words—they would stop attacking mines and haciendas (chapter 5). Furthermore, conversion would increase the size of the labor force available to the colony. This, in turn, would attract colonists to unsettled areas. Of course, Spain expected to benefit economically from all of this—from the additional taxes she could collect; from the discovery of new mines; from the profits of commercial agriculture. And the crown greedily encouraged the northward advance of the missionaries. Franciscans and Jesuits spearheaded the movement.

Missions in New Mexico

The first missionary effort on the far frontier took place in New Mexico. The mission of San Bartolomé was founded in 1581, almost two decades before Juan de Oñate led his small band of colonists into the territory (chapter 6). In that year, three Franciscan friars—Agustín Rodríguez, Francisco López, and Juan de Santa María—entered New Mexico. They were accompanied by eight soldiers and sixteen Indian servants (Peñuelas, p. 135). They built their mission at the edge of a village, leaving the Indian community intact and thus establishing a policy that would be followed in New Mexico for generations to come. But the first mission was doomed. The eight soldiers returned home after the buildings were finished and Indians attacked and destroyed the mission, killing the friars.

Juan de Oñate rebuilt San Bartolomé when he established the Kingdom of New Mexico. It continued to exist until 1711 when it was again destroyed by Indians. But by that time, San Bartolomé was only one of many missions in New Mexico. One, San Miguel de Santa Fe, completed in 1608, is the oldest church building still in use in the United States. Using this chain of missions as a basis for their operations, the Franciscans worked zealously to convert the Pueblo Indians. Later friars used the "pacified" Indians to escort them into remote areas.

The power of the Roman Catholic Church in New Mexico grew steadily. No one could escape its absolute authority. The Church controlled not only the Indians but the Spanish and mestizo populations as well. It was, in part, a spiritual control—control over the souls and consciences of the people. The colonists, isolated as they were from the outside world, were especially susceptible to this control. In the villages, they relied heavily on the Church for their social contacts and recreation. The Church was the center of community life and the friars were often the only educated persons in the community. Their influence was felt perhaps even more strongly on the haciendas and farms of New Mexico. There people were cut off from the daily ministerings of the priests. The infrequent visit of a priest to the hacienda became an important spiritual highlight and, since he brought news and conversation, a social event to be talked about for weeks afterward. But Church control in colonial New Mexico is best illustrated by the economic burden imposed on the people. Exorbitant fees and tithes were extracted from church members in a land where money was scarce. The fact that few people tried to avoid the financial burden is evidence of the Church's overwhelming authority.

For all this, New Mexico was basically a secular rather than a monastic colony. Religion was important. But the colony was not geared exclusively to religious matters, and only a small percentage of its people—the friars—concerned themselves with the conversion of the Indians. Most New Mexican colonists thought first of survival and concentrated on growing crops, building homes, and raising livestock; in short, on building a life for themselves in the wilderness.

Missions in Arizona and Texas

Even before the end of the seventeenth century, the crown could clearly see that the struggling New Mexican colony would survive only with the support of other settlements to the east and west. But the burden of expense and trouble that it had experienced over the colonization of New Mexico was too great to be repeated. This, it felt, might be avoided by using the Church as an instrument of colonization. The crown relied on the zeal of the priests to pursue Indians for conversion. Missionaries would move into an area and pacify the Indians. Civilian settlement of the region would then replace the mission at some future, undisclosed date. Thus Spain never considered mission settlements as anything more than a temporary measure. On this basis, the crown promoted missionary efforts in the North with increased energy.

However it was seldom a successful venture. The first critical areas to be pacified were those lands bordering the Kingdom of New Mexico—Arizona and Texas. An Italian-born Jesuit, Father Eusebio Francisco Kino, began moving north about 1687, establishing a chain of missions between Sonora and Arizona. He founded San Xavier del Bac (near modern Tucson) on April 28, 1700. Father Kino contributed a great deal to Spanish knowledge of the northern frontier. He explored much of Arizona and charted part of the Colorado River for the first time. But as a missionary, he was something of a failure. None of his missions survived for long. Arizona was not conducive to any kind of settlement. It was hot and arid. Its Indian population was small and scattered and, more important, extremely ferocious. Conditions in

Arizona were so unfavorable that the Spaniards finally wrote it off, believing that no one would ever be able to colonize the region. And except for a few courageous hacendados, Spanish settlers avoided Arizona throughout the entire colonial period.

Missionaries in Texas met with a greater degree of success than their counterparts in Arizona—but scarcely enough to fill the crown with enthusiasm. Their effort was well underway before the end of the seventeenth century. We know that the mission of Our Lady of Guadalupe at El Paso had been founded before 1680, when New Mexican colonists sought sanctuary there following the Pueblo Indian revolt. But El Paso, on the Rio Grande, was situated directly on the road to the New Mexico colony; the mission there might easily be considered part of New Mexico, an extension of that colony rather than of Texas.

Franciscan friars moved eastward across Texas from the Rio Grande. In 1690 they founded San Francisco de los Tejas, and by 1731 they had created a chain of a dozen missions. The most prosperous was San Antonio de Bejar, in the center of Texas. Generally, however, the friars faced almost insurmountable difficulty in maintaining their missions. Much of Texas, like Arizona, was rugged land. Dry and dusty plains did not attract settlers and offered the missions little reason for building a foundation for later colonization. Moreover, most Texas missions were surrounded by hostile Indians. Few of them welcomed the missionaries and most friars were too busy fighting for their lives to concentrate on Christianizing the region. Worst of all, the Spanish crown, which gave little support under the best of conditions, repeatedly abandoned the floundering Texas missions. Without this minimal support the missions had no chance of succeeding.

Missions in California

Only in California did the mission system really succeed. The California missions fulfilled the dream the crown had for all its missions in the New World. They were an economic success—profitable for both friars and the crown. They pacified the Indians as completely as anyone could have hoped. And they provided the social foundation for the colonization of the region.

The Jesuits had founded missions in Baja California by 1697. The priests gathered the Indians into mission communities, often far from their own villages; pressed the new religion on them, and turned them into loyal, if subdued, subjects of the crown. Zealous priests in Baja California, as in other areas, were often brutal in their treatment of the Indians. One nineteenth-century Indian recorded that he was dragged into captivity "lassoed as I was with their horses running; after this they roped me with my arms behind and carried me off to the Mission San Miguel" (Forbes, 1964: pp. 62–63). The same Indian continued his story: "When we arrived at the mission, they locked me in a room for a week, the father...talked to me by means of an interpreter, telling me that he would make me a Christian, and he told me many things that I did not understand....One day they threw water on my head and gave me salt to eat, and with this the interpreter told me that now

Mission of San José de Guadalupe, California, 1813

I was a Christian.... I tolerated it all because in the end I was a poor Indian and did not have any recourse but to conform myself and tolerate the things they did with me" (Forbes, 1964: p. 63).

The Jesuit missions in Baja California were well established by the time Franciscan friars moved into upper California. In 1769 Father Junipero Serra, a Franciscan from the island of Mallorca in the Mediterranean, founded Mission San Diego de Alcala, the first of twenty-one California missions stretching north as far as Sonoma. These were to be the most successful (and profitable) of all the Spanish settlements on the far northern frontier. But then, California had the supreme advantage, with its fertile soil, its mild climate, and its docile coastal Indian tribes. In this atmosphere the friars became one of the most powerful forces in colonial Spanish America.

The Franciscan missions were as totalitarian as the Jesuit missions of Baja California. The friars gathered the Indians about them in tightly controlled mission communities. Each mission, simple and austere, was built around a large central courtyard. The church was the prominent feature of this structure. All the other structures of the mission faced the plaza: quarters for both Indians and friars, stables and coach houses, laundry facilities and kitchens, and a variety of workshops. Some—Mission San Carlos Borromeo at modern Carmel, for instance—were closed communities, all buildings adjoining one another, like the villages of New Mexico. Others—like San Juan Bautista, the largest of the missions—were open, their buildings separate.

Most of the missionaries were apolitical. The crown's main motive in promoting the missions may have been to create a peaceful corps of Indian taxpayers and laborers, but the friar's main purpose was to support and protect the Indians. They would do so even at the risk of defying the crown. The friars loudly protested the exploitation of Indians in the mines and fields of Spanish America. They even went as far as excommunicating civil servants who robbed Indians or forced them to work.

Yet the friars themselves were often not totally exemplary. They were often guilty of working the Indians of their missions too hard. And in many instances they whipped Indians who objected or were too slow at their work. If an Indian found a way to escape, the friars tracked him down and punished him severely. Torture was not uncommon. And the death rate in the California missions was exceedingly high. Between 1769 and 1835 the Indian population of coastal California dropped from about 70,000 to about 15,000 (Forbes, 1964: p. 76). Part of this can be attributed to the Indians' susceptibility to European diseases, part to the fact that they were worked beyond the limits of human tolerance.

The California missions, to the joy of the crown, developed into elaborate economic complexes. The friars began by building each mission into a self-sustaining operation. The mission was built by the Indians, under the direction of friars. The Indians constructed all the buildings, cultivated the land, and made the mission self-sufficient. Whatever the community needed, it provided for itself. All the cloth the mission used was woven by the Indians, who made clothes, sheets, table linens, and blankets. They made their own shoes, soap, and candles. The blacksmith's shop was one of the busiest places in the mission complex. Laundries and kitchens hummed with activity all

Junipero Serra

Junipero Serra (1713–1784), known as the Apostle of California, was a Franciscan priest who came to Mexico from Spain in 1750 to work among the Indians. After spending nearly 20 years in Mexico, he founded a mission near present-day San Diego, California. This was the first mission of many he established in California, some of which are still manned by Franciscans such as Mission Santa Barbara and Mission San Antonio (near King City, California).

With sixteen other missionaries he converted over 3,000 Indians. Father Serra, as Father Las Casas, was a vigorous protector of the Indians. He helped them to raise livestock, such as sheep and cattle, and to farm their lands, raising grains and growing fruit.

---

day long. From the time it was established, a mission was a busy place.

The California missions grew quickly to extremely profitable corporations. The mild climate of coastal California is ideally suited to large-scale agriculture.

Within a few years the friars had planted orchards; the fruits they grew were far in excess of the needs of the missions and the surplus could be sold at a profit in New Spain and even in Spain itself. The friars imported grape vines; soon vineyards dotted the countryside and a thriving wine industry developed. The crops of the friars foreshadowed twentieth century commercial agriculture that has made California the prime producer of fruits and vegetables in the United States. By 1834 the mission holdings were valued at about $78 million—an incredible sum in those days—although the total area farmed by the Franciscans probably did not exceed 10,000 acres (McWilliams, 1949: p. 33).

Decline of the Mission System

Despite the apparent financial success of the California missions, the power and status of the Church on the far northern frontier declined steadily during the final years of the colonial period. Its defenses and its authority crumbled. The crown began to fear the California missions because they were becoming too wealthy and, consequently, too independent. The Franciscan order, tasting success, became greedy. The friars cheerfully defied the crown and began trading with nations other than Spain. Soon ships out of Boston began calling in California ports to load the produce of the missions and to drop off cargoes of luxury items from the Far East. The friars ignored the rules of Spanish mercantilism and in so doing undermined the absolute authority of the crown.

By the middle of the eighteenth century, the king viewed the missions as a threat to his own position. Later, after independence in 1821, Mexico felt that the missions were representative of the hated Spanish crown and completed the destruction of the system, which had begun when Spain chose to follow a course of ignoring the northern Church. (During the seventy years between 1760 and 1830, not one bishop visited the New Mexico colony [Horgan, 1954: p. 547].) Then too, since many settlers lived far from the villages and the churches, they relied less on the Church for their spiritual and social needs. Besides these factors, the ideas of the Age of Enlightenment had begun to gain favor in America: the scientific approach to life began to displace the spiritual.

The early independence era was marked by conflict, often violent, between Church and state. As a result, the Church in Mexico was separated from the state, and the political strength of the Church collapsed. The missions of the northern frontier provinces were secularized by 1835. Secularization resulted in the ouster of the friars and the loss of their power. All mission possessions came under civil authority and a large share of mission landholdings fell into private hands. Some civil servants made fortunes for themselves by selling off the mission lands. It was a chaotic time for all, but the disintegration of the mission system had its greatest effect on the Indians. They were declared free and independent and turned out of the missions that had protected them for so long. Many Indians reverted to their old religions. Most, unprepared to fend for themselves after being overprotected by the friars, were reduced to a state of poverty and despair. Their only chance of survival, in many cases, was to join the throngs who sought the protection of the haciendas, ready to trade their new-found independence for a life of debt peonage.

The secular priests who replaced the friars came to the northern frontier in fewer numbers than their predecessors. They were less zealous than the friars and generally less willing to devote themselves to the needs of Indians and the small number of colonists. After the last Franciscan friars had been expelled from the missions, a handful of priests remained to provide for religious needs of many. Only a few parishes—generally the wealthier ones—had resident priests; most communities were lucky if a priest visited them two or three times a year. The priests could hardly be blamed for not wanting to serve on the isolated frontier. Whereas the friars had been cared for by their orders, the secular priests had to live on what their parishioners could contribute, which was very little. Thus most frontier priests ended their lives as paupers.

After secularization, the status of the Church on the frontier declined rapidly. The churches and abandoned missions decayed and no one bothered to repair them. This, at the end of Spain's American colonial experience, was the fate of the greatest medium of Spanish culture.

In one respect, however, the missions had succeeded. They did provide a basis for colonization, especially in California. Settlers, moving north in small numbers, gravitated to the missions and built their own colonies nearby. Even after the missions had been abandoned and the Church's power declined, these little colonies remained. And they formed a core for the continued settlement and growth of the region.

REFERENCES

Forbes, Jack D. *The Indians in America's Past.* Englewood Cliffs: Prentice-Hall, 1964.

Horgan, Paul. *Great River: The Rio Grande in North American History.* 2 vols. New York: Holt, Rinehart and Winston, 1954.

McWilliams, Carey. *North from Mexico.* Philadelphia: J. B. Lippincott, 1949.

Peñuelas, Marcelino C. *Lo Español en el Suroeste de los Estados Unidos.* Madrid: Ediciones Cultura Hispánica, 1964.

PART TWO

The Foreign Intrusion

CHAPTER **8** | # Threatened Colonies I: European Competitors

Slowly, between the sixteenth and eighteenth centuries, Spain extended her control over the northern reaches of New Spain. By the end of that period she had established a chain of settlements across the northern frontier—some civilian, some religious, some military. Thus Spain transformed a vast area of the present-day United States, and by her actions set the stage for further transformation. Today that area is neither Spanish nor American nor Indian but a unique blend of cultures and institutions. The society of the modern Southwest was born out of conflict between its various elements and matured as a unique fusion of those same elements.

The general state of the frontier colonies by the eighteenth century was one of hardship, but there was always a desire for a better life. These settlements lacked the goods and services other European settlements in the New World took for granted. This was true especially in New Mexico, isolated as it was from the rest of the so-called civilized world. The colony struggled along without the craftsmen it so badly needed—carpenters, blacksmiths, and the like. Nor were personal

services available in New Mexico: there were no barbers, for instance—a service that European settlers in Mexico City or Jamestown, Virginia or Pernambuco, Brazil, might have taken for granted. The New Mexican colonists had to perform virtually every task for themselves. Moreover, manufactured goods were in short supply and luxury items very rare. At intervals, traders with carts traveled north from Chihuahua with goods and supplies. But the Chihuahua merchants charged exorbitant prices: early in the nineteenth century, a yard of calico—a crude, cotton cloth—sold for two or three dollars in New Mexico (Gregg, 1967: p. 7). Tools like axes and hoes sold at prices only the wealthiest colonist could afford.

Most colonists had little if any money to spend. They could not afford the prices the merchants asked and, at any rate, they had long learned to survive without the help of manufactured goods. They wove their own cloth and worked with homemade, crudely fashioned axes and hoes. They lived, for the most part, not in a money but in a barter economy. To get things they needed and wanted, the people of New Mexico attended fairs, like the one at Taos. At the fair a man might trade a horse for a homemade axe, the wool from his sheep for a bolt of finished cloth. Given this tradition, the Chihuahua merchants found that the trade with New Mexico was far from lucrative. Often they returned home with a good portion of the merchandise they had brought to New Mexico. The carts, always sporadic in their arrival, came less and less frequently and finally gave out altogether. New Mexico remained an impoverished colony.

The northern colonies badly needed the services their isolation denied them. The people needed doctors and surgeons and carpenters and blacksmiths. And although they could survive without many of the manufactured goods available only at high prices, they dreamed of owning these things. They dreamed also of luxury items—perfume, spices, silk cloth.

It became obvious very early in the colonial experience that Spain would not make goods available to the northern colonies. It was, therefore, natural that the colonists should welcome foreigners who might provide them with the things they wanted. Thus began the first really severe threat to Spanish sovereignty in the American possessions.

Spain, from the first, had done everything possible to isolate her colonies from foreign influences. She prohibited trade with other countries and forbade the immigration of foreigners to Spanish America. Spain planned to consume all the raw materials the colonies could produce and to supply all the goods the colonies could use. The system, designed to bring the greatest possible amount of capital into the royal treasury with the least possible effort, never worked. In the first place, Spanish merchants, selling to what they believed was a captive market, asked unreasonably high prices for their finished goods. Secondly, after Spanish sea power was desperately weakened by England in 1588, the fleets came less often to the New World. In all the population centers of Spanish America, the colonists developed a thriving black-market trade with men of other nations—England, France, the Netherlands. Smuggling continued to grow throughout the colonial period, totally undermining mercantilistic principles and creating in Spain fresh hysteria over the "foreign threat."

However, the frontier colonies of the far north benefited little from the black-market trade. Yet it was the northern frontier, bordering as it did on the territory of the rival nations, that most concerned the Spanish crown in this instance. There was reason for the concern. The northern frontier had the weakest defenses of all the Spanish colonies; but it was most in need of defense, for foreign interest in the area was very real.

The French Threat

France was the first nation to threaten Spain's hold over the frontier. French explorers and colonists had moved southward from Canada into Louisiana. That territory, like all of southern North America, had originally been claimed by Spain. In a series of eighteenth-century continental wars it passed back and forth between the two rival nations. But the French were well established in Lousiana before the end of the seventeenth century and their presence effectively split

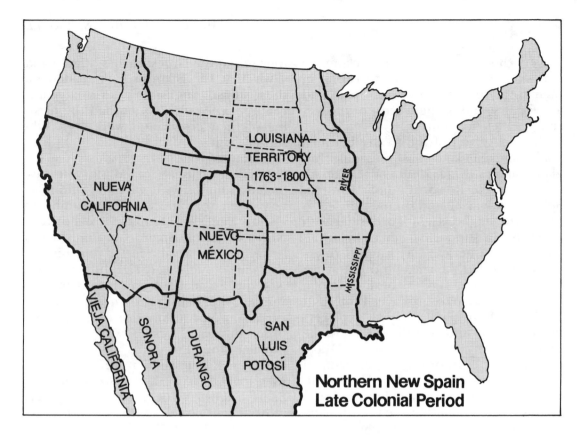

**Northern New Spain
Late Colonial Period**

Spanish territory in North America by separating Florida from Texas. The Spanish crown, quite naturally, feared French designs of additional territorial conquest. Indeed, the French were moving westward from Louisiana by the 1680s. They crept into Texas, finding little to hold them there, and on to New Mexico. Before many years had passed, New Mexican colonists realized that the French had some very useful skills to offer; they could fill the void in personal services. A few New Mexicans—mostly colonial officials—began to import French barbers and cooks, ignoring the regulations against the entry of foreigners into Spanish territory. The French, for their part, saw New Mexico as a territory ripe for trade and began looking for ways to develop a share in that trade. Beginning about 1714, Louis Juchereau de Saint Denis led the first of several French expeditions attempting to reach Santa Fe from Louisiana (Loomis and Nasatir, 1967: p. 11). The unsuccessful effort ended when Louisiana reverted to Spain in 1763, the spoils of victory of the Seven Years War. The French threat was temporarily relieved. But Spain could not yet relax.

The British Threat

The British in North America posed a more constant and more pressing threat. England and Spain were traditional enemies, long-time contenders for world power. Both sought to lay claim to America and increase the territory in their royal domain. However, Spain had arrived first and brought most of the territory under her control.

Another aspect of the rivalry between Spain and England was religious. England, under King Henry VIII, broke away from the Roman Catholic Church. Subsequently, England simply refused to recognize the Treaty of Tordesillas with which Spain supported her claim to almost all of America. The English rulers maintained that the treaty did not affect them; it was, they said, the brainchild of a Pope who had no control over Protestant England. On this basis English explorers sailed willfully into Spanish waters. In the sixteenth century, Sir Francis Drake explored the coast of California, claimed by Spain but as yet unsettled. English pirates like John Hawkins harassed the Spanish fleet on the high seas and made off with a fair share of the New World treasure. (The Dutch, who threatened Spanish sovereignty in the Caribbean were even more successful as pirates;

they seized the largest caches of gold and silver that the Spanish ever loaded on their ships.) English pirates—sixteenth-century renegades—often had the blessing of their crown and were even subsidized by it.

England's rout of the Spanish Armada in 1588 further served to increase Spanish animosity. It gave England mastery of the seas and was the preamble to all-out English colonization of eastern North America. Spain could only stand by while her rival created colonies in lands she thought were rightfully Spanish. Nor did Spain have any means of preventing the British expansion that occurred in North America over the next two centuries. England won control of Canada from France as an outcome of the French and Indian War and established outposts as far west as Oregon. Soon English settlers and adventurers moved southward to the Texas coast. Thus, by the mid-eighteenth century Spain was feeling the pressure of English expansion on both sides of the North American continent.

The Russian and Indian Threats

Still a third party compounded the threat of foreign invasion of shaky Spanish frontier possessions: Russians, enjoying an era of unparalleled expansion themselves, crossed the Bering Strait and claimed Alaska. From there they began to move southward along the coastline, profiting from fur trapping and trade with the Indians. They established settlements and outposts along the way. By the time the southernmost Russian settlement had been founded at Fort Ross, California, a few miles north of San Francisco Bay, frightened Spanish au-

thorities had decided something had to be done to halt the advance of the foreigners.

Added to the foreign intrusions, of course, was the Indian threat that had always plagued the frontier colonies. Thus the Spaniards decided that mission settlements in California and Texas (chapter 7) would perform two important tasks. Settlement of the frontier would discourage foreigners seeking virgin territory; and the missions, by pacifying the Indians, would leave Spanish frontier authorities free to deal with the more insidious foreign threat. Spain, therefore, went all out in an effort to subdue the hostile Indian tribes.

Pacification involved, first of all, missionary efforts designed to impose Spanish culture on the Indians. But the Spaniards also used diplomacy in dealing with nomadic, and often hostile, tribes. They sent pacified Indians as colonists among the non-Christian tribes, hoping that hostile Indians would follow the example of their more peaceful brothers. These ef-

forts were subsidized by royal funds and the program was, to a large degree, successful. By 1800, Spanish efforts had generally overcome the Indian threat to the more settled parts of the northern frontier. Pacification of unsettled regions—Arizona, for instance, and parts of Texas and New Mexico—was never successful, and it was hampered by colonists who, in an effort to enrich themselves, willingly sold weapons to the Indians.

The Spanish Defense System

The Spaniards, as part of the effort, created a defense system for the northern frontier. It was based on the model of protection for the mining areas of New Spain (chapter 5)—forts and garrisons intended more to protect the mines and population centers of New Spain than the northern colonies. A chain of forts eventually stretched from Texas to California. Defense of the frontier colonies was divided between two forces. The burden of defense lay with the militia, an ill-equipped civilian force called up in time of emergency. All men between the ages of sixteen and forty were required to serve in the militia for a period of ten years. They had to supply their own horses and arms; as a result, their forces had few of either. The civilian soldiers were given periodic training, but the militia was generally poorly trained and lacked discipline.

The second force, the regular army, was not much better off. Spanish colonial armies were made up of volunteers and there was very little to attract recruits to the ranks. Soldiers received minimal wages and faced long duty at isolated forts. They had little chance of advance-

ment, for officers' commissions were restricted to the peninsulares and a few creoles. Poor discipline and morale disrupted the regular army and limited its efficiency. Desertion was a common offense and was rarely punished. Defense of the frontier was further hindered by poor communications, poor transportation, and inadequate finances. By 1776, twenty-two *presidios* (forts) stretched from Texas to California, manned by a total of only 907 soldiers. Needless to say, the defense of the colonies depended on the ragged militia rather than on a few unhappy soldiers.

Spain reorganized the northern frontier and with it the defense system in 1776. The frontier was made a separate military unit, independent of New Spain. The authorities felt that by this action they could better deal with the foreign threat, which had replaced the Indian threat as uppermost in the Spanish mind.

The crown appointed Teodoro de Croix as chief administrator of the northern colonies and charged him with the task of strengthening frontier defenses. De Croix relocated some of the presidios and garrisons, established new

Los Angeles

In 1769 a Spanish expedition of 63 men led by Protolá left their ships and marched four hundred miles through California terrain that had never before been traversed by Europeans. They camped near asphalt pits on a site which they felt had all the requirements for a large settlement. They named it for Our Lady of the Angels—El Puebla de Nuestra Señora la Reina de Los Angeles de Porciuncula.

In 1771 two Franciscan priests, Fathers Somera and Cambón, founded a mission at this location after another site farther south proved unsuitable. The hostile Indians made peace with the Spaniards when a painting of the Virgin was shown to them. Soon afterward, however, a soldier insulted a chieftain, who fired an arrow at the Spaniard. The soldier shot the Indian dead and cut off his head. This severely hampered the padres in their efforts to make conversions.

In 1781 the *pueblo* of the Los Angeles was founded by Governor Phillipe de Neve. The first settlers were eleven families recruited from Sonora and Sinaloa who were of mixed ancestry—European, Indian, and Negro. Due to their indifference the first church was not erected until 1822, and then only with the help of the other California missions. Ten years later a resident priest was appointed.

Mexicans remained the major population group in Los Angeles until Anglos began pouring in following the Gold Rush of 1849. Today, three-quarters of a million people of Mexican descent live in the Los Angeles metropolitan area—the greatest urban concentration of Mexicans outside of Mexico City, Guadalajara, and Monterrey.

---

ones, and abandoned others—a process that would be repeated many times during the remaining years of the colonial period. Most important, though, he increased the number of soldiers manning the frontier outposts. By the end of his administration, the number of soldiers stationed on that portion of the frontier from Sonora to Texas alone had risen to 4,686 (Jones, 1966: p. 12). During the period of de Croix's tenure, Spain made a real effort to strengthen the defense system. Unfortunately, the mother country was directing the effort from a distance of thousands of miles and had little understanding of the real needs of the colonists. The crown's main interest continued to be the creation of a chain of forts to protect New Spain, not the frontier colonies. As a result, the new forts stretched along the same Texas-to-California line as before and continued up the coast of California to protect the ocean frontier. New Mexico was left outside the perimeter of the system and forced to continue defending itself, as much as possible, with a rough militia.

The presidios represented still another economic burden for the northern colonies. Soldiers and their families (who usually followed them to their duty stations) had to be fed and housed. Their needs presented a problem even in agriculturally rich California. The missions, while large-scale agricultural enterprises, concentrated on the cultivation of orchards and vineyards. They grew crops to feed themselves but were in no way prepared to feed the swelling population of the presidios as well. Therefore, Spain ordered the settlement of various civilian communities. These settlements were to have a dual purpose: to feed the presidios and forestall the advance of the English and Russians down the coast of California. It is amazing that any of the communities survived. The *pueblo* (village) of San Jose was founded in 1777 by only fourteen men—five civilians and nine soldiers (Clark, 1959: p. 9). Its purpose was to grow grain and vegetables to feed nearby Mission Santa Clara and the military outpost at San Francisco. Los Angeles was founded on a similar basis in 1781. Its twelve founding families (a total of forty-four persons) had been recruited to raise cattle and crops to supply the four California presidios (Forbes, 1964: pp. 148–49). But in its earliest days, the pueblo never did more than support itself.

(Incidentally, the racial composition of early Los Angeles has been regarded as representative of the frontier colonies as a whole. Records show that of the twelve family heads who founded the pueblo, two were Spaniards, four were Indians from the province of Nueva Viscaya in Mexico, one mestizo, two Negroes, two mulattos, and one Chinese [ibid.].)

Most of the civilian settlements were too small to support and protect themselves, much less aid the presidios. In the 1780s, Governor Juan Bautista de Anza tried to remedy the situation by reorganizing the settlements. He ordered that each Spanish town across the frontier should have a minimum of twenty families and all homes should be equipped with gunports. This was really important only in New Mexico, still under attack by Indians. It was an effort to consolidate the settlements and it did not work. The settlers ignored the order, refusing to give up their homes and farms and be herded into the confines of a village. Those who already lived in villages objected to being relocated to other, larger communities. And so, by the end of the eighteenth century, life on the frontier was little changed from what it had been a century or two before.

But drastic change was just around the corner. It was a change wrought by a foreign threat more severe than any Spain had yet experienced and it would end with the transformation of the frontier colonies. The seeds of modern southwestern society were about to be planted.

REFERENCES

Clark, Margaret. *Health in Mexican American Culture: A Community Study.* Berkeley: University of California Press, 1959.

Forbes, Jack D. *The Indians in America's Past.* Englewood Cliffs: Prentice-Hall, 1964.

Gregg, Josiah. *The Commerce of the Prairies.* Lincoln: University of Nebraska Press, 1967. A facsimile reproduction.

Jones, Oakah L., Jr. *Pueblo Warriors and Spanish Conquest.* Norman: University of Oklahoma Press, 1966.

Loomis, Noel H., and Nasatir, Abraham P. *Pedro Vial and the Roads to New Spain.* Norman: University of Oklahoma Press, 1967.

CHAPTER 9 | Threatened Colonies II: The Anglo Invasion

The United States began to pose a new threat to Spanish sovereignty on the northern frontier before the end of the eighteenth century. It was a threat more active and more complex than the British, French, or Russians had presented. Before many years had passed, the threat was translated into an invasion of the Spanish frontier and that invasion changed the character of the culture and the society of the land. Anglo-American met Spanish American in the borderlands; the conflict and the blending of the two cultures provided the foundation of modern society.

The westward movement of English-speaking people had begun soon after England established her first colonies on the Atlantic seaboard. Like the Spaniards, Englishmen came from a country where few had owned land. They came to America filled with an all-consuming desire to own property. Land—vast expanses of it—would provide the basis for building a colony and a new life in a New World. As the lands along the coast were claimed, English colonists began to move inland. This movement characterized the English colonial period and continued, unabated,

after the United States had won its independence.

Before the end of the eighteenth century, American settlers in Ohio and Kentucky had begun to exert tremendous pressure on the Spanish authorities in Louisiana. They demanded of Spain the right of passage down the Mississippi River; the river was the only way for them to transport goods back and forth between their homes and the eastern cities. Overland routes were barred by mountains. The United States government, fearing that lack of communication might destroy the loyalty of the western territories and encourage settlers there to create a nation of their own, supported the Ohio and Kentucky settlers. But President Thomas Jefferson, who believed that rivers, like oceans, should be free for men of all nations to travel, took the argument one step further; he demanded of Spain the use of a port (New Orleans) at the mouth of the Mississippi.

That the American settlers won these rights from Spain is a moot point. France regained Louisiana after their armies had defeated Spanish forces on the European continent. Napoleon Bonaparte, seeking new funds to finance his schemes for military conquest, sold Louisiana to the United States.

The Louisiana Purchase dealt a harsh blow to Spanish security. It brought the United States up to the very borders of Spanish territory. An aggressive young nation looked westward from Louisiana to the Pacific Ocean. Increasing numbers of Americans began to dream of occupying the entire continent. Only 2,000 miles of Spanish territory separated the Americans from fulfillment of that dream. They were encouraged by the few people who had already moved in that direction; for by the time the United States had bought Louisiana, the Anglo invasion had already begun.

Invasion of New Mexico

The Americans in Kentucky found more to their liking in Spanish territory than just a river which provided an ideal means of transportation. These frontiersmen saw a great opportunity for self-enrichment in Spanish territories. During this period, beaver fur, used to make men's hats, was in great demand in the eastern United States and in Europe. Beaver were plentiful along the upper Rio Grande in New Mexico. But the colonial government allowed only permanent New Mexican residents to trap beaver and required them to buy special hunting licenses. Into this setting came the mountain men from Kentucky. They began entering New Mexico to trap beaver about 1790, creating untold turmoil among Spanish administrators. They trapped without licenses or purchased licenses from legal residents. Many were arrested and stripped of thousands of dollars worth of furs and supplies. But still they came, encouraged because others escaped and made immense fortunes from the sale of the beaver skins.

Every year the trappers came to Taos, New Mexico, to organize their supplies and prepare for the long trapping season ahead. And when the season was ended, they returned to Taos—filthy, bearded creatures, starved for contact with other

Fur trappers recounting their experiences around the campfire

human beings after a lonely winter in the mountains. In this fashion, the people of the Spanish frontier had their first encounters with the Americans. All too frequently they were appalled by what they saw. This Anglo, they said, is a wild man, an animal. Indeed, the trapper often was a wild man. He made his own laws and his manner was coarse and crude. He dressed in animal skins that became covered with the grime of many seasons. He was a fighter—a violent man who killed just for the pleasure of it, and it made little difference to him whether his victim was a wild animal or a man. He raised havoc in all the towns of New Mexico. And with the trapper as their model, the people of the frontier formed their impression of what all Americans—the Anglos—were like.

The trappers, for better or for worse, added yet another element to the growing diversity of the frontier populations. The beaver trade came to an abrupt end in the 1830s, when the fashion in men's hats changed. The trappers were cast adrift and many of them remained in New Mexico. Some eked out a living in the mountains. But others settled in colonial villages.

Merchants and the Santa Fe Trail

Trappers opened the road to New Mexico, but it was the merchants who really spearheaded the Anglo invasion of Spanish territory. New Mexico offered a lucrative market to any who wished to exploit it by offering goods at reasonable prices. But the trade probably evolved by accident. It began with trailblazing and led to the establishment of an easy route from Missouri to Santa Fe—the famous Santa Fe Trail. This route allowed mer-

chants to enter New Mexico while avoiding the hazards of illegal east-west travel through Spanish territories; by coming down from the north, they could sneak past most of the Spanish authorities. One John Peyton followed the trail as early as 1773 (Peñuelas, 1964: pp. 91–92), but little came of his efforts. Establishing the route of the Santa Fe Trail was left to Captain Zebulon M. Pike, who led an expedition to Santa Fe in 1806.

In the years that followed, a few traders with mules made their way from Missouri to New Mexico. But once they reached New Mexico, the traders faced merciless harassment by Spanish administrators. In 1812, colonial officials seized traders as spies, confiscated their wares, and threw them into jail in Chihuahua where they remained for nine years (Gregg, 1967: pp. 5–6).

However, a few merchants continued to brave the dangers, drawn by the great chance for profit which trade with New Mexico offered. Soon, the prevailing mood shifted in their favor.

Mexico began her struggle for independence in 1810. For the next eleven years both Spain and the revolutionary leaders generally ignored the frontier. Soon, American merchants discovered that they could sneak into New Mexico undetected, and even if they were discovered, little was done to halt their progress. They had made great inroads into the colonial market by the time the Mexicans won their independence. Almost immediately, the Mexican government took steps to ease the restrictions on commerce with foreign countries; and a group of people from Santa Fe traveled north to seek trade with American merchants. Early signs of willingness to trade were so encouraging that by 1826 the U.S. government was surveying a road

Early Sante Fe trade

from Missouri to Santa Fe (Branch, 1962: p. 113).

The volume of trade that developed soon surpassed the expectations of even the most optimistic merchants. The first serious traders started out with about five thousand dollars' worth of merchandise, carried on pack horses (Gregg, 1967: p. 7). By 1824, they were using wagons and carrying goods valued at up to thirty thousand dollars (Gregg, 1967: p. 10). And by 1846, the Santa Fe trade was valued at about one million dollars per year (Horgan, 1954: p. 503).

A Changing Community

The merchants provided goods that New Mexicans had done without for more than two centuries. But the traders provided New Mexico with much more than mere finished goods. They changed the entire life style of a community that, for two centuries, had been isolated from the lack of outside influences, a community that had changed little over the years for lack of external stimuli. Now, suddenly, the traders brought excitement and different ideas. The people of Santa Fe flocked to meet the arriving wagon

trains. Santa Fe was momentarily transformed from a quiet village to a lively market town.

In the bustle and excitement of the marketplace, Anglo-American traders and Santa Fe residents took another look at one another and added to the store of impressions that had developed since the first Anglo trappers entered the territory. For their part, the Mexicans—and of course, the people of the northern frontier were now Mexican citizens rather than Spanish subjects—still found the Anglos very strange characters. In appearance, the traders—who came to town dressed in their Sunday best—were the exact opposite of the early fur trappers. But their actions often intimidated the reserved and formal New Mexicans. The traders, adventurers every one, were boisterous and casual in their dealings with people, and during their stay they transformed quiet Santa Fe into a rowdy town. More than one anxious Santa Fe husband locked his wife and family in the house while the traders were in town. The people of Santa Fe never knew quite what to expect of their visitors, and so they usually expected the worst.

On the other hand, the traders thought

the Mexicans were outlandish creatures, too. They considered them idle, even to the point of laziness. Few traders could understand the language of the New Mexicans. But more important, few understood or sympathized with the people of a different culture. Almost all the customs of New Mexico were foreign to the Anglos. And the trader, aggressive and profit-oriented, developed a feeling of superiority toward the New Mexicans he met. Generally, he saw them in much the same light that the Spaniards had seen the Indians of Mexico three centuries earlier—as innocent, childlike people who needed to be educated in the ways of "civilized" society. It was hardly a good foundation for friendly relationships between the two peoples.

The Santa Fe trade grew much faster than anyone had expected. More and more Anglos poured into New Mexico and some of them stayed. The business represented power and profit for aggressive traders, but the Mexicans were not prepared for so many people or so much merchandise.

The Mexican government soon began to worry about the long-term effects of the trade and the consequences of Anglos moving into Mexican territory. Mexican authorities backed off from their original position favoring the trade. They ceased supporting the efforts to build a road from Missouri to Santa Fe. They stopped encouraging the trade and slowly developed a policy of actually hindering it. Soon, traders found they were being subjected to strict and thorough customs inspections at the Mexican border. They were repeatedly stopped at other towns along the trail and the whole customs examination repeated. Finally, in 1843, the president of Mexico, Antonio López de Santa Anna, outlawed the trade. But he had failed to take into consideration the reliance of the New Mexicans on merchandise from the north. They had suffered for centuries from lack of goods; now that the goods were available, they refused to give them up. Faced with a shocked and protesting population, Santa Anna was forced to rescind the law in 1844.

Anglo economic domination of New Mexico, based on the Santa Fe Trail trade, was virtually complete by the 1840s. Yet few Americans settled in New Mexico. Rather, it was Texas that bore the full weight of an invasion of Ameri-

Colonial family in New Mexico

can settlers. Especially inviting was East Texas, with its vast unsettled lands, its rich soil and mild climate. East Texas, not cut off from the United States by mountains or deserts, was open to invasion. And more Americans settled there than in all the other Spanish frontier areas combined.

Invasion of Texas

Americans began making their way into Texas before the end of the eighteenth century, perhaps as early as 1785. They first came with filibustering expeditions—private armies—fighting Indians and the few Spanish friars and families who had settled there. Soon, they were looking for plots of land and demonstrating a desire to settle down and make their homes in the region. Spanish colonial government, desperately anxious to establish settlements that would deter Indian attacks and French and English intrusions, willingly allowed a few Americans into the territory. It hoped such action would encourage Spanish colonization of Texas. Thus Spain issued a few land grants to Americans. In 1795, for example, three traders were granted 207,000 acres of land in Texas. But Spanish friendship soon gave way to fear.

The situation was in no way helped by the actions of Philip Nolan, a dashing, Irish-born adventurer. Nolan apparently dreamed of conquering Texas. He made his first recorded trip to the territory in 1791, when Spanish authorities arrested him as a spy and confiscated his wares (Loomis and Nasatir, 1967: p. 207). A few years later, in 1801, he led an armed expedition into Texas. Nolan, whose actions considerably damaged Spanish-American relations, was killed in a chance meeting with Spanish soldiers.

Despite the antagonism created by men like Nolan, the Spaniards did not halt Anglo immigration and the invasion of Texas began in earnest after the Louisiana Purchase brought the United States to the very edge of Spanish Texas.

The Austin Colony

In 1820, Moses Austin of Missouri obtained a charter from the Spanish government to settle three hundred American families in Texas (Peñuelas, 1964: p. 97). Under the charter's terms, the colonists agreed to become Spanish subjects, renouncing their American citizenship, and to accept the Roman Catholic faith. Moses Austin died before the effort got off the ground, but his son Stephen carried on with plans for the colony. Meanwhile, Mexican revolutionaries succeeded in winning their long-fought struggle for independence. The government delayed approval of Austin colony. Texas was still sparsely populated and the government, therefore, decided to permit Anglo colonization if the settlers would become Catholics and Mexican citizens.

By the time the Mexican government made its decisions in 1823 (Horgan, 1954: p. 459), approval of the Austin colony was immaterial. Stephen Austin had already, in 1821, led the settlers into Texas and founded the community of San Felipe de Austin. After that, Anglo settlement in Texas mushroomed. By 1835, there were probably between twenty-five and thirty-five thousand Americans living throughout Texas (Manuel, 1965: p. 16). In contrast, only about five thousand Mexicans lived there, and most of them had concentrated in the south, along the Rio Grande (McWilliams, 1949: p. 99).

The Mexican government quite naturally began to fear that the Americans might take over Texas by default, possession being nine-tenths of the law. Moreover, the Anglos nominally accepted Mexican citizenship, but more often than not ignored the requirement that they become Roman Catholics. This introduced an element of religious heterogeneity that the Mexican authorities considered potentially disruptive.

The Anglo settlers created further confusion by doing as they wanted, with little respect for Mexican law. The most important example of this occurred over the issue of slavery. Mexico emancipated the slaves when independence was declared and, consequently, slavery was illegal in Texas. But most of the American settlers had migrated to Texas from the southern states. Their whole life style depended on maintaining the institution of slavery and they brought black slaves with them into Texas. In 1830, the frantic Mexican government forbade both the importation of slaves and further American immigration to Texas. But the steps were taken too late. The Anglos, vastly superior in numbers, paid little heed. Their overwhelming invasion had made the Mexican government a force without authority in Texas.

Invasion of California

California presented a third attractive target for American invasion. During the eighteenth century clipper ships sailing between Boston and the Far East had stopped in California ports. The sailors, on returning to New England, marveled over the California climate, scenery, and vast fields farmed by the friars and mission Indians. Snowbound victims of an eastern winter began to dream of a fairyland they had never seen. Soon, the dream was reinforced by the rapidly spreading idea that it was the Americans' God-given right to possess all the continent from Atlantic to Pacific—their Manifest Destiny. California and the Pacific Coast became the ultimate goal of American expansionists.

Mission Santa Clara in California, about 1840

Owing to its distance from the thirteen original colonies, American penetration of California was considerably behind that of Texas. About the time of Mexican independence, a few Anglo fur trappers were hunting in the mountains of eastern California. They were the trailblazers; they established routes across the mountains and the pioneers followed. Soon, a few Anglo men migrated to the larger towns of California, especially to San Francisco. These first immigrants were not guided by the ideals of Manifest Destiny, the goal of winning California for the United States. Instead, they came in search of opportunity and a new life for themselves. Most of them married the daughters of California's *gente de razón*— the wealthy and socially prominent families of the territory. They became Mexican citizens and (unlike the settlers in Texas) willingly accepted the Catholic faith. Many even adopted Spanish names. They were soon assimilated into Mexican society and played no part later in the American invasion.

The Anglo invasion of California really got underway in the 1840s. It was based on an advertising campaign. Most newspapers and popular magazines published in major East Coast cities carried advertisements extolling the virtues of California, the magnificent opportunities California could offer. Attracted by the real or imagined glories of the distant land, thousands of urban Americans dreamed of migrating. Some made the dream a reality by packing up their belongings and setting off across the continent.

Sutter and New Helvetia

One who backed the advertising campaign was John Sutter, a German wanderer who had immigrated to the United States and eventually landed in California. Sutter dreamed of becoming a feudal lord and he proposed that he be given a tract of land in the Sacramento Valley where he might establish a settlement. The area suited his needs, for that part of California was quite barren of European settlement; the friars had never succeeded in pacifying the Indians of the interior and Spanish settlement clung precariously to the narrow coastal shelf. Governor Alvarado of California, making the same error in judgment as the authorities in Texas, saw in Sutter's proposal a chance to create a buffer colony which would protect the coastal settlements. John Sutter was granted 50,000 acres of land.

Sutter called his little kingdom New Helvetia. He set out to build a strong military post and to encourage Americans and Europeans to settle in his colony. He was successful to some extent, but Anglo settlement of Mexican California never did reach the proportions it had in Texas. By 1845, there were only about seven hundred Americans in California— scarcely ten percent of the total white population, with New Helvetia boasting the greatest concentration of settlers (Cleland, 1962: p. 107). The full-scale invasion would not take place until after California had fallen to the United States (chapter 11).

The American invasion of Mexican territories would have far-reaching implications. It brought together peoples of different cultures and societies, people whose ideas and approaches to life were radically different. As we have seen, both thought the other group to be made up of the strangest possible creatures. Their initial timidity toward each other was intensified by the basic and growing animosity between Mexican authorities and Anglo settlers. Good relationships between the Anglos and the people of the frontier were marred by lack of communication—the inability to speak each other's language—and by the ruthless violence of fur trappers and the aggression of men like Philip Nolan.

Yet not all the early contacts were disagreeable. Indeed, they were more often friendly. In some areas, Mexicans and Anglos were drawn together to make a success of their farming and each learned from the other. Many of the American men who migrated to the frontier married Mexican women. Thus from the earliest days the two cultures began to fuse.

This peaceful blending process was interrupted by an era of conflict—and war. Texas, California, and New Mexico were to be a breeding ground for a conflict of cultures. And a wound that was opened a century ago has never healed.

REFERENCES

Branch, E. Douglas. *The Hunting of the Buffalo.* Lincoln: University of Nebraska Press, 1962.

Cleland, Robert Glass, *From Wilderness to Empire: A History of California.* New York: Alfred A. Knopf, 1962.

Gregg, Josiah, *The Commerce of the Prairies.* Lincoln: University of Nebraska Press, 1967. A facsimile reproduction.

Horgan, Paul. *Great River: The Rio Grande in North American History.* 2 vols. New York: Holt, Rinehart and Winston, 1954.

Loomis, Noel H., and Nasatir, Abraham P. *Pedro Vial and the Roads to New Spain.* Norman: University of Oklahoma Press, 1967.

Manuel, Herschel. *Spanish-Speaking Children of the Southwest.* Austin: University of Texas Press, 1965.

McWilliams, Carey. *North from Mexico.* Philadelphia: J. B. Lippincott, 1949.

Peñuelas, Marcelino C. *Lo Español en el Suroeste de los Estados Unidos.* Madrid: Ediciones Cultura Hispánica, 1964.

CHAPTER 10 | Frontier in Conflict

Conflict spread rapidly in the first few years that Mexicans and Americans shared the frontier. The conflict was multifaceted—between Mexican and Anglo, between Anglo and the Mexican government, between Mexican and Mexican government.

The conflict between Mexican and Anglo began as a result of the attitudes the two people developed during their earliest contacts. As we have seen, the relationships between the two were generally friendly. But early impressions are difficult to erase and certain stereotypes evolved and hardened. Americans often thought of Mexicans as lazy, cowardly, and backward; Mexicans saw Anglos as arrogant, rude, aggressive, and dishonest. Many people accepted these unfair generalizations rather than judging a man on his own merits and accomplishments. The result, of course, was a growing animosity.

Rebellion in Texas

The conflict between the people and the Mexican government evolved, on one hand, out of the Americans' lack of respect for Mexican law (chapter 9) and, on the other, out of the lack of any tradition of self-government on Mexico's northern frontier. Mexicans and Anglos alike wanted self-determination and were willing to fight for it. These combined factors of conflict created a situation that would eventually lead to violence.

The first violence, occurring in Texas, was directed against the Mexican government. Both Mexicans and Americans participated in rebellion against the government, but the Anglos, because of their numerical superiority in Texas (chapter 9), led and controlled the movement.

Anglo-Texan settlers became involved early in revolutionary activities. Trouble began soon after Spain was ousted from Mexico in 1821. After a brief flirtation with monarchy, independent Mexico adopted a democratic system of government. Self-governing states united under a central authority and the old Spanish

78

provinces of Nuevo León, Coahuila, and Texas were all united as one vast state.

Drive for Separate Statehood

The story of the Texans' rebellion against the federal government was, first of all, the story of a drive for separate statehood in Mexico. In May 1824, the province of Nuevo León won separate statehood. The Texans demanded the same status. They believed the territory as far south as the Rio Grande should be separated from Coahuila and should take its proper place among the states of Mexico.

Other factors soon compounded Mexico's problems with her northern province. In an era when new nations were forming and American people were breaking their ties with distant European mother countries, the people of Texas began to think of breaking their ties with a distant government in Mexico City. Many Mexicans and Anglos alike began to dream of building a new and independent republic. Moreover, as early as 1825, some Anglos began to think of bringing Texas into the United States. The Mexican government may have dealt calmly with demands for separate statehood, but ideas of total separation from Mexico were tantamount to treason and would have to be suppressed.

Land problems which the Anglo settlers created in Texas further complicated the situation. Newspaper advertisements in U.S. cities offered land for sale in Texas, vast expanses of it, and thousands of Americans purchased property. They flocked to Texas only to find that most of the advertisers had no claim to the land they sold. Many of the disappointed immigrants settled on lands that the Mexican government had set aside as part of the national domain, a sort of national forest or park not open to colonization. Agitated Mexican officials met with little success in driving the squatters off the land. The situation became still more explosive as some Anglos began seizing lands actually held by Mexican settlers; they attempted to force Mexicans off property that, in some instances, had been held by the same family for generations.

Edwards' Colony and the Fredonia Rebellion

New action was quickly introduced. The government of the state of Coahuila-Texas granted an American named Haden Edwards the right to settle eight hundred families near the old Spanish town of Nacogdoches. The grant encompassed a vast territory; to the west it stretched as far as the boundary of the Austin colony. When established, it would be far larger than the original Austin colony. The contract between Edwards and the government required that he respect the rights of settlers already living within the territory of the grant so long as they could prove ownership of the land. Therein lay the seeds of rebellion.

In September 1825, Haden Edwards demanded that all the people living in the territory of his grant produce proof of land ownership. He offered those who could not do so the option of either leaving or purchasing from him the territory they claimed. Almost none of the Anglos who lived near Nacogdoches owned the land they had settled; many were among those who had purchased land from dishonest Anglo real estate agents. Even fewer of the Mexicans possessed the title—the piece of paper—to their property, although the families may have held the land as far back as the eighteenth century. But all these people, having established their claim by virtue of their physical possession of the land, steadfastly refused to bow to Edwards' demands. He then threatened to drive them off the land by force.

The settlers, first the Mexicans and later the Anglos, turned to the state government as their only recourse against Edwards' demands. A barrage of complaints and grievances was directed at officials in the capital city of Saltillo. The complaints finally became so frantic and the popular opposition to Edwards' authority so intense that the government realized it would have to take some action. The alternative would be a rebellion of united Mexican and Anglo settlers against the government, with the possibility of much bloodshed and the establishment of an independent state. Consequently, government officials decided to cancel Edwards' colonization contract.

Haden Edwards and his brother Benjamin responded with their own little rebellion. They declared independence, proclaiming the establishment of the "Republic of Fredonia." Benjamin led a small force into Nacogdoches, where his men barricaded themselves behind walls and prepared to fight it out. But the Fredonians never had a chance. In the first place, the rebellion included, at most, only about thirty men (Hollon, 1968: p. 112). Independence, particularly under Edwards' leadership, failed to win support from either Mexican or Anglo settlers. In the second place, Stephen Austin supported the Mexican government, demonstrating that Anglo-Texans, despite separatist ideas that might be gaining favor among a few colonists, were not yet ready to break the bond with Mexico. Austin called up his militia to join the Mexican forces marching to put down the Fredonian Rebellion. In the face of strong military opposition, the Republic of Fredonia collapsed and Edwards and his settlers were expelled from Texas.

Mexican Reaction

The rebellion, futile and easily suppressed, seems scarcely worthy of the prominence it achieved. But the Mexican government saw it as a sign of things to come, and Anglo settlement in Texas suddenly appeared to be dangerous. The potential for a full-scale Anglo rebellion combined with growing U.S. interest in Texas to increase problems for Mexican officials. In 1827, U.S. Secretary of State Henry Clay authorized an offer of one million dollars to Mexico if that nation would recognize the Rio Grande as the border with the United States (Horgan, 1954: p. 478). (As American interest in Texas increased, the offer eventually rose to five million dollars.)

The Mexican government reacted by imposing tighter controls on the Texans. This certainly had a great deal to do with the closing of the frontier to Anglo-American immigration in 1830. It also meant new, heavier taxes and stricter laws governing Texas. Quite naturally, the Anglos were the specific target of these measures. For instance, the state government of Coahuila-Texas made trouble for American shipping interests on the Rio Grande with a new law taxing only American-owned ships. Anglo resentment toward Mexican authorities was further augmented when, in 1830, General Manuel de Mier y Téran of the Mexican army led a force into Texas with the intention of expelling Stephen Austin and all the Americans who had settled in the Austin colony. The effort did not succeed, for General Mier led a vagabond

Stephen F. Austin

Stephen F. Austin (1793–1836) received permission from the Mexican government in 1823 to establish a settlement in Texas, provided the American colonists became Mexican citizens, practiced the Catholic religion, and observed all Mexican laws, including the prohibition of slavery. Fifteen other *impresarios* soon founded their own settlement. The Mexican government hoped the colonies in Texas would provide a barrier against American expansion.

When Austin parceled out land to his colonists, each family interested in farming was given 177 acres, and stockraisers were eligible for 4,428 acres. Most of the families declared that they intended to raise cattle. Austin himself received 97,416 acres because he was the founder. By the end of 1824, 297 titles to land were issued. These first settlers selected the best land along the Brazos, Colorado, and Bernard rivers. They came to be known as the "Old Three Hundred." Austin later enlarged his colony considerably.

Within ten years there were from twenty to thirty thousand Americans in Texas. Many, including Austin, had slaves working their cotton fields, at a time when slavery was becoming an important issue in the United States. The Texans did not get along well with Mexican authorities and rarely fulfilled the conditions of settlement set by Mexico.

With the continuous turbulence and instability of the Mexican government, officials of the Mexican state of Coahuila were unable to maintain law and order in Texas. Austin was sent to Mexico City in 1833 with a petition that Texas be made a separate state of Mexico. Thinking that Austin advocated rebellion, the Mexicans jailed him for eighteen months. Conditions remained tense when Austin finally was released. When he returned to Texas his speech in favor of independence marked the beginning of war between Texas and Mexico. Texas became the Lone Star Republic because the northern states opposed the admission of another slave state into the Union.

After the war Austin lost the election for president of Texas to war hero Sam Houston. He died shortly thereafter in 1836. Today Austin is remembered as the father of Texas.

---

army that was not interested in fighting. He established some military posts in Texas and then led his men back to Matamoros on the south bank of the Rio Grande.

The Campaign Intensifies

With the benefit of more than a hundred years' hindsight, we see clearly now that the attitude and actions of the Mexican government created negative reactions. As controls tightened, discontent intensified among both Mexicans and Anglo settlers, and by 1832 Texas was in a state of rebellion. Anglo Texans had built up a supply of weapons and a fleet of river schooners. In June, this little "navy" attacked the fort on Galveston Bay and defeated the Mexican force posted there. It was the first incidence of antigovernment violence since the Fredonian Rebellion. But unlike the Fredonians, these Texans were not asking for independence. They wanted only two

things: both Mexican and Anglo settlers wanted Texas established as a separate state (independent of Coahuila) within the Mexican federation; in addition the Anglo Texans, the majority of the population, asked for relief from laws prohibiting further American immigration. The Mexican government, although petitioned repeatedly by its Texas citizens, took no action on either issue.

Finally, in September 1832, the Texans decided to take matters into their own hands. A convention was called to discuss separate statehood. It met in defiance of an 1824 law denying the people the right of assembly. Among its delegates were Mexicans, Americans, and European settlers.

Meanwhile, a revolution in Mexico had brought an old familiar figure to power: Antonio López de Santa Anna. The Texans generally supported Santa Anna, feeling that he would be more sympathetic to their cause. They were soon to discover that he was not a friend but an implacable enemy who viewed every action that was not in the interests of his government as a personal affront. This became evident after the Texas statehood convention reconvened in April 1833. The delegates framed a petition appealing for statehood and drafted a state constitution. Communication between the capital and the provinces was still haphazard at best. For a time the Mexican government erroneously believed the Texans had declared independence. When the misunderstanding was corrected, the government refused the Texans' appeal.

Stephen Austin traveled to Mexico City in a futile effort to persuade Santa Anna to change his mind and allow Texas its separate statehood. After several frustrating months waiting for an appointment to see the president, he wrote home saying that Texas should go ahead with plans for separate statehood, no matter what the government said. Santa Anna eventually met with Austin and made a number of concessions to the Texans. But when Austin's letter was discovered, he revoked the concessions and held Austin in prison for several months. The positions of both camps hardened. The hope of peaceful settlement was extinguished. Texas chose to fight.

First Skirmishes

Early in the summer of 1835, thirty Texans under the command of William Travis captured the customs garrison at Anahuac (Horgan, 1954: p. 517). A retaliatory Mexican force, commanded by General Martín Perfecto de Cos, sailed up the Rio Grande from Matamoros in small boats and was soundly defeated. A few months later the Texans seized the garrison at Goliad with its vast store of supplies.

Even while these skirmishes were taking place, the convention met again to form a state government and the new government once again swore the loyalty of Texas to Mexico. Then, on December 5, Texan armies seized the Alamo Mission (which was then a military supply depot) and all of its provisions. Thus San Antonio, the chief city of Texas, fell to the rebels. The Mexican government was forced to sign a treaty with the Texans agreeing to all their demands.

Antonio López de Santa Anna was enraged by the Texans' action. He took it as a personal insult which he was determined to avenge with his last ounce of strength. But because of his strong reaction, the Texans, floundering through their first difficult days of self-government with weak-willed officials and undefined goals, were drawn together in a common cause. The inevitable result of the continued conflict would be a complete and final break with Mexico.

Santa Anna began raising an army, thousands of men strong, to attack Texas. He decided he would command the forces himself. The Texans countered by preparing to invade Mexico at Matamoros. In doing so, they withdrew all but a few men from the Alamo garrison—at the very time General Santa Anna prepared to attack the Alamo. He was in no hurry. While he waited for more troops, he placed his guns and spent several days casually lobbing shells at the old mission. While Santa Anna thus pinned a few Texans inside the Alamo, fifty-eight delegates (including only three Mexicans) met at Washington-on-the-Brazos. On March 2, 1836, they declared Texas an independent republic.

It seemed the Texans would have to fight for all they were worth to secure their independence. But in reality, the war was short. Texas suffered a major

Fall of the Alamo

fect. The hatred engendered among Anglos by their defeat at the hands of Antonio López de Santa Anna was directed not only at Mexico but also at Texans of Mexican descent, a fact which promised ill for the future of the territory.

Santa Anna had won a decisive victory. At that point Texas was his; he could have exacted whatever terms he chose with all the traditional harshness of a conqueror. Instead, he made a fatal strategic error. He withdrew from San Antonio and, reaching a place called San Jacinto, ordered his troops to stop for rest.

Santa Anna should have known—must have known—that the Texan forces which had gone to Matamoros would be hard on his heels. Indeed, to assure a victory over Texas, he should have hunted them down and attacked as soon as he had finished with the Alamo. Instead the Texans, led by Sam Houston, attacked Santa Anna's weary and unprepared army at San Jacinto. The battle was over quickly, leaving six hundred of Santa Anna's men dead. Only nine Texans were killed (Hollon, 1968: p. 123). Santa Anna was taken prisoner and the war was, in truth, over. The Texas victory cost Santa Anna his presidency. The dictator was soon overthrown—although later he returned to office more powerful than ever. The Mexican government, however, secured Santa Anna's release and withdrew its armies. Independence was an accomplished fact, although Mexico refused to recognize the Republic of Texas.

Thus ended the first major conflict between settlers and government. It was largely a revolt of Anglo-Texans against a government they had never chosen to respect. The part played by Mexicans in

defeat and followed it with a major victory; the whole episode was finished with only two days of battle.

The Alamo

Mexican forces, ranging between 2,500 and 5,000 men, depending on the source one reads, attacked the Alamo before dawn on March 6. Within an hour they had killed the 182 Texans barricaded behind the mission walls. The rout of the Alamo united Texans against a common enemy. No matter what their personal views on politics, they all agreed that Mexico was the villain. But the episode of the Alamo had a more far-reaching ef-

Texas was necessarily small because they were vastly outnumbered by the Anglos. But the real importance of the event is that the fragmentation of Mexican terri- tory began with the loss of Texas. It was a process that would occupy most men's thoughts throughout the course of the next decade.

Conflict in New Mexico

The people and the government came to blows in New Mexico, too, But whereas the Anglos had played the major role in the fighting in Texas, the New Mexican conflict was between Mexicans and Mexi- can government.

New Mexico had no tradition of self- determination. From its earliest days it had been governed from afar. Colonial administrators sent there from Spain and Mexico City had little in common with the settlers and followed the directives of superiors who had even less understand- ing of the needs of the northern colony. When Mexico won her independence, the Kingdom of New Mexico became a state of the new republic, and the people, briefly, saw a chance to gain a voice in government. For a time, native New Mex- icans held the top posts in the state. How- ever, in 1824, New Mexico was demoted to the position of territorial department, part of the larger State of Chihuahua.

Like the Texans, the New Mexicans re- sented their lack of autonomy. They had had a taste of self-government and liked it. Moreover, they were rapidly absorbing the ideas of freedom and state autonomy held by American traders and the few Anglo settlers who had come to New Mexico. Throughout the colonial period, the New Mexicans had accepted being governed by outsiders. Now they were resentful when Santa Anna appointed an outsider, Colonel Albino Pérez, to rule the territory. The political cauldron was beginning to boil.

But political discontent was only one aspect of the New Mexican conflict with the government. Another was economic, and this affected the entire population on the most basic level—that of personal sur- vival. The Mexican treasury was increas- ingly in need of money during the first years of independence, and one way to get it was to levy taxes and duties. The government felt that the northern prov- inces were especially susceptible to these measures because distance would prevent them from effectively fighting back.

1837 Revolt

We have seen some of the influence of taxation on the Texas revolution. A similar situation developed in New Mexico. Like the Anglo-Texans, the New Mexicans felt that they had been singled out for eco- nomic discrimination when direct taxes were imposed. The government instituted various new taxes in 1837. A woodcutter, for example, was required to buy a license costing five dollars a month, and shep- herds had to pay twenty-five cents a head to take their sheep through Santa Fe (Horgan, 1954: p. 552). As rumors of additional, heavier taxes spread, the agitated New Mexicans finally revolted.

The first victories went to the New Mexicans. Aided by Indian allies, they forced Colonel Pérez and his troops to beat a hasty retreat. The Indians caught Pérez and beheaded him. Flushed with success, the rebels then repudiated Governor Manuel Armijo and elected José Gonzáles in his place. But in time the rebellion became its own victim, for New Mexico was plagued by internal disorder and dissension even within the rebel forces. Armijo, after remaining in Santa Fe for a time to try working with the new government suddenly fled to Albuquerque. There he began gathering a force of loyal supporters to oppose Gonzáles. At the same time, a hardy opposition to the new government emerged in Santa Fe. Its leader, General José Caballero, threw his support to Armijo. And in late September 1837, less than two months after the revolt erupted, Armijo led a volunteer army north. He captured Santa Fe and proclaimed himself governor. The New Mexican revolt collapsed totally in January 1838, when loyalist forces defeated the rebels and Gonzáles was killed in battle. New Mexico, after a few skirmishes, was once again firmly in government hands.

The angry Mexican government steadfastly believed that the Americans were responsible for the revolt, as they had been in Texas. In quick and arbitrary reaction, Governor Armijo placed a tariff of five hundred dollars on each wagonload of merchandise that came down the Santa Fe Trail (Gregg, 1967: p. 104). Unfortunately, the New Mexicans suffered most from this act, for prices soon reflected the additional cost of bringing goods into New Mexico.

Texans Intervene

But a few years later it appeared that Mexico was justified in its attitude. In 1841, the Texans took it upon themselves to "save" New Mexico from the tyranny of Governor Armijo. Their real purpose, however, was undoubtedly the annexation of New Mexico to the Republic of Texas. Northern New Mexico, the center of the 1837 rebellion, was still resentful, and the Texans imagined that the discontented elements of New Mexican society would soon join their forces. Volunteers from Texas, calling themselves the "Santa Fe Pioneers," set off for New Mexico. Their expedition, however, was a dismal failure. They were poorly prepared. No one knew the route to New Mexico; they traveled slowly and were often lost; their food ran out and hunger threatened to force them back to Texas. Moreover, they were mistaken about the attitude of the New Mexicans.

Most New Mexicans saw the Texas volunteers as a threat to their security. Once split by dissension, New Mexicans now united to face the invaders from Texas—much as the Anglo-Texans themselves had united after the battle of the Alamo. To be on the safe side, Governor Armijo tightened his security network and when the Texans arrived at Santa Fe they were unceremoniously thrown into jail. Thus the New Mexican revolt dissipated, leaving the territory little changed politically from what it had been a few years earlier, or even a few centuries earlier.

For all that the Mexican government accused Americans (and through them the United States) of fomenting the revolts in New Mexico and Texas, those uprisings could not be explained so simply. More realistically, they were bred of centuries-old problems that had plagued the frontier: the lack of communication with the capital and the failure of officials to understand the needs of people far removed from the centers of authority and the lack of goods and services which could have made frontier living less difficult. In themselves, these problems were enough to create dissension and a desire for independent action among the people of isolated provinces. Indeed these were the problems that sparked the first defiant actions by frontier citizens.

But Mexican fears were not without basis, as was shown within a very few years. Texas, with its overwhelming majority of American settlers, pulled the United States into the center of the political arena. Soon a new and more serious conflict shook the frontier—a conflict between Mexico and the United States. Its outcome would be the ultimate violence: war between two sovereign nations.

REFERENCES

Gregg, Josiah. *The Commerce of the Prairies*. Linclon: University of Nebraska Press, 1967. A facsimile reproduction.

Hollon, W. Eugene. *The Southwest: Old and New*. Lincoln: University of Nebraska Press, 1968.

Horgan, Paul. *Great River: The Rio Grande River in North American History*. 2 vols. New York: Holt, Rinehart, and Winston, 1954.

CHAPTER 11 | The Ultimate Violence

The presence of large numbers of American settlers in Mexican territory was bound to create interest in that territory on the part of the U.S. government. But at least three other factors augmented that interest: American expansionism, the Monroe Doctrine, and the slavery issue.

Expansionism

Expansionism was an integral part of nineteenth-century American life. From the earliest days of English colonization, land hunger and population pressure had driven people westward, away from the settled regions of the Atlantic seaboard. Within a few years of independence, American citizens had come to believe that they had an unalienable, God-given right to occupy all the territory between the two great oceans, and that it was essential for them to do so.

This dogma, soon to be named Manifest Destiny, was in part the outgrowth of the aggressive nationalism of a young and still weak nation. But it was also based on myth. The population of the United States grew by leaps and bounds during those first few decades of independent life. It was thought that if the rate of population increase continued the existing territory of the United States would not be sufficient to house and feed the nation.

This frightening thought turned the eyes of the nation westward, toward vast expanses of sparsely populated or even uninhabited land. The fact that the land was held by Indians or, in the Southwest, Indians and Spanish-Mexican colonists, made little difference. The early nineteenth-century American quite simply believed that people inhabiting the land he wanted would have to move out of the way to make room for the multiplying millions. His attitudes were much like those of European colonists—Spanish as well as English—of an earlier century: the land, if he could conquer it, was rightfully his; and if he won it, he had proven his innate superiority over the conquered people.

Thus the Americans moved slowly westward, pushing the Indians farther and farther toward the interior of the continent, finally reaching territories held by another sovereign nation,

Manifest Destiny

In 1845 the summer issue of *United States Magazine and Democratic Review* contained an article which defended the annexation of Texas by the United States. The anonymous author upheld "our manifest destiny to overspread the continent alloted by Providence for the free development of our multiplying millions."

The phrase "manifest destiny" became a popular catchword in American history. With it people expressed their view that the territory of the United States should stretch from the Atlantic to the Pacific oceans.

Politicians of both the Democratic and Republican parties, journalists, and others used this phrase in the nineteenth century to stir up the imagination of the American people to make other territorial annexations appealing to them. The acquiring of Mexican territory after the Mexican War (1846–1848), the dispute with Great Britain over Oregon boundaries, the Alaska Purchase of 1867—all fell under the call of Manifest Destiny—the belief the United States was destined by the will of God to expand its boundaries to their natural limits.

Mexico. The Americans began settling on Mexican lands in large numbers during the 1820s. The early Anglo settlers often accepted Mexican citizenship, became Roman Catholics, even adopted Spanish names. But the U.S. government did not accept this renunciation of its authority and soon began to seek ways of bringing the territories under its own control.

The Monroe Doctrine

The Monroe Doctrine further contributed to U.S. interest in Mexican territory. Proclaimed by President James Monroe in 1824, it pledged U.S. protection for newly independent Latin American republics. It stated that the United States would never allow a European power to intervene in the affairs of the American nations or to establish new colonies in the Western Hemisphere. Monroe promised that the Latin Americans could count on the United States to defend their freedom from that day forward. This was the essence of Latin American-U.S. relations for many years to come; indeed, it still plays a definite role in those relations.

European powers tested the Monroe Doctrine repeatedly during the nineteenth century, and until late in the century, the United States was rarely strong enough to keep them from doing exactly as they pleased. In the 1840s, this testing served to further U.S. interest in Mexico's frontier territories. England negotiated the armistice between Texas and Mexico in 1843 and it was soon evident that she had designs for bringing Texas under her own protection. The United States, which had shown interest in purchasing Texas as early as 1827 (chapter 10), saw England as a rival. British activity in Texas was a violation of the Monroe Doctrine and, more important, a threat to U.S. security. The threat of European colonization, whether fanciful or realistic, quickly renewed American interest in Texas.

The Slavery Issue

Perhaps the most powerful motive behind the U.S. desire for the acquisition of new territory was the slavery issue. By the early years of the nineteenth century, the United States was rapidly being divided into two opposing camps: those who would abolish slavery and those who favored perpetuating it. As it turned out, the division occurred on a regional basis—the industrial, free-labor North versus the plantation, slave-economy South. The Constitution of the United States had given slave states the right to count three-fifths of the slaves (who, of course, could not vote and had no rights of citizenship) in determining the number of representatives each state would send to Washington. As a result, the southern states dominated the House of Representatives. They had an equal voice in the Senate (where each state has two senators) as long as the number of slave and free states remained equal. Naturally, it was important to both South and North to bring new states into the Union on their side and so increase their political power.

Texas—Mexican Texas—soon became the center of the controversy. The early Austin settlers had come from Missouri, a slave state. They brought their slaves with them, in defiance of Mexican law. Shortly, as the cotton kingdom moved westward, other southerners settled in east Texas. And they, too, brought slaves to tend and pick the cotton. Anglo Texans, frustrated in their dealings with the Mexican government (chapter 10), had sought to join the United States in the 1830s. But if Texas entered the Union it would do so as a slave state, giving proslavery forces an advantage in the Senate as well as the House. Northern opposition, combined with desire to avoid conflict with Mexico, led the United States to refuse the Texans' request for annexation. But in the next few years, as abolitionist power increased, it became very important to the South to bring Texas into the Union. Texas as a slave state represented security for the South, a deterrent to any House or Senate vote to abolish slavery. By 1842, this was a critical issue—the predominant issue in American politics.

Annexation of Texas

Texas acted as a catalyst. All the elements which argued for U.S. takeover of the region were present in Texas: Manifest Destiny, the Monroe Doctrine, and the slavery issue. But Texas statehood presented a problem very different from any the United States had so far experienced. New states to the east and north were simply attached to the United States without fanfare. American settlers had moved into the territory, driven out or subdued the Indians, and claimed basically unsettled, unattached lands for their country. Such areas were generally homogeneous, strictly American territories by the time they entered the Union. But Texas was an independent republic, claiming sovereignty in its own right. Moreover, it was a republic still claimed by Mexico, the mother country, which refused to recognized its independence. Nor was Texas homogeneous. Its population, while overwhelmingly American, also contained blacks, Mexicans, and Indians. The United States government hesitated to adopt this melee of peoples and their social and political problems.

While the Senate and House of Representatives pondered, the Republic of Texas became increasingly nationalistic. Once independence was won, in 1836, the Anglo Texans considered it less important to become part of the United States. The desire for U.S. protection faded. The feeling that they could make it on their own gained favor after Texas tried to borrow money from the United States and was refused. As the weeks and months passed, the Texans found themselves less and less in need of U.S. support. Indeed, in some quarters, anti-U.S. sentiment was growing. After all, if the Texans really needed aid, it was evident that they could turn to England. But few Texans expected to need assistance. They were a self-assured lot, confident that, having defeated Mexico once, they had nothing to fear in the future.

Independence had not brought peace, however. The vast territory between the Nueces and the Rio Grande was still in dispute, claimed by both Texas and Mexico. Neither country was strong enough to assert itself and make good its claim. Some Texans actually wanted to wage war on Mexico. They thought their chances of victory good, for Mexico was shaken by civil war in the years immediately following the battle at San Jacinto. But in reality, the Texans—disorganized and inefficiently governed—were not strong enough to prevent even a seriously weakened Mexico from using the disputed territory. The inability of the Republic of Texas to pursue its aims was clearly demonstrated when, in a single day in 1842, Mexican troops captured three garrisons held by the Texans. They withdrew two days later, but the warning was clear: Mexico, weakened though she was, possessed greater military power than the fledgling republic. Threats and attacks and ugly words passed between the two countries in the early 1840s. But it was apparent to most outsiders that Mexico and Texas were mere lambs pretending to be lions.

In the U.S. annexation became the central campaign issue of the 1844 presidential election. The election of the annexation candidate, James K. Polk, was seen as a victory for the expansionists—a mandate from the American people to bring Texas into the Union. Mexico had declared that any attempt to annex Texas would be considered an act of war, but Americans paid little attention. On February 25, 1845, the House of Representatives voted to offer the Republic of Texas statehood. A few days later the Senate agreed, and on July 4, the Texas Congress accepted the offer. To some people—anti-expansionists—it seemed sheer folly: the United States daring Mexico to go to war.

Whether Mexico would have gone to

war for Texas alone—a Texas already lost—is a question that cannot be answered. Some compromise might have been reached, diplomacy might have averted the sword. Mexico declared she did not want to engage in a war, but events in California damaged relations between Mexico and the United States to a point beyond repair.

California: Prelude to War

The United States had long been interested in acquiring California, a territory with rich agricultural potential which could also provide a window to the Pacific. During the 1830s, this desire took the form of a diplomatic campaign in which the United States sought to negotiate to purchase the territory. But in 1842, progress in that direction halted abruptly, thanks to the activities of Commodore Thomas Catesby Jones of the U.S. Navy.

Relations between Mexico and the United States had already been strained to the breaking point over Texas. Commodore Jones, in Callao, Peru, received a false report that war had broken out. His source further claimed that Mexico planned to cede California to England, thus keeping the terriory out of American hands. On the basis of this information, the commodore ordered his fleet north to join the war effort. On October 18, 1842, he captured Monterey, California, with its presidio and customshouse, and raised the American flag. Only at that point, evidently, did he learn that his country was not at war. Jones withdrew, apologizing profusely. The governor of California accepted the apology and there was little ill will felt in the province. However, the incident infuriated officials in Mexico City and the Mexican government immediately broke off all negotiations for the sale of California to the United States. In so doing, Mexico perhaps underrated American determination.

The U.S. government, it seemed, was willing to employ subversion to bring California under its control, and this activity further deteriorated relationships between the United States and Mexico. The first effort was an attempt to create a group of supporters, in effect a fifth column, among the Californians themselves. In 1845, the State Department sent an agent, Thomas O. Larkin, to California "to encourage the Californians to look to the United States for counsel and assistance" (Cleland, 1962: p. 98).

Larkin won leading Californians Mariano Vallejo and General José Castro over to his cause. Together they plotted to make California an independent republic. Larkin probably planned to create a second Texas and thought beyond independence to the time when California could be convinced to join the Union. Many Californians, and there were relatively few Anglos in the population, supported the notion of independence. But they soon shifted their position and Larkin's efforts proved worthless.

The change in sentiment was the direct result of the aggressive activities of John C. Fremont. We may never know how much support Fremont had from the U.S. government. It seems probable that he at least had unspoken, official approval. It also seems likely that he had the financial backing of John Sutter (chapter 9). At any rate, Fremont was an adventurer par excellence. He led armed expeditions into California and few Californians doubted what his main purpose was—conquest and self-aggrandizement. He aroused their fear and suspicion more than any other single man or government had done, and fear of Fremont soon became fear of all Americans.

For a time Fremont wandered about the valleys of central California, since he had promised the governing elements in California he would stay away from the coast—the militarily strategic coastline. But he soon chose to ignore the pledge. In February 1846, he marched to the Salinas Valley and established his camp within striking distance of the presidio at Monterey. General José Castro ordered Fremont to leave the province. Instead, the adventurer moved his camp to a stronger position. Castro gathered his cavalry and militia and prepared for battle, but neither force attacked. On March 9, during the night, Fremont broke camp and silently stole away to Oregon. The whole incident merely served as another irritant. The Californians were angered, alienated from the Americans, and any chance of peaceful annexation of California by the United States disintegrated. Moreover, Anglos and Mexicans living in California were now at swords' points.

The clash came on June 10, 1846. On that date the Anglo settlers of the Sacramento Valley, led by Ezekiel Merritt, revolted against the government of California. The uprising was very efficiently organized and it seems likely that John C. Fremont, returned from Oregon, had a role in planning it. The rebels marched under a banner with the crude figure of a bear on it, a standard which gave the incident its name: the Bear Flag Revolt. They seized a band of horses General Castro had gathered and raced to the town of Sonoma. There they captured Mariano Vallejo and carried him to Sutter's Fort, where he was imprisoned for the next several months. This accomplished, the rebels declared independence and proclaimed their Bear Flag Republic.

Mexican-American War

The Bear Flag Revolt was little more than a diversion. By the time it broke out, Mexican authorities in California were occupied with a far more serious problem. Mexico, pressed to the extreme by U.S. subversion, had declared war on the United States two months earlier. The threat of American armies and the prospect of hard-fought battles left the authorities all across the frontier little time to deal with internal disorders.

Both sides began to prepare many months before war was declared. In March 1845, after the U.S. Senate approved statehood for Texas, Mexico broke diplomatic relations with the United States and declared that she considered the annexation of Texas a hostile act. The United States added insult to injury when President Polk began to entertain the idea of acquiring all the land to the west of Texas—unwarranted aggression in Mexico's eyes. Then, in July, Polk ordered General Zachary Taylor to lead his army to Corpus Christi, Texas, on the Nueces River.

Officially, General Taylor was sent to Corpus Christi on a nonaggressive mission—to guard Texas against attack. Unofficially, the mission was a show of power, intended to frighten Mexico. But what a strange show of power! Taylor led one of the most motley armies imaginable. Mid-nineteenth-century armies were generally made up of volunteers. The U.S. Army paid its regular soldiers a paltry seven dollars a month (Horgan, 1954: p. 666) and attracted the dregs of society—escaped criminals, vagabonds, and adventurers. These soldiers were generally crude and tactless, seldom clean, and always arrogant. Their personal habits aside, they had one major failing as a fighting force: very few were trained in the arts of warfare. No wonder, then, that the Mexican government, hearing reports of Taylor's army, refused to be intimidated.

War fever spread rapidly in Mexico. Then a coup d'état brought an out-and-out warmonger, General Mariano Paredes y Arillago, to the presidency. The Paredes government sneered when the United States, still attempting to purchase the territory, offered Mexico $25 million dollars for a Rio Grande boundary and all lands west to the Pacific, and furthermore agreed to pay Mexican claims against Texans (Horgan, 1954: p. 606). Diplomacy had reached an impasse.

Polk's reaction was swift. He ordered Taylor's army to proceed to the Rio Grande, across the disputed territory claimed by both Mexico and Texas. Obviously, Mexico might consider this a violation of her territorial rights, an invasion by foreign troops. Still Mexico did not declare war. Taylor arrived at the Rio Grande in late March 1846, and the two armies settled down to wait, facing each other across the river. Each examined the other, measuring fighting capabilities.

Like cats stalking a mouse, they paced their respective sides of the river, waiting for the other to make the first move. The soldiers themselves developed a sort of friendly rivalry, shouting back and forth across the river, sometimes even socializing. But for the officers, the wait was a battle of nerves. Each side hoped to provoke the other and Taylor finally succeeded in causing the Mexicans to attack. On April 11, General Pedro de Ampudia of the Mexican Army arrived at Matamoros and demanded that the Americans retreat to the Nueces River. When Taylor refused, Mexican troops crossed the river. In retaliation, the U.S. Navy blockaded the mouth of the Rio Grande, thus cutting off Ampudia's access to the sea. On April 23, Mexico declared that a state of "defensive" war existed. The long-sought war had begun.

The Mexicans entered the war confident of victory. The troops Mexico had massed on the frontier were superior in numbers—three or four times as many men as in Taylor's army. And the Mexicans knew the desert terrain while the Americans did not. But they did not count on the fantastic effort the United States would put into this "little war." The U.S. Congress, in declaring war, authorized a volunteer army of fifty thousand men and appropriated ten million dollars to pay the costs of war. It soon became apparent that Mexico had no chance against the military machine of the United States.

Many Americans had wanted war. Most wanted to fulfill the dream of Manifest Destiny. But a few intellectuals began to see Mexico as a lamb being led to the slaughter and led the first antiwar protest in American history. Future leaders like Abraham Lincoln and Ulysses S. Grant protested that the war was unfair and unjust—a case of a strong nation bul-

Santa Anna

Antonio López de Santa Anna was born into a bourgeois Mexican family and trained at an early age for a military career. He was seventeen when he was first sent to the northern provinces to fight Indians. He advanced rapidly through the ranks while putting down the forces of Hidalgo, Morelos, and other rebels who fought for independence from the weak Spanish government in the years between 1811 and 1821.

When a harsh government came into power in Spain, Santa Anna quickly changed his allegiance to the rebel cause and was promoted to general. He acquired a reputation for bravery, daring, and ruthlessness in defeating the Spaniards and through taking part in many of the squabbles and internal uprisings that beset the early years of the Mexican republic. During his first term as president of Mexico he personally led Mexican troops at the battle of the Alamo, but was later captured by the Texans and eventually was returned to Mexico temporarily shorn of his power.

The loss of a leg in 1838 while repelling French invaders once again made him a national hero, and propelled him to the dictatorship of the country. In his up and down career he was the Mexican head of state on four different occasions. Whenever he fell from power, such as after losing the war with the U.S. from 1846–48, Santa Anna would retire to his ranch until he slowly became embroiled in another political intrigue.

He spent many of his later years in exile, but died on Mexican soil in 1876 at the age of 82.

---

lying and taking advantage of a weak one. Lincoln, a young man, refused to serve in the army that would fight the Mexicans. Henry David Thoreau, the philosopher, went to jail rather than pay taxes to support the war effort. When his poet friend Ralph Waldo Emerson asked what he was doing in jail, Thoreau responded by asking Emerson what he was doing *out* of jail. But the protesters were in the minority. The majority of Americans, like the Mexicans, were stricken with war fever. They fervently believed that Mexico, by standing in the way of the goals of Manifest Destiny, had wronged the United States and must be punished.

California Contest

The war was short, as wars go. The first decisive U.S. victory was in California. Early in July 1846—just weeks after

General Winfield Scott in Mexico City

the Bear Flag Revolt broke out—a U.S. naval force, under the command of Commodore John Sloat, captured Monterey and declared California an American possession. American forces occupied San Diego and Los Angeles, forcing California leaders (including the nimble General José Castro) to flee to Mexico. Bewildered Mexicans fought bitterly to save Los Angeles. Some five hundred to six hundred patriots, led by José Maria Flores, forced the Americans to withdraw from the city, and Los Angeles was not really subdued until after the war was over. But by the end of summer Mexico realized she had lost California.

Occupation of New Mexico

The war in New Mexico was similarly short. American forces marched to Santa Fe, the captial city, and raised the American flag. The occupation was bloodless, meeting little resistance. Few New Mexicans greeted the arriving troops; most stayed hidden in their homes and Santa Fe that day was a quiet town, the silence broken only by the sound of marching feet. Some have speculated that the New Mexicans may have welcomed American forces since these forces would provide a measure of protection against advancing Texans (chapter 10). Moreover, it is possible that any resistance was squelched by Governor Manuel Armijo, who reportedly received a large sum of money from an American agent in return for promising to hand New Mexico over peacefully. In any case, the Americans quickly established a military government in Santa Fe, promising to honor the civil and religious rights of New Mexicans. General Kearny, in charge of the American force, kept his word. But the peace was short-lived.

Despite their apparent apathy, the New Mexicans did manage to organize a revolt at Taos in January 1847. The rebels killed Americans and any Mexicans who accepted American rule. The first American civil governor, Charles Bent, was assassinated in the uprising. It was a bloody affair, but quickly suppressed. Donaciano Vigil, a wealthy New Mexican appointed acting governor, soon restored order. The priest who allegedly instigated the revolt, Father José Antonio Martínez, was suspended and later excommunicated, for other reasons. New Mexico, like California, was firmly in American hands.

Fighting in Mexico

The United States pursued the war to the very heart of Mexico. Indeed some Americans were beginning to believe that Mexico itself should be annexed to the United States. After all, they said, Mexico is part of North America; since it is our Manifest Destiny to control the entire continent, this necessarily includes Mexico. The U.S. government was unwilling to go quite so far, its main goal being merely to bring Mexico to her knees and conquer the Mexican frontier provinces. To achieve this, Mexican ports—especially the chief port of Veracruz—were blockaded. The action cut off Mexico from trade and overseas assistance and served to destroy the country's already shaky economy.

War brought severe economic hardship to Mexico as well as renewed political chaos. In 1847, President Paredes was ousted and Antonio López de Santa Anna once more returned to power. Internal disruption was so great that Mexico was ready for peace by the time General Winfield Scott led the American armies into the Valley of Mexico in the summer of 1847. The United States was also ready to end the conflict, as war was becoming an ever heavier burden.

An armistice was announced on August 24, 1847. But the Mexicans, fighting for survival as a nation, used the cease-fire to reinforce their troops and fortify their positions. Consequently, General Scott chose to end the armistice. On September 14, his troops stormed the fortress of Chapultepec Castle on the outskirts of Mexico City.

Chapultepec Castle was manned only by military cadets—mere students. These brave young men barricaded themselves behind the heavy walls, and from that position fought a heroic and bitter battle. Outnumbered by the enemy in both men and ammunition, the students literally fought to the death. And when it was clear that their cause was lost, those who had survived jumped from the windows of the castle, preferring to die on the rocks below rather than accept defeat and imprisonment by the Americans. Thus the cadets, the *niños heroes*, earned their place among Mexico's most honored patriots.

To all intents and purposes the war was over. Scott led his victorious army into Mexico City and Santa Anna's government fell, heralding the end of all resistance. Scarcely a year and a half had passed since Mexican troops had crossed the Rio Grande at Matamoros. And the American dream of controlling all the territory from the Atlantic to Pacific was about to be realized.

REFERENCES

Cleland, Robert Glass. *From Wilderness to Empire: A History of California.* New York: Alfred A. Knopf, 1962.

Horgan, Paul. *Great River: The Rio Grande in North American History.* 2 vols. New York: Holt, Rinehart, and Winston, 1954.

Rosenbaum, Robert J. *Mexicano Resistance in the Southwest.* Austin: University of Texas Press, 1981.

CHAPTER 12 | Heritage of Bitterness

The Mexican-American War created unparalleled bitterness and hostility toward the United States, not only in Mexico but throughout Latin America. The overwhelming U.S. victory and American treatment of the defeated nation showed Latin Americans a new image of the United States as the Colossus of the North, a great power firmly and arbitrarily imposing its will on weaker, defenseless Latin American nations. All of Latin America, but especially Mexico, was bitter and the bitterness would last well into the twentieth century. Even today, Latin American relationships with the United States are often marred by suspicion and distrust.

The basic instrument of this long-lasting bitterness was the treaty that ended the Mexican-American War.

Negotiations for peace between Mexico and the United States began, tentatively, before the last battles had been fought. Both parties wanted desperately to reach an agreement and began to seek a means of doing so as soon as the outcome of the war was apparent. But it would not do for the United States to send a high-ranking diplomat to open talks with a nation rapidly and systematically being thrashed on the battlefield. Thus President Polk ordered the chief clerk of the State Department, Nicholas P. Trist, to proceed to Mexico City. Trist's mission was to initiate peace talks with President Santa Anna of Mexico. But before he could make much headway, General Winfield Scott's troops entered Mexico City and Santa Anna's government collapsed.

Treaty of Guadalupe Hidalgo

Trist, ordered to return to Washington, refused to obey. Perhaps he saw a chance to earn recognition, to make a name for himself which would be remembered by future generations. Perhaps he was quite simply an idealist who believed that he could be the architect of a satisfactory and lasting peace between two warring nations. At any rate, he chose to remain in Mexico City. He

98

immediately started negotiating a peace settlement with the new government, and the treaty that finally settled the war was largely the work of this insignificant State Department clerk.

The talks continued throughout the autumn of 1847 and into the winter. The resulting treaty was signed at Guadalupe Hidalgo, a suburb of Mexico City, on February 2, 1848. Nicholas Trist had succeeded in his self-assigned task of creating an agreement between the United States and Mexico. Unfortunately, he is remembered not because of the lasting quality and success of that agreement but because of its failure. For the Treaty of Guadalupe Hidalgo contained the seeds of bitterness.

The United States, like most nineteenth-century nations, viewed victory in war as synonymous with territorial gain. Indeed, adding to one's territories had been the chief purpose of war by "civilized" nations throughout many past centuries. Consider, for instance, the way Spain and France had traded Louisiana back and forth at the conclusion of each war between them (see chapter 6); the acquisition of Canada by England as an outcome of war with France in the eighteenth century; or American takeover of Puerto Rico and the Philippines following war with Spain in 1898. The spoils of victory were almost always territory. Mexico, had she won the war, probably would have demanded similar concessions from the United States. But Mexico lost the war and the first purpose of the Treaty of Guadalupe Hidalgo was to turn a vast area of Mexican domain over to the United States. With the goal of officially gaining the new territory, the U.S. Senate ratified the treaty on March 10, 1848.

From our point of view today, the ratification seems a farce: only those articles which won the approval of the senators were ratified and the document that remains is a patchwork of deleted paragraphs. Thus the treaty ratified by the United States was not the treaty signed by the Mexicans. Mexico, in defeat, had little choice but to go along.

By the terms of the treaty, Mexico approved the prior (1845) U.S. annexation of Texas, thus ending twenty years of squabbling and warfare over the future of that territory. Furthermore, Mexico ceded a vast expanse of territory, long coveted by Americans, to the United States. The Mexican Cession fulfilled the goals of Manifest Destiny, including modern California, Arizona, New Mexico, Nevada, Colorado, Utah, and a bit of Wyoming. In return, the United States agreed to assume the war claims of Americans against Mexico and to pay Mexico the sum of $15 million. (This was later amended to $10 million, to be paid in two installments of $7 million and $3 million, respectively [Faulk, 1967: pp. 133–34].) Mexico thus lost more than half the territory which had been hers at the time of independence in 1821. Loss of territory was a bitter pill to swallow, made additionally so by the discovery of gold in California and subsequent economic development of the region (chapter 13).

The Treaty of Guadalupe Hidalgo, designed to end the war and increase the territory of the United States, made certain provisions for future relationships between the two countries. Its weakness in this respect, instead of smoothing the path into the future, created new problems, new animosity. Its architects left loopholes which would lead to future conflicts. Furthermore, Anglos living in the ceded territories cared little for documents. They were going to live as they chose, do as they pleased without regard for a piece of paper. Thus violations of the Treaty of Guadalupe Hidalgo, in spirit and in fact, were a common occurrence from the day it took effect.

"New Citizens"

The U.S. government, in assuming the new territories, also assumed responsibility for thousands of Mexicans living there. These people were given the choice of either leaving the conquered territory within one year or becoming American citizens. A few, very few, packed up their belongings and trekked south to land still held by Mexico. Most chose to stay in their established homes, seeing very little difference between one government and another. After all, the frontier had always been isolated from the machinery of government and it seemed likely to remain so. By staying, these people, whose ancestors had first been Spanish subjects and later Mexican citizens, now became American citizens. They became a new element in U.S. society—the Mexican Americans.

The Treaty of Guadalupe Hidalgo bound the United States to protect these newly acquired citizens and to guarantee their civil rights. It gave the Mexican Americans the right to retain their language, thus, in theory, compelling the government to publish its documents and conduct its business in both Spanish and English and necessitating the establishment of Spanish classes for Spanish-speaking schoolchildren. It gave them the right to retain their religion, to worship according to the rites of the Roman Catholic Church. And it gave them the right to retain their culture, to follow customs their families had practiced for generations and to celebrate the traditional fiestas without interference.

Even these basic civil guarantees were soon violated. As we have seen, the Anglos on the frontier had long before developed a superiority complex. They generally considered the Mexican a lazy, uncivilized person, reduced to a state of inferiority by his language, his religion, and his culture. In this atmosphere, the Mexican Americans were allowed to worship as they chose, but they were often ridiculed for doing so. And, in some areas, aggressive Anglos made it difficult for them to get to church or worked to drive the Catholic priest out of town.

Soon, English replaced Spanish as the language of the territory. The Mexican American who did not understand English was completely out of touch with the powers that controlled his existence. Since he could not understand, the Anglos were reinforced in their belief that all Mexicans were inferior. They felt justified in denying an inferior people equal rights. The provisions of the treaty were first violated and ultimately ignored. The Mexican American found he was, at best, a second-class citizen of his new country. The Mexican government, bitter but weak, was powerless to do anything but complain. Defeated, Mexico had no means of forcing the United States to enforce the guarantees of the treaty.

Under the terms of the treaty, the United States also accepted the task of policing the hostile frontier Indians. But the U.S. government was no more prepared or able to tackle the problem than

Treaty of Guadalupe Hidalgo
(February 2, 1848)

"Mexicans now established in territories previously belonging to Mexico, and which remain for the future within the limits of the United States, as defined by the present treaty, shall be free to continue where they now reside, or to remove at any time to the Mexican Republic, retaining the property which they possess in the said territories, or disposing thereof, and removing the proceeds wherever they please, without their being subjected, on this account, to any contribution, tax, or charge whatever.

"Those who shall prefer to remain in the said territories may either retain the title and rights of Mexican citizens, or acquire those of citizens of the United States. But they shall be under the obligation to make their election within one year from the date of the exchange of ratifications of this treaty; and those who shall remain in the said territories after the expiration of that year, without having declared their intention to retain the character of Mexicans, shall be considered to have elected to become citizens of the United States.

"In the said territories, property of every kind, now belonging to Mexicans not established there, shall be inviolably respected. The present owners, the heirs of these, and all Mexicans who may hereafter acquire said property by contract shall enjoy with respect to it guarantees equally ample as if the same belonged to citizens of the United States."—Article VIII, Treaty of Guadalupe Hidalgo

Although this treaty guaranteed the property rights of the former Mexicans, U.S. officials were reluctant to recognize the validity of Spanish and Mexican land grants. Newly arrived Americans were accustomed to Anglo-Saxon legal forms, surveys, and careful documentation. They disregarded the Mexican system of property laws and settled on the most desirable agricultural lands. The original landowners were forced to file claims to land their ancestors had owned for generations. They had to pay surveyors and hire lawyers who often demanded huge tracts of land for their services. Federal officials appointed to the territory undermined land grant claims by allowing documents in colonial and Mexican archives to decay or be sold for scrap. Many disputed land claims were tied up in the courts for decades and were generally decided in favor of powerful ranching and mining interests over land-grant holders.

Spanish or Mexican authorities had been in the past. For a time, the United States chose to ignore the Indians of the ceded territory, thus violating the treaty and incurring the wrath of Mexican officials. This article of the treaty was of special concern, for the Indians, generally peaceful for long periods of time, had taken advantage of the chaos and confusion brought about by war and the transfer of territory. Their attacks grew more fierce, more devastating. Unchecked, they raided farther south into Mexico.

The Mexican government refused to share the responsibility for control when Indians attacked deep in Mexican territory. Under the terms of the treaty, the United States was held responsible for damages. The United States, on the other hand, was also harassed by the attacks and felt that Mexico should take a part in the struggle to pacify the Indians, especially since much of the Indian activity took place well outside of American jurisdiction. The Indian threat remained a problem until the 1870s and contributed to strained relations between Mexico and the United States.

Continuing violations of the treaty and a sequence of events not covered by treaty complicated the situation that developed in the territory of the Mexican Cession. Loss of territory to a conqueror is always cause for bitterness. But much of the animosity that developed between conqueror and conquered after the Mexican-American War might have been avoided.

A Permanent Boundary

A major loophole in the Treaty of Guadalupe Hidalgo left room for further disagreement between Mexico and the United States. It concerned the establishment of a permanent boundary between the two nations. The treaty did not set that boundary, but merely provided for a joint Mexican-American commission to undertake the task. It is likely that this was left open because the United States, represented by Nicholas Trist, knew very little about the territory in question. Doubtless, the U.S. government wanted to fix a boundary that would be most advantageous to the Americans. This could be done only after a complete study of the area had taken place.

John B. Weller, appointed chief U.S. delegate to the commission, was instructed to make that study. Before meeting with Mexican commissioners in San Diego, California, he was directed to collect what information he could on the precious metals the region offered and on the flora and fauna. He was instructed to make a map and to recommend sites for a railroad, road, or canal—whichever would offer the most efficient means of transportation. All this took many months and produced volumes of documents on the nature of the territory—documents which had to be carefully examined in Washington before the commission could proceed.

The joint commission was scheduled to meet in May 1849, more than a year after the war had ended. But the Americans, traveling from the East Coast, were stranded in Panama for a month, unable to secure passage to California. They finally reached San Diego in July and settled down to the tedious process of carving out a boundary agreement with the Mexican delegates.

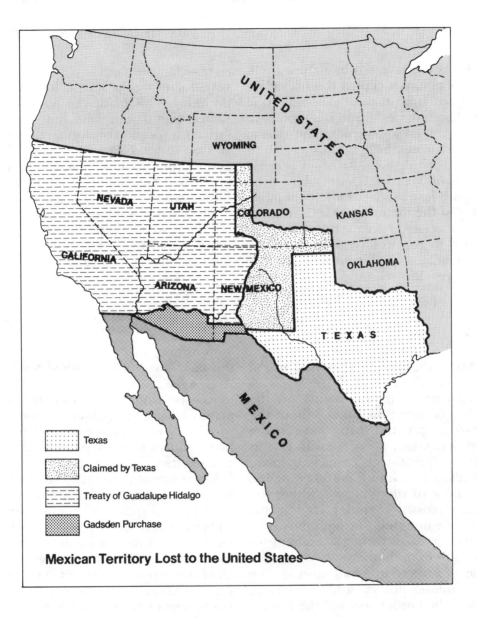

Mexican Territory Lost to the United States

Legend:
- Texas
- Claimed by Texas
- Treaty of Guadalupe Hidalgo
- Gadsden Purchase

The border that the two countries finally agreed upon used the Rio Grande as its basis. It was decided that the international boundary between Mexico and the United States would follow the course of the river from the Gulf of Mexico to El Paso, Texas. (This gave the United States the territory between the Nueces and the Rio Grande, so long disputed by Mexico and Texas.) From El Paso, where the river turns north, an imaginary line was drawn straight across and up to the Gila River. The boundary followed the Gila to the Colorado River. From that point, another imaginary line was drawn straight across to the Pacific Ocean.

The boundary settlement seemed a logical one to the commissioners who drew it on the map. It satisfied the Mexicans because it followed, as much as possible, barriers presented by nature itself. Both delegations accepted the prevailing philosophy that nations should have "natural boundaries"—and if a mountain chain or an ocean were not available, then rivers would have to do.

The Americans were satisfied because the goals of Manifest Destiny had been achieved. The boundary settlement made a reality of the dream of American territory from ocean to ocean. But the agreement led to confusion and formed the basis for heated border disputes in later years. The Rio Grande—a whimsical river—changed course repeatedly in the years following the war, as it continues to do today. This made the border a fluid rather than a stationary line. It also affected the location of the line drawn from El Paso to the Gila River. When the Rio Grande moved south (and it should be noted that the change was often only a foot or so), Mexico could protest that the United States was unfairly adding to its territory. But when the river moved north, the United States could use the same argument against Mexico.

Continued Dispute

As far as the people who lived in the area were concerned, the border was an artificial barrier, merely a line on the map. People living on either side of the line passed back and forth between the United States and Mexico easily and at will. Rivers present no obstacle to man. The shallow Rio Grande could be waded during most of the year and where the boundary crossed over dry land it was even less meaningful. The boundary line, in places, passed through buildings— stores and even homes—or down the middle of streets in small towns. The people whose homes and businesses straddled the border scorned the foolish decision of some far-off officials who relegated Americans to one side and Mexicans to the other side of the imaginary line. They continued to live on both sides, visiting their friends and families, conducting their business, farming their land.

Life went on as it had for generations. Neither government could control the entry of "aliens" into its territory. The U.S. Border Patrol, intended to assume this task, was not established until 1924. And in the more than seventy years prior to its establishment, the easy flow of humanity back and forth across the border provided a constant source of conflict between bureaucracies headquartered in distant cities.

Expansionist propaganda in the United States soon compounded the growing boundary dispute by demanding an additional territorial gain. A significant number of Americans still believed that the United States should have annexed all of Mexico at the end of the war. Several additional factors led to the development of fevered anti-Mexican sentiment during the middle of the century. In the first place, Americans grew increasingly resentful of Article XI of the Treaty of Guadalupe Hidalgo, which held the United States financially liable for Indian raids in Mexico. Secondly, the gold rush was on in California (chapter 13) and one of the choice routes for reaching the gold fields was to sail south from New York or Boston, journey by foot across the Isthmus of Tehuantepec in southern Mexico, and board a ship for California on the Pacific side. But Mexican officials, bitter over the outcome of the war, were less than friendly to American gold prospectors. They either denied the Americans permission to land in Mexico or harassed them throughout their overland journey, confiscating goods and supplies, arbitrarily jailing the travelers.

The gold rush added still another, more compelling motivation for U.S. expansion. Americans demanded quick, effective transportation to California. The logical solution to the problem of getting to the gold fields was to build a railroad across the continent. And the most sensible route for a railroad was across terrain with no mountains, few rivers and few hills. The ideal route included a direct line across a stretch of land to the south of the Gila River—land that belonged to Mexico. By the early 1850s, acquiring that stretch of land had become of primary importance for the United States.

The Gadsden Treaty

The U.S. government sent James Gadsden to Mexico in 1853. His mission was to settle the boundary dispute with Mexico and all other difficulties. Through this man the United States negotiated the purchase of that sandy strip of land south of the Gila River (Hicks and Mowry, 1956: p. 312). (Incidentally, the Gadsden Purchase included the town of Mesilla, founded by Mexicans who had chosen to leave the territory won by the United States in the Mexican-American War.)

But the Gadsden Treaty represented far more than a mere purchase of land. It was, in essence, a renegotiation of the Treaty of Guadalupe Hidalgo. It included settlement of a number of new issues, such as establishing the rights of Americans to cross the Isthmus of Tehuantepec and the resumption of trade between Mexico and the United States. But its real importance was in its amendments to the Treaty of Guadalupe Hidalgo. On the one hand, the Gadsden Treaty reaffirmed the civil rights of the Mexican Americans and pledged the United States to guarantee their land titles. On the other hand, it reduced the payment due Mexico for the ceded territory. Whereas the original treaty had set the U.S. debt at $15 million, the Gadsden Treaty reduced that to $10 million (Faulk, 1967: p. 134).

Santa Anna—once again returned to power in Mexico—needed money so badly that he agreed to the new terms. Gadsden had been instructed to secure the release of the United States from Article XI of the Treaty of Guadalupe Hidalgo—the article making the United States financially liable for Indian raids on Mexico. But some compromise was necessary. Gadsden therefore agreed that the United States should accept $5 million in Mexican claims for Indian damages (ibid.). When it came up for ratification, the U.S. Senate struck the clause from the Gadsden Treaty and extinguished all Mexican claims while at the same time retaining American claims against Mexico. The Mexican government accepted the revised Gadsden Treaty. It had little choice. Rejection would likely mean another war and Mexico, still weakened from her previous encounter with the United States, could scarcely risk another defeat.

Thus the United States reduced Mexico to the status of a conquered, ineffective nation. The bitterness of defeat would mar relationships between the two countries for many years. More importantly, the bitterness was transferred to the people who shared the ceded territory—the Mexicans and Americans who now found themselves citizens of the same country.

REFERENCES

Faulk, Odie B. *Too Far North, Too Far South.* Los Angeles: Westernlore Press, 1967.

Hicks, John D., and Mowry, George E. *A Short History of American Democracy.* 2nd ed. Boston: Houghton Mifflin, 1956.

CHAPTER 13 | The New Southwest

Agreements between governments meant little to the inhabitants of the lands Mexico ceded to the United States. The people were isolated as they had always been. Few of the men who created the agreements had ever visited the frontier, nor did they wish to do so. Few of them understood the people or the needs of the frontier; their main concern was the relationship between officials in Mexico City and Washington, D.C. The agreements could solve conflicts between governments, they could not solve the growing personal conflict between Mexican American and Anglo American in the ceded territory.

Anglos flooded into the territory that the Treaty of Guadalupe Hidalgo transferred to the United States. Their way had been prepared by the thousands of American settlers who had lived in the territory for a generation or more. But unlike earlier colonists, these new settlers came as conquerors. In most areas they were vastly outnumbered by Mexicans who had recently been given citizenship and, supposedly, equal rights. The Anglo settlers most likely felt insecure as a minority and so they, the conquerors, set out to subdue the conquered. Mexican Americans soon found that they were discriminated against and treated like aliens in lands they felt rightfully belonged to them. Their land was taken from them; their political power, or the potential for it, usurped, and their social position threatened.

Only in New Mexico did the Mexican Americans retain the veneer of their prewar prominence. And even in New Mexico lands which had been in families for centuries soon began to fall into Anglo hands—the traditional owners unable to document ownership or unable to pay the heavy taxes charged against them. In many instances unscrupulous Americans systematically set out to separate people from their land for their own profit and power. Even the U.S. government was less than fair as it set out to acquire land for the public domain. Throughout most of the Southwest, the Mexicans were supplanted, left with only the most menial tasks. A new stereotype emerged—a stereotype of the Mexican American as an unskilled worker, uninterested and incapable in politics or education.

Arizona town in 1864

Anglo Superiority

As we have seen, Anglos on the frontier had frequently demonstrated feelings of superiority toward the Mexicans. Their arrogance engendered feelings of hostility and bitterness among Mexicans who were the target of Anglo prejudice. Mutual animosity was increased by the transfer of Anglo prejudice against Negros to the Mexican Americans. This happened early in Texas, where American settlers brought black slaves with them to the new colonies. The prevailing attitude was summed up by an Anglo Texan when he stated in 1856: "The people are as bigoted and ignorant as the devil's grandchildren. They haven't even the capacities of my black boy.... You can't drive them out, because there ain't nowhere to drive 'em...and it'll be fifty years before you can outvote 'em" (Forbes, 1964: p. 17).

Not infrequently, American immigrants did try to drive Mexicans out of the territory as they had driven out the Indians. In 1853, a "citizen's committee" of Austin, Texas, forced twenty-five Mex-

ican families out of town (Forbes, 1964: p. 86). By 1856, there were no more than three hundred Mexican families in all of Arizona—a substantial reduction even in such a sparsely populated region (McWilliams, 1949: p. 82).

After the Civil War, prejudice became all the more prevalent. A large number of men and women, loyal to the defeated Confederacy, fled to the territories of the Mexican Cession—especially to Texas and Arizona. These southern immigrants treated the Mexican American with contempt. They saw a chance to create an all-white colony in unsettled Arizona. The Mexican Americans were subjected to new extremes of discrimination. Governments in Arizona went so far as to pass ordinances outlawing Mexican fiestas which had been guaranteed by the Treaty of Guadalupe Hidalgo.

In the midst of growing hostility and bitterness, a new society began to develop in the Southwest. Like the society of post-conquest Mexico and the society of the same frontier three centuries earlier, it was born of conflict between two peoples. And like those earlier societies, the conflict would lead to a unique fusion of cultures—a fusion often overlooked by those who see only the existing conflict. The meeting of Mexicans and Anglos changed the lifestyle and culture of both. The new society began to emerge in the violence of the postwar period and matured with the building of an economic empire—the New Southwest.

California: Forty-Niners

Events in California provide a dramatic example of the processes that created the New Southwest. The discovery of gold in California—the treasure that had eluded Spanish explorers and Mexican settlers for so many centuries—did little to ease the tensions between Mexico and the United States. The gold of American California was of no value to Mexico. But its discovery and the subsequent gold rush did much to mold the new society.

Small amounts of precious metals had been found throughout the frontier regions from the earliest days of Spanish settlement. The Spaniards, and later the Mexicans, operated a highly profitable mercury mine at New Almaden (near San Jose) in California. Arizona was known to have rich silver deposits and only the ferocity of the local Indians had prevented the development of these mines. Settlers in New Mexico and California continually panned the rivers and streams, finding small quantities of gold. The search for gold had provided the initial motivation behind the settlement of the bleak desert of New Mexico. It began in earnest when Juan de Oñate led his colonists to a new home on the shores of the Rio Grande. But neither Oñate nor any of the men who followed him found the mythical treasure that would have ended forever the Spanish crown's multiplying financial worries. The amounts discovered never seemed to be sufficient to meet the needs of governments who sponsored the exploration. Reportedly, a Mexican herdsman named Francisco López discovered sizable quantities of gold near Los Angeles in 1842 (McWilliams, 1949: p. 134). But the real bonanza continued to elude the Mexicans as it had the Spanish.

Then, in the winter of 1848, James Marshall contracted to build a sawmill for John Sutter's settlement in the Sacramento Valley. On January 24, he noticed some shiny yellow rocks in the millrace that ran from the river to the mill. On closer examination, the rocks proved to be gold nuggets and there were more—many more. The mother lode, the richest gold-bearing area the world has yet known, had been discovered.

Sutter and Marshall tried to keep the discovery a secret. In Mexico City, the treaty to end the war was still being negotiated. The two men believed that if the knowledge of gold in California leaked out, Mexico would be unwilling to sign away her rights to the province and the peace would be jeopardized. Moreover, they were selfish; they did not want to share the fortune the gold would bring. They succeeded for a few days—long enough for Mexico to sign the

Treaty of Guadalupe Hidalgo. But it was futile to expect such a discovery to remain secret. The news was spread by word of mouth, first among the families of the Sacramento Valley and later in cities all over the continent. Newspapers picked up the tale and published the news. Soon a full-scale gold rush was on.

Men came to California from all over the world to claim a share of the seemingly inexhaustible supply of gold. The population grew rapidly. In 1848 there were only an estimated 15,000 non-Indians in all of California (Cleland, 1962: p. 134). A federal census of 1850, while most certainly inaccurate, placed the population at 93,000 and a state census two years later counted 260,000 non-Indian Californians (ibid). Almost without exception, the newcomers headed for the gold fields.

The first immigrants, Chilean and Peruvian miners, sailed up the Pacific Coast and arrived in the summer of 1848 (McWilliams, 1949: p. 127). They were soon followed by miners from Sonora in Mexico. Before long, men from Europe and the eastern United States began to head for California. They faced a long journey and a difficult one, no matter which route they chose. They could travel overland, across the North American continent, but the journey took many months (giving other gold prospectors a head start) and the travelers faced constant danger of attack as they passed through Indian territories. At the other extreme, the gold prospectors could sail south from New York, around the tip of South America and up the Pacific Coast to California. But the Straits of Magellan made for dangerous sailing and the journey often took longer than the overland route. A few adventurous souls crossed the Isthmus of Tehuantepec in southern

Mexico, where they faced harassment by Mexican officials (chapter 12), the dangers of malaria and yellow fever and an unpleasant trip through unfamiliar jungle and across hard-to-scale plateaus.

It soon became apparent that the Isthmus of Panama offered the best route to California. Prospective miners sailed from East Coast ports to Panama and trekked across the narrow strip of land uniting two continents. Once on the Pacific side, they secured passage on a ship bound for California. Greedy men fought and even killed for hard-to-get space on the ships. Many of the less ferocious were stranded for weeks, even months, in hot and humid Panama where malaria was a constant threat and boredom dulled their spirits.

The Anglos who finally reached California were tough, aggressive men, somewhat reminiscent of the fur trappers of an earlier era. They flooded into the territory and soon outnumbered the Spanish-speaking miners who had preceded them. Initially, the Anglos were at a disadvantage in the gold fields. Whereas some Spanish-speaking immigrants brought mining skills with them, the Anglo prospectors had little or no mining experience. They were mostly young men, some barely out of their teens. They had worked at various trades except mining, and so they had to learn that skill from the Spanish-speaking miners. In this way they learned of the *batea,* a flat-bottomed pan with sloping sides used to take gold from the rivers and streams. Later, when large gold deposits were discovered and miners began to take gold from dry mines, the Anglos learned of the *arrastra,* a mill that pulverized rock so that the gold could be removed from quartz. And they learned of using mercury to refine the gold—the same patio

Discovery of gold in California. From an old painting.

process that the Spaniards had used to refine silver three centuries earlier.

Thus the success of California mining was directly linked to the knowledge imparted by Mexican and South American miners. Even California mining law followed the Spanish and Mexican traditions, in that a man's right to a property depended not on purchase but on the discovery and development of a mine: merely "staking a claim" and working it established ownership of the land.

Anglo prospectors probably resented their dependence on the knowledge and techniques of Spanish-speaking miners. Such dependence must have been a blow to the pride of men who considered themselves superior to the men who taught them. Then too, the Anglos saw the Mexicans—and they considered all Spanish-speaking people as Mexicans—as undesirable competiton in this matter of making one's fortune. They claimed that California was American now and the yield of its gold fields belonged solely to Americans. The Mexicans, on the other hand, were not willing to give up

the claims they had staked and the profitable mines they had developed.

For a time the conflict seethed beneath the surface. The two groups were separated by distance, as Spanish-speaking miners had concentrated in the southern part of the mother lode and Anglos in the northern part. But eventually, the Anglos began to invade the southern mines, forcing a confrontation. When California passed a discriminatory foreign-miners' tax, compelling all who were not American citizens to pay heavier taxes on their claims and on the yield of their mines, violence erupted. Mexican miners revolted, expressing in their actions all the pent-up bitterness and hostility they felt. The Anglos, superior in numbers, retaliated with equal violence. During the next few years, scores of Mexican miners were lynched and murdered. Many of the survivors abandoned their claims and fled.

Those who remained in the mother lode found new barriers raised against them. Mining camps were split into two sections, Mexican and American. Segregation had come to the gold fields. From that time on, Mexican and Anglo miners regarded each other as enemies. The contradiction of this trend could be seen in isolated camps. Mexican-driven mule trains brought supplies to the communities. Anglo miners greeted the Mexican drivers as the dearest of friends. The discrimination and mutual hostility of the more densely populated mining towns was unknown.

The gold rush affected all of California, not just the mother lode. The prosperity of the area certainly meant that California was granted statehood earlier than it would have been had gold not made the territory so profitable. This served to make the transition to American rule easier for many wealthy Californians who had an opportunity to participate in forming the new government. The citizens of California went over the the head of their military governor and called a convention to draft a state constitution. Among the delegates were men like Mariano Vallejo, José Antonio Carrillo and Pablo de la Guerra—all wealthy ranchers. The constitution was ratified by popular vote in November 1849, and California was admitted to the Union on September 9, 1850.

More important, the focal point of the new state shifted from south to north with the gold rush. San Francisco was transformed almost overnight into a sprawling and boisterous city. It was the port of entry for all those mad dreamers who rushed to California in search of gold. New arrivals set up their tents on the hills or built temporary shelters from cast-off wood. From a distance, this San Francisco must have looked more like a huge army encampment than an established city. Permanent housing was in great demand and real estate values and rents soared. It cost as much as a thousand dollars a month to rent one room (Cleland, 1962: p. 143). San Francisco pulsated with activity; it soon became the new cultural center of California and the new crime capital as well. It developed a reputation for wickedness that lived on for a century after the gold rush ended.

Cattle Barons

In southern California, previously thriving towns were virtually abandoned. But the ranches of the area flourished. The food needs of the gold fields proved an economic boost to hundreds of Mexican-American ranchers. Mushrooming populations created a tremendous demand for meat in the gold country. Ranchers, driving their cattle north, soon discovered that they could demand and receive anywhere from twenty dollars to a hundred dollars a head (Cleland, 1962: p. 150). Wealth was new to most of the ranchers, who for years had struggled just to survive. Suddenly, many of the ranchers began to spend everything they earned. They lavishly adorned their homes—in the manner of the hacendados two centuries earlier. They spent fantastic sums of money on their clothing—as much as three thousand dollars for a single outfit—giving rise to the statement that the rancher "wore his whole *rancho* on his back." They continued to live from day to day, giving little thought to the future. They achieved great heights and when the bubble burst they had a long distance to fall.

The bubble did burst, and very soon. Cattle ranchers in the plains states began to ship beef to California. It was of better quality than that offered by southern California ranchers. Moreover, it was cheaper, for the midwestern promoters knew they would have to undercut the price of California cattle in order to sell. Soon the demand for local beef dwindled and died. By 1853, the California ranchers could not *give* their beef away in the mining areas. The ranchers, reduced to poverty, found that nature also conspired against them. In 1861 floods killed thousands of head of livestock (Cleland, 1962: p. 156). The wet year was followed by two years of drought, which may have killed up to three million cattle (McWilliams, 1949: p. 91). During these same years, swarms of locusts devastated the pastures.

This series of catastrophes ruined many of the ranchers. It furthered the break-up of the great land grants. The process had begun shortly after the end of the Mexican-American War. The Treaty of Guadalupe Hidalgo forced the United States to recognize the legitimate land titles of Mexican Americans. But the Federal Land Grant Act of 1851 violated the spirit of the treaty. It ordered that all land titles held under Spanish or Mexican grants must be submitted to a board for verification and stated that claims not submitted within two years would be automatically forfeited. California, with its rich agricultural lands, was the chief target of this act. Between 1852 and 1857 the board examined more than eight hundred claims, involving some twelve

million acres of land (Cleland, 1962: p. 151). Of these, five hundred were approved; the remainder, either rejected or withdrawn, became the property of the U.S. government and were sold at auction to the highest bidder.

Verifying a claim was a long, involved process, for most of the grants were vaguely described, seldom recorded on paper, fragmented by inheritance. Many of those who could verify their title to the land were ruined by the expense of doing so. If they managed to avoid bankruptcy and keep their land, the ranchers faced stiff, unrealistic laws which were designed to force them off the land. In the early 1870s, a new law compelled them to fence their property, thus ending the tradition of the open range and imposing on the rancher the added burden of buying feed for the livestock. In 1886, the California Supreme Court further injured the ranchers by upholding the English law of riparian water rights—that is, the law proclaiming water is owned by the individual landowner rather than by the community. It meant that an owner could dam up the water, literally parching his neighbor, who was often forced to sell his land for next to nothing.

These laws, combined with increasingly heavy taxes, completed the destruction of Mexican-American ranchers in southern California. Only a very few held on. Most lost their land—which was bought at low cost by Anglo speculators—and were left to drift, aimless and poverty-stricken. It was a story repeated time and again across the frontier.

A Violent Land

The result was hostility, bitterness and violence. Lawlessness was a common state

of affairs in the years following the war. Both Mexicans and Anglos turned to vio-

Joaquín Murieta

In the 1850s a Mexican-American bandit-hero roamed through Calaveras County in California. His name was Joaquín Murieta. According to legend Murieta had been a peaceful gold miner until Anglos jumped his claim and killed his brother.

In his attempt to avenge himself on the "gringos," Murieta was soon credited with nearly every crime committed in California. He was often compared to Robin Hood. However, his activities often brought retaliation against innocent Mexican Americans.

The California legislature posted a $1,000.00 reward for his capture and sent a special force to track him down. After months of chasing bandits across the mining region the rangers killed a Mexican American who was thought to be Joaquín Murieta, although there was some question as to the identity of the dead man.

---

lence to vent their anger—violence directed against their own groups as well as against each other. Robbery, murder, torture, intimidation were daily occurrences in nearly every town. For a time, the mining camps of California held the dubious record of being the most violent communities in the land. They attracted criminal elements from many countries. They offered asylum and anonymity far from the reach of police in New York or Mexico City, London or Buenos Aires. San Francisco, the gold rush port of entry, was notorious for its gambling dens and saloons and boasted an appallingly high crime rate. Arson was common in the mining areas and devastating fires raged through mining camps. In 1851, fire completely gutted Stockton, and a year later, a large part of Sacramento burned to the ground (Cleland, 1962: p. 142).

In many of these towns, fearful citizens, in desperation, took the law into their own hands. As early as 1849, citizens of San Francisco formed a court and seized and tried the leaders of one lawless band. In 1851, the first vigilance committee was formed. Its members, the vigilantes, acted as a sort of citizens' police force. They ran down criminals, real or imagined, and brought them to trial before the committee. The vigilance committee pronounced sentences and carried them out. It executed some criminals, exiled others, and jailed or whipped still others. In time, the vigilance committee became almost as fearsome as the lawless elements.

Lawless men among the Anglo immigrants had their counterparts among Mexican elements of frontier society. Some Mexicans also took the law into their own hands. They were feared, as bandits, by both the Mexican and Anglo-American citizens of the borderlands. The governments of both Mexico and the United States sent troops to track down the Mexican outlaws. But the bandits were usually successful in eluding their pursuers. Some earned fame as folk heroes in the history of the Southwest.

Joaquín Murieta was such a person. With his lieutenant, Three-Fingered Jack, Murieta terrorized the Mexican population of southern California ranches and towns from 1851 to 1853. He was eventually killed in an ambush. His death reduced the terror in the region but by no means ended it.

Texas: The Lawless Society

The entire frontier was a lawless place in the aftermath of the Mexican-American War. But Texas experienced the most severe eruptions of violence of any of the territories.

Tensions, always so much a part of Texan history, came to a head with the so-called Cart War of 1857. Mexican ox carts had been hauling several million dollars worth of goods a year between San Antonio in Texas, and Chihuahua, Mexico. Anglo Texans, wanting to take over the lucrative trade, systematically tried to force the Mexicans out of business. They harassed the cart trains and stole the goods. Eventually, a few of the more persistent cart drivers were killed. The Mexican government protested and the Cart War ended abruptly when U.S. troops began to escort and protect the carts. The incident, short-lived but brutal, added to the existing taste of bitterness.

But violence continued to disrupt Texas. In July 1859, a Brownsville deputy sheriff arrested a Mexican American

Cart War of 1857

who was a vaquero on the ranch of the Cortina family. Juan Cortina saw the arrest and the beating and chose to avenge it. He shot and wounded the deputy and freed the prisoners from the local jail.

In 1877, on the heels of Cortina's capture, still another war broke out—the Salt War. The difficulty arose over a salt mine, located a hundred miles east of El Paso. For years, the mine had been worked by Mexicans and Mexican Americans and the workers had been allowed to gather, without charge, enough salt for their personal needs. But the mine changed hands and its new owners, Anglo entrepreneurs, decided to charge for the salt. The news was greeted by threats of assassination and accusations of discrimination. When the Texan who claimed ownership of the mine killed an Italian politician who was fighting for the rights of the salt gatherers, the Mexicans revolted. An angry mob killed three Anglos and caused thousands of dollars worth of damage. The Anglos, in retaliation, killed many Mexicans. The revolt was futile, for in the end the Mexicans had to pay for the salt they gathered. But

it was typical of the Mexican-American experience in the years following their adoption as American citizens.

Mexican Americans and Anglos shared the responsibility for the violence that plagued the frontier following the Mexican-American War. However, there can be no doubt but that the Mexican Americans were frequently pushed into violent actions as a last resort as they became victims of a discriminatory and hence oppressive Anglo society. They were soon outnumbered and outpowered. As a minority in his own homeland, the Mexican American became fair game—an appropriate scapegoat to take the blame for lawlessness and an appropriate target for further violence. As we have seen, the Anglos drove the Indians out of Texas, or exterminated them. They tried to drive Mexicans out of Arizona and Texan towns. They also found means of running Mexican ranchers off their lands in Texas, New Mexico, and California and there harassed the Spanish-speaking miners.

These tactics were not enough to satisfy people bent on completely subduing the Mexican Americans. After mid-century, lynching became a common outlet for anti-Mexican sentiment, justified, according to its adherents, as the only means of dealing with Mexican banditry. The vigilance committees of California and the Texas Rangers gave lynching a semiofficial status—an aura of official support for this most lawless act. The tragedy was that many victims were labeled as bandits and then were lynched for minor crimes or crimes they had not committed at all. The Texas Rangers became famous for their wanton killing and lynching of innocent Indians and Mexican Americans.

Anglo immigrants to the territory of the Mexican Cession made a conscious effort to rid the territory of most Indians and Mexican Americans and to reduce the remaining population to a fearful state. But these same Anglos soon found that they needed the Mexican American, for he was to be the backbone of the economy that emerged in the New Southwest—the backbone of an agricultural empire.

The New Economy

The agricultural empire began to develop in the years immediately following the Civil War. It was the direct result of the urbanization of the Atlantic seaboard. Industry drew thousands of Americans to the cities. Small farms were abandoned—the very farms that had long supplied meat and vegetables to urban markets—and the household gardens that most families had maintained disappeared. The cities, forerunners of the sprawling megalopolis, could not provide food, and traditional sources were drying up.

Some areas of the Mexican Cession boasted ideal agricultural land: particularly East Texas and the central valley of California. Irrigation promised to reclaim thousands of acres in other regions. A few men saw that these regions had the potential for feeding the nation. They saw that they could build immense fortunes from agriculture, if only a few problems could be solved.

The first problem was to find a means of transporting agricultural products from the frontier to distant cities. This need added impetus to the demand that railroads be built to connect the two extremes of the continent. Soon, the plan was put into action. But the building of a railroad across the Southwest created a tremendous demand for labor. That labor was provided by Mexican Americans. Most of these laborers living on or having been separated from their land, worked for wages on the construction of the railroad. This same course would solve the second problem: where to get enough labor to meet the needs of large-scale commercial agriculture. For when the railroad was finished in the 1880s, few of the men who had worked on it could return to their old way of life. Instead, they sought jobs on the new commercial farms or in the mines.

There were still problems to be solved. Railroads offered a means of transportation, but until the refrigerator car was introduced, the produce of the southwestern farms often spoiled before it reached the distant cities. Moreover, the Southwest, in the last decades of the nineteenth century, was sparsely populated as it always had been. The existing labor supply

was not large enough to grow and harvest the volume of crops demanded by
eastern cities. Thus commerical agriculture developed slowly; only the introduction of a large body of cheap labor would
get it off the ground.

By the end of the century the outlines
of the dominant new economy were
evident—an agricultural economy, with
farms owned by Anglos and based on
Mexican labor.

REFERENCES

Cleland, Robert Glass. *From Wilderness to Empire: A History of California.* New
York: Alfred A. Knopf, 1962.

Forbes, Jack D. *The Indians in America's Past.* Englewood Cliffs: Prentice-Hall,
1964.

McWilliams, Carey. *North from Mexico.* Philadelphia: J. B. Lippincott, 1949.

Samora, Julian, Joe Bernal, and Albert Pena. *Gunpowder Justice: A Reassessment
of the Texas Rangers.* Notre Dame, Ind.: University of Notre Dame Press, 1979.

PART THREE

The Mexican Heritage

CHAPTER 14 | Invasion from the South

The cultural outlines of the New Southwest were formed by 1900. It was an agricultural society, a society managed by Anglos. The Mexican Americans, relegated to menial positions, provided the labor essential to making the commercial farms a success. But as we have seen, a labor shortage curtailed the expansion of commercial agriculture. There simply were not enough people in the Southwest to meet the growing demand for farm labor.

Shortly after the turn of the century, the labor situation was changed by events in Mexico. A great Mexican Revolution was about to begin. It changed the direction of Mexican government and society. And it altered the history of the Southwest.

The stage for the Mexican Revolution was set many years before it occurred. Benito Juárez, Mexico's benevolent mid-nineteenth-century dictator, died in 1872, shortly after his forces had driven French empire builders from the country. Juárez was a reformer, but he died before he could implement many of the social and political changes he envisioned and had, in fact, outlined. Mexico floun-dered without any effective leadership for four long years. Then, in 1876, a Mixtec Indian from Oaxaca assumed the presidency. His name was Porfirio Díaz and he had been a local caudillo, or political boss, before he won national power. Díaz would rule Mexico with an iron hand for nearly four decades.

The new president was a classic example of the nineteenth-century Latin American dictator. He was a tyrant schooled in oppression. He ruled not because people wanted tyranny but because of the strength of his personality and his ability to organize and control. Díaz covered his oppression with a patina of good deeds. He rescued Mexico from the throes of civil war and restored political order. But he did so with the help of the *rurales,* his personal police force, which had become within a few years the strong right arm of the dictator, relying on terror tactics to squelch any opposition to the regime.

Díaz also straightened out the economy of Mexico. He balanced the budget and began the long overdue economic development of the country. However, he let most of the nation's natural resources fall into foreign hands and he and his friends grew rich while the poor of Mexico became poorer.

Land concentration was already a problem when Díaz came to power. Indeed, this was one of the ills of Mexican society that Benito Juárez had helped to correct. Under Díaz, land became increasingly concentrated in the hands of a few wealthy owners. Díaz divided up the church lands and parceled them out among his cronies. He gave public lands to his loyal supporters in return for their continuing favor. Communal land, the traditional land tenure system of Mexico, fell into private hands. Rural people in ever growing numbers were driven off these communal lands and forced to choose between debt peonage and migration to the cities. Before the end of the Díaz regime, somewhere between 82.4 percent and 96.9 percent of all heads of rural families had no land (Wilkie, 1967: p. 42). They were farmers without farms.

Opposition to Díaz

By the end of the nineteenth century a liberal opposition to the tyranny of Porfirio Díaz was emerging in Mexico. The dissident liberals, forced underground by the dictator's strong-arm methods, were mostly intellectuals and idealists. They demanded that the aging president voluntarily retire at the end of this current term of office, that the government guarantee the communal lands, and that fair pay and work conditions be established for Mexican laborers. But the liberals more often met with failure than success. They lacked effective leadership or any real cohesion. They were fragmented into an array of nervous little groups. They could not agree enough to marshal the forces they needed to protect themselves against Porfirio. If they did speak out, the government ordered their arrest. Leading liberals, more often than not, spent their most productive years in prison or in exile.

The United States, with its large Mexican population, inevitably became involved in the political uproar developing in Mexico. Dozens of fleeing liberals sought asylum in the Southwest, where they expected to find sympathy and support to carry on their work of opposing the Mexican government. From time to time they tried to involve Mexican Americans in their liberal activites. One of these men was Ricardo Flores Magón, editor of a fledgling liberal newspaper, *Regeneración*. The Díaz government arrested and jailed Flores in 1900, but he soon escaped. He fled to Texas, where he joined his brother and other exiled liberals.

Flores continued to publish *Regeneración* in San Antonio, Texas, and later in St. Louis, Missouri. He was seldom more than one step ahead of Díaz agents and U.S. authorities who frowned on exiled liberals printing subversive newspapers on American soil. But Flores continued to publish sporadically. He had considerable success in sneaking his newspaper into Mexico as well as in distributing it among the Spanish-speaking people of the Southwest. However, the success was short-lived. When the liberals began organizing a revolution in Texas, the authorities closed in. Subsequent events read something like a movie plot. Ricardo Flores Magón and his brothers were jailed but soon escaped. During the ensuing months they led Díaz agents and American police on a wild chase all over the Southwest, until they were finally captured and jailed in Los Angeles.

The intellectual liberals were dedicated and energetic men. But they had little support among the masses of Mexico. The liberals' tools were presses, ink and newsprint. But the written word was meaningless to hundreds of thousands of illiterate peasants—the very people the liberals hoped to win over to their side. The liberals talked of abstract goals, of political change and democracy. The masses wanted land and food—concrete improvements to their lives that they could see and feel. Yet out of the liberal opposition to government a revolutionary movement emerged and new leaders surfaced.

Porfirio Díaz

Zapata and Villa

The peasants of southern Mexico found a leader in Emiliano Zapata, a sharecropper from Morelos. He could communicate with the landless, illiterate masses as the liberals had never been able to do. Zapata himself was a peasant and his rallying cry, "Land and Liberty," united the people he led in a common cause. In the early years of the twentieth century, Zapata organized guerrilla bands and led devastating attacks on haciendas and sugar refineries. The peasant guerrillas burned and looted the haciendas, killed the owners, destroyed the cane fields and refineries, and terrorized the countryside. They ambushed the rurales and stole their guns and horses. Zapata's aim was to break up the haciendas. He threw himself wholeheartedly into this task and soon replaced the

liberals as the predominant threat to the Díaz government.

The second great revolutionary leader was Pancho Villa. Born Doroteo Aranga, he called himself Villa after a bandit famous in the folklore of northern Mexico. The twentieth-century Villa was as violent as his hero. Whereas Emiliano Zapata was an idealist, Villa was an opportunist. To him, the revolution was merely an episode which offered a chance for personal advancement, a chance to win fame and fortune.

Whatever his shortcomings, Villa contributed a great deal to the revolutionary effort. He provided efficient leadership and unparalleled organizational ability, both of which were sadly lacking among the supporters of the revolution who preceded him. Pancho Villa created a private army and soon gained absolute control over the important northern states of Chihuahua and Durango. Like Zapata, Pancho Villa made his presence felt by looting and burning. His forces wantonly destroyed crops and livestock, railroads and roads, homes and businesses. Like Zapata he expressed his feelings about the government in the only way he knew: through violence. But both Pancho Villa and Emiliano Zapata were regional leaders. Neither had interests common to all Mexicans; neither could forge a national revolutionary movement.

Madero

The task of uniting the forces of revolution was left to Francisco Madero, the third great leader and, strangely enough, a man who counted himself among the discredited liberals. Madero was an unwilling revolutionary, yet he provided the catalyst for revolution. The son of a wealthy landowning family, he had long opposed the continuing dictatorship of Porfirio Díaz and supported liberal demands for political change as well as for social reform. Madero was more of an idealist and a dreamer than most, but he won mass support through his apparent honesty and his sympathy for the multitudes of Mexican people.

Francisco Madero moved slowly and cautiously. In 1908 he merely suggested that if Díaz did run for reelection, the people should be allowed to choose the vice-president. (Madero, like hundreds of others, probably believed that Díaz would die of old age before the end of the next term. Although elections were inevitably fixed, the dictator always ran for office, thus maintaining the illusion that he had been chosen by the voters and had popular support. If the people had the chance to choose the vice-president and if Díaz died in office, then his successor would be a true popular choice.) The masses, however, clamored for Madero to run against Díaz in the election of 1910, and he finally succumbed to the popular wish. When Madero announced his candidacy, Díaz had him arrested for sedition. Francisco Madero fled to exile in El Paso, Texas, and from there planned reforms for Mexico. His popularity among the Mexican people increased as a direct result of his suppression by the Díaz government.

The revolution, in fact, might be dated from Madero's arrest. For the first time, Mexicans united behind a common leader and for a common cause. Even Pancho Villa and Emiliano Zapata announced their support of Madero. Violence and dissension increased during the months that followed the arrest until, on May 24, 1911, an angry mob surrounded the dictator's home and demanded his resignation. Porfirio Díaz, realizing he had lost control and fearing for his life, resigned the next day. He was eighty-one years old and had been dictator of Mexico for thirty-five of those years. He was destined to lasting fame as Mexico's most hated president. He would die in exile four years after his fall, a broken and bitter man.

Francisco Madero easily won the presidential elections that were held in November 1911. But he failed to solve national problems and thus drove the country farther and farther along the

Emiliano Zapata

Emiliano Zapata (1883–1919) was born into a poor Indian peasant family. Without benefit of a formal education he became a daring and determined revolutionary who led his followers, untrained peasants, in an attempt to bring about a just agrarian reform with the motto "land, liberty, and death to the *hacendados* [landowners]." His efforts involved him in the political turmoil of his day.

It was a time when various generals, presidents, and ex-presidents of Mexico had followers who fought one another in trying to bring about what each considered the best government for Mexico.

Zapata joined forces with the politician Francisco Madero in 1911 to rid Mexico of the dictator Porfirio Díaz. This they did, but then Zapata could not accept Madero as president of Mexico, nor his successor Venustiano Carranza, so that Zapata soon found himself allied with Francisco (Pancho) Villa in marching on Mexico City to depose Carranza.

The fortunes of battle favored Carranza, and Zapata was confined to a struggle for reform in an area south of Mexico City. This apostle of agrarian reform was eventually assassinated by his enemies.

road to full-scale revolution. Madero was, after all, a liberal, affected by the same lack of understanding of the masses that had made earlier liberals ineffective. He offered the people democracy when they wanted food and land. His main interest was continuity and stability in government. To this end he made compromises with old Díaz supporters and refused to break sharply with the financial policies of the old regime (Wilkie, 1967: p. 35). Moreover, he was as guilty of nepotism as his predecessor, bringing into government his own friends and relatives, many of whom were greedy and incapable men.

But Madero's greatest failure was that he tried to ignore Mexico's most pressing problem, the matter of the landless peasants. He sincerely believed that redistribution of land must wait until after political stability had been achieved. The peasants were not willing to wait and this decision lost him the support of Emiliano Zapata. Once again, Zapata began to lead guerrilla raids against the haciendas. In the north, Pancho Villa had never stopped raiding and destroying. Thus the collapse of the Madero government was inevitable. It came during a mass uprising in February 1913—a ten-day bloodbath known as *la decena trágica*. Those ten tragic days saw the true beginning of the Mexican Revolution and a violent civil war that nearly destroyed Mexico in the decade that followed.

Civil War in Mexico

The details of the Mexican Revolution are not really important for our purposes. Volumes have been written on the subject and anyone interested in the dramatic course of the revolution can read any one of a number of excellent books. What is important to this study is the effect of revolution—on Mexico and, particularly, on the southwestern United States. The revolution changed the course of the history of the Southwest to a far greater extent than any previous event.

Civil war threw Mexico into a state of chaos. Struggles for power destroyed what little political stability had existed under Madero. One president after another was overthrown. The people never knew, from moment to moment, what figure represented authority. It was a disturbing era. (But anarchy had its comic moments, too. During one period, Pancho Villa and Emiliano Zapata seized the presidency. Neither was willing to let the other rule and so they traded the office back and forth between them for several months.) Presidents, to stay in power, resorted to tactics as brutal as any that Díaz had used. Assassinations were common. Francisco Madero, murdered while supposedly trying to escape, remained in the hearts of the masses; he became the first and greatest martyr of the revolution.

Economic depression reflected the political chaos. Villa and Zapata continued their war of destruction. Within a few years, Mexico's railway network had been virtually demolished, largely due to the activities of Villa's army. Bridges were blown up, tracks sabotaged, trains attacked. Transportation systems ground to a halt. Zapata's guerrillas destroyed a large part of the nation's crops and livestock in the agriculturally productive south. The consequent shortage of food led to starvation. Undernourished Mexicans were susceptible to disease, and epidemics decimated entire towns, much as they had after the Spanish conquest.

U.S. Involvement

Eventually, the Mexican Revolution embroiled the United States. When a number of liberals fled to exile in Texas, their presence and their antics involved American authorities, willing or not. Then, Porfirio Díaz sought the aid of the U.S. government in his battle against the liberals. President William Howard Taft agreed on the condition that Mexico renew the leases on U.S. naval facilities in Baja California. When Díaz refused, Taft withdrew his promise of assistance (Horgan, 1954: pp. 908–9). But the United States was soon to become directly involved in Mexico's affairs.

The justification for involvement was to be found in U.S. foreign policy. The United States had long opposed European intervention in the affairs of American nations and, under the Monroe Doctrine, pledged to protect the nations against such intervention. But by the end of the nineteenth century, many of the Latin American states were deeply in debt to European powers. Threatened invervention by these powers led President Theodore Roosevelt to announce the Roosevelt corollary to the Monroe Doctrine. Basically, this stated that the United States, rather than allow Europeans to intervene, would intervene itself and force the American nations to honor their commitments.

Thus the United States undertook the role of policing the hemisphere—a sort of big brother whipping small, recalcitrant children into shape. For the most part, the Roosevelt corollary affected the nations ringing the Caribbean Sea. It led, during the first decades of the twentieth century, to outright American occupation of nations like Haiti, Cuba, and the Dominican Republic, and strengthened the Latin American view of the United States as the Colossus of the North (chapter 12).

Mexico became a target of the Roosevelt corollary after the civil war began in 1913. Mexican revolutionaries began receiving arms from European nations—arms they certainly could not pay for. Moreover, the chief supplier was Germany and, on the eve of World War I, this threatened to involve Mexico and all the nations of the hemisphere in the European conflict. To prevent German intervention, President Woodrow Wilson ordered an arms blockade against Mexico. Ships of the U.S. Navy—part of the "great white fleet"—blockaded Mexico's ports.

Then, in April 1914, a group of U.S. Marines landed at Tampico to pick up supplies and were arrested by Mexican officials. Although the marines were soon released, Admiral Henry T. Mayo demanded that the Mexican government apologize formally and honor the American flag with a twenty-one gun salute. President Wilson, who had not been consulted, felt compelled to back Admiral Mayo as a representative of the government. When Mexico's president, Victoriano Huerta, refused to salute the flag, Wilson ordered the fleet to Veracruz (the marines seized the city) and the army to march overland from Texas to join it. War between Mexico and the United States

Pancho Villa (hand on Howitzer) with his revolutionaries

Francisco (Pancho) Villa

Francisco (Pancho) Villa (1878–1923) became an outlaw and bandit after killing a man when in his early twenties. He roamed the mountains of northern Mexico, robbing trains and banks and raiding mines.

This experience gave him the skills necessary to be a successful guerrilla fighter. For Pancho Villa threw in his lot with the revolutionaries of 1910 who fought the regime of Porfirio Díaz. Villa was a courageous fighter and gained fame for his bravery.

He fought with the other revolutionaries for the presidency of Mexico, yet lost an important battle to a supporter of Venustiano Carranza. Villa became angry with the United States over its support of Carranza, and he raided an American town in New Mexico, killing 17 Americans. For this the United States sent General John J. Pershing with an American army to capture Villa. The Americans failed to do so, and the expedition made a hero of Villa.

The Mexican government retired him as a general in 1920, but three years later he was assassinated. Pancho Villa made a great impression on his countrymen. Although a tough revolutionary who did not hesitate to kill in battle, he also sympathized with the peasants and the weak.

was averted only through the good offices of the ABC Powers—Argentina, Brazil, and Chile. But U.S. involvement in the Mexican Revolution was just beginning.

The Tampico incident toppled the Huerta government. The deposed president fled to Europe but shortly made his way back to America. Like so many exiled revolutionaries before him, Huerta settled in Texas and soon began plotting an attack on Mexico. For a while it was easy for the U.S. government to ignore a seemingly harmless exile. But Huerta soon began soliciting the aid of Germany, and by 1915 Huerta was holding secret meetings with German agents in Texas. The United States openly sided with England and France against Germany in the European war. When it was revealed that Huerta and the Germans had developed a plan for Mexico to seize the border states, U.S. authorities arrested Huerta, who died while in their custody.

The Pershing Expedition

The United States was still merely observing the Mexican Revolution. The U.S. president's policy was to watch and wait, but to be on the alert so that if intervention was deemed necessary he could order it without delay.

One more incident turned observation into active participation. When the chaos of civil war reached across the border into the American Southwest, the U.S. government felt compelled to take action. Raiders frequently crossed the border and rounded up American cattle. By February 1916 at least thirty-six American citizens had been killed in raids by Mexican revolutionaries. Then, in March, Pancho Villa and his army attacked Columbus, New Mexico, killing sixteen people. The U.S. Congress and the American people demanded intervention. President Wilson, determined to retaliate against Villa, ordered an expeditionary force into Mexico under the command of General John Pershing. President Carranza of Mexico reluctantly consented to the expediton; it was obvious to him that Wilson would send it whether he agreed or not.

The expedition proved as futile as government sanctions against Villa had been in the past. Pancho Villa was at home in the desert of northern Mexico. For months the expeditionary force tried to track him down. But Villa was always one step ahead, leading the thirsty, dusty Americans on a merry chase. This comedy of errors ended early in 1917, when Wilson withdrew the expeditionary force. Pershing's forces had failed to track down the elusive Pancho Villa, who still roamed freely in northern Mexico. They had succeeded only in intensifying anti-American feeling in Mexico. From the official American point of view, it was an incident—and an embarrassing one—to be forgotten.

But the people of the Southwest could not turn their backs on the revolution quite as easily as their government. Border citizens continued to face the threat of raids by Mexican revolutionaries, but the effects of revolution went far deeper. The Mexican Revolution changed the character of the Southwest and altered its course for the future.

Refugees in the Southwest

The basic cause of this change of character was a great migration of Mexicans to the Southwest. Thousands upon thousands fled the ravages of civil war, leaving Mexico for relative safety north of the border. The immigrants came from all levels of Mexican society. Many of those who fled to the United States were peasants—the Mexicans hardest hit by the revolution—but some were from middle- and upper-class families. The majority, poor and illiterate, were like the answer to a prayer in the Southwest: they represented the large body of cheap labor that southwestern agriculture and industry so badly needed. Indeed, many of the peasants were attracted "by the shine of the dollar" (Peñuelas, p. 19). The low wages they could earn as unskilled laborers on commercial farms seemed a fortune to people who had spent their lives as peons and tenant farmers, living outside the money economy.

And so the peasants came north, carrying with them what few possessions they could manage. They came mostly to Texas, wading across the shallow Rio Grande, and to California, journeying for miles on foot to cross the border. It has been estimated that nearly ten percent of Mexico's total population emigrated during the years of civil war (McWilliams p. 163). By 1925, Los Angeles had the largest community of Mexicans in the world outside of Mexico City.

We have no real knowledge of how many Mexicans migrated to the United States during the course of the revolution. There was little if any attempt to count or control the numbers until the mid-1920s. The U.S. government had no means of controlling Mexican entry until after the Border Patrol was established in 1924. However, we have relatively accurate figures for legal immigration after 1930, and these figures show a steady increase. Between 1931 and 1940, an average 2,200 Mexicans sought permanent residence in the United States each year, but by 1955 this number had climbed to 61,368 (Lewis, in Council on Foreign Relations, *Social Change,* 1961: pp. 291–92). Since political order had been restored to Mexico by the mid-1920s, the figures seem to indicate that something more basic than a desire to escape the chaos of civil war has been pushing Mexicans northward. Nor do the figures give us any real indication of how many Mexicans have immigrated in the last forty years; for they do not account for the thousands of migrants who have entered the United States illegally (chapter 15).

The great migration has had a tremendous effect on the United States as a whole and the Southwest in particular. Most apparent to even the casual observer, the migration has revived the "Mexican" character of the Southwest. It has brought fresh blood into a Spanish-Indian-Mexican society that had its roots in the sixteenth century. In some areas it has once again given Spanish-speaking people a numerical advantage. But the migration also introduced new conflicts into a society already riddled with conflict. The Mexican who fled the revolution was a different person from the Mexican American whose family had lived in the Southwest for generations. In broad terms they had a common heri-

The Sacramento Barrio, 1910

"For the Mexicans the barrio was a colony of refugees. We came to know families from Chihuahua, Sonora, Jalisco, and Durango. Some had come to the United States even before the revolution, living in Texas before migrating to California. Like ourselves, our Mexican neighbors had come this far moving step by step, working and waiting, as if they were feeling their way up a ladder. They talked of relatives who had been left behind in Mexico, or in some far-off city like Los Angeles or San Diego. From whatever place they had come, and however short or long the time they had lived in the United States, together they formed the *colonia mexicana*. In the years between our arrival and the First World War, the *colonia* grew and spilled out from the lower part of town.

"Crowded as it was, the *colonia* found a place for these *chicanos*, the name by which we called an unskilled worker born in Mexico and just arrived in the United States. As poor refugees, their first concern was to find a place to sleep, then to eat and find work. In the *barrio* they were most likely to find all three, for not knowing English, they needed something that was even more urgent than a room, a meal, or a job, and that was information in a language they could understand. This information had to be picked up in bits and pieces—from families like ours, from the conversation groups in the poolrooms and the saloons. Beds and meals, if the newcomers had no money at all, were provided—in one way or another—on trust, until the new *chicano* found a job. On trust and not on credit, for trust was something between people who had plenty of nothing, and credit was between people who had something of plenty. Because the *barrio* was a grapevine of job information, the transient *chicanos* were able to find work and repay their obligations."—Galarza, pp. 200–1.

---

tage, religion, and language. Yet there were specific differences and language provides a graphic example.

The Spanish spoken in the Southwest generally retained the flavor of the sixteenth-century Spanish. This was the heritage of centuries of isolation (chapters 4 and 5). In contrast, the Spanish spoken in Mexico had changed considerably in the same three centuries, influenced by contact with Europeans, Africans, the Indian groups, and other

Spanish-speaking peoples. The great migration, by bringing greater numbers of Spanish-speaking people to the Southwest, accentuated the differences between Anglos and Mexicans. But the differences between the immigrants and the Mexican Americans introduced a new prejudice—the prejudice of old Spanish- and Mexican-American families against the newcomers.

The Job Market

The immigrants, willing to work for pennies a day at unskilled jobs, represented competiton to the old inhabitants. Although labor had been in short supply prior to the Mexican Revolution, southwestern agriculture and industry had not yet grown to the point where they could accommodate the tremendous numbers of people who wanted jobs. True, this situation would once again reverse itself in a few years as the labor pool made it possible for commercial farms to grow and operate at peak capacity. But early in the century, the migration exerted tremendous pressures on the land and labor market.

The pressure, in turn, created an internal migration. People who could not find jobs in the Southwest began to migrate northward in search of employment. As a result, Mexican Americans began to disperse throughout the United States rather than remaining exclusively in the Southwest. Today large Mexican-American communities are to be found in the nation's midwestern and western sections—indeed, in every part of the country.

During and after the revolution, Mexicans immigrated to the United States in search of opportunity. They sought escape not only from the chaos of revolution but from poverty and the chains of debt peonage. They dreamed of earning enough money to support themselves and their families with an improved standard of living. They chose the Southwest because it was accessible; because, having once been part of Mexico, it would be more like home, and because they hoped to fit in easily in a society which already had a large Mexican-American element.

The illusion soon shattered. The Mexican migrant had failed to take into account the strength of anti-Mexican sentiment in the Southwest, to realize that Spanish-speaking people had been relegated to the most menial jobs and the lowest rung of the social ladder. Moreover, the immigrants had failed to consider the opportunities available. A few went to work in the mines of Arizona. Others found employment with the railroads. And in these positions, they contributed to the industrial development of the Southwest. But most knew little besides farming. They were skilled farm workers and they quickly filled the jobs available in agriculture. Thus they became trapped by low wages and a system of debt peonage not very different from what they had known in Mexico. The farm workers, and their children after them, were tied to the job by debts, trapped by the need to survive. Within a few years of immigration the "shine of the dollar" had dulled and the dream corroded.

REFERENCES

Council on Foreign Relations, Inc. *Social Change in Latin America Today.* New York: Vintage Books, 1961.

Galarza, Ernesto. *Barrio Boy.* Notre Dame, Ind.: University of Notre Dame Press, 1971.

Horgan, Paul. *Great River: The Rio Grande in North American History.* 2 vols. New York: Holt, Rinehart and Winston, 1954.

McWilliams, Carey. *North from Mexico.* Philadelphia: J. B. Lippincott, 1949.

Peñuelas, Marcelino C. *Lo Español en el Suroeste de los Estados Unidos.* Madrid: Ediciones Cultura Hispánica, 1964.

Wilkie, James. *The Mexican Revolution: Federal Expenditure and Social Change Since 1910.* Berkeley: University of California Press, 1967.

15 | Cheap Labor

In the last chapter, we examined the effects of immigration from Mexico to the Southwest at the turn of this century. We have seen that the events of the Mexican Revolution tended to push many Mexicans toward the Southwest. At the same time, other factors acted as a magnet which pulled people to the United States.

Chief among these forces were conditions created by the entry of the United States into World War I. The Great War required a vast input of manpower in the armed services and the blossoming defense industries. This created a demand for labor in other, more traditional areas of endeavor. Since work in war-related industries usually pays higher wages than many other occupations, the general labor force moves into these industries and lower paying jobs, however essential, often go unfilled in wartime.

During World War I, the labor shortage was particularly severe in agricul-ture. Farm laborers left the fields in droves to seek the higher wages of the defense industry. At the same time, the United States experienced a great period of economic expansion. In the Southwest, this meant the expansion of commercial agriculture, the establishment of railroads and the development of a number of industries, including mining. Thus at the very time the war was taking people away from the Southwest, the need for labor was increasing in the region. Mexican immigrants, driven by the revolution and attracted by the prospect of employment, filled the gap.

A number of other events help explain why Mexico has become the chief supplier of labor in the United States during this century. Even today, these events provide reasons for the fact that Mexicans constitute the main source of cheap labor in this country. And the roots of the matter are found in the past.

Land Grants

In the early period of colonization and settlement of the Southwest (1600–1850), the people settled on land that was taken from the Indians. This land, which then

134

"belonged" to Spain and later to Mexico, was often parceled out to the settlers in the form of land grants. These grants, some of them covering hundreds of thousands of acres, were awarded to individuals or were given in common to a group of people. Those who did not settle on land grants would settle in the "public" domain.

The Treaty of Guadalupe-Hidalgo, which ended the war between Mexico and the United States, guaranteed the conquered people a number of rights, including that of possession of their land. But the Anglo-Americans, utilizing a number of legal, illegal, and sometimes unscrupulous means, soon separated most Mexicans from their land. It must be noted that while Americans consider land as a capital commodity to be owned, bought, sold and exploited, many other people hold a different view. The Mexicans—and Spaniards and Indians before them—believed the land was to be used, obviously, but not necessarily as a capital commodity.

Moreover, the American system of land ownership involved accurate surveys and complicated titles of ownership and deeds of transfer. The Mexican system, dating from the Spanish colonial period, was not always that accurate or substantiated by legal documents. Land grants, if recorded on paper, were often loosely described. A property might be said to extend from the peak of such a mountain to the mouth of such a river, encompassing so many acres more or less. This kind of description, typical of the colonial period, is very different from an exact geographical survey measured in degrees and feet. Furthermore, locating the records proved difficult. Many of the land grants were deposited and recorded in Spain, others in Mexico and still others in Santa Fe, New Mexico. To further complicate the situation, one of the territorial governors of New Mexico, William Pile, sold a large portion of the colonial and Mexican archives as wastepaper in 1869. It is also reported that William Arny, acting governor in 1866, placed the archives in an "outhouse," letting the documents rot.

Consequently, many people could not produce legal title to the lands they owned. Even though the United States did establish a land claims court, many of the lands passed into the United States public domain for lack of adequate documentation of ownership. Of the more than thirty-five million acres claimed under land titles, the Court of Private Land Claims had approved a little over two million acres when it adjourned in 1904. The result of this situation was that many people lost their land and were thus pushed out into the labor supply and a wage economy.

Immigration Laws

Immigration laws offer another reason for Mexico's important role in supplying cheap labor. The United States is a nation of immigrants. After its formation as a nation, the great majority of people who came to U.S. shores came from northern Europe. This has been known historically as the old immigration. After 1850 new waves of immigrants came to this country. In increasing numbers, they migrated from southern Europe. All of these immigrants, seeking a better life in one way or another, supplied labor for a rapidly growing nation. When new sources of labor were needed, particularly in the Southwest, the United States turned to China and later to Japan. But Americans soon came to believe that Orientals would not make good citizens and, in fact, constituted a threat to national security. The Chinese were blocked by the exclusion acts of the 1880s and the Japanese immigration was curtailed by the Gentlemen's Agreement of 1907. The Philippines and Korea as well as Mexico then became chief sources of cheap, immigrant labor for the United States.

The first formal U.S. immigration laws establishing quotas were passed in 1921 and codified in 1924. These nationality acts set quotas stipulating the number of immigrants who could enter the United States from any given country. These quotas favored people from northern Europe and disfavored, to a degree, people from southern Europe. People from Asia were almost entirely excluded. The nationality acts, however, did not establish quotas for people from the Western Hemisphere. Thus, unlimited numbers of people could enter the United States from Canada, Mexico, Central and South America. Since Mexico is contiguous to the United States, Mexico then became the chief source of cheap labor.

It must be noted that between 1849 and 1924 the border between Mexico and the United States was not policed and people of both nations tended to go back and forth to either country without difficulty. In 1924, however, the Border Patrol was established and now that imaginary line called the border became a real barrier for people going back and forth between Mexico and the United States. The need for documentation suddenly became a bothersome reality. And although large numbers of Mexicans were admitted legally to the United States, others, in increasing numbers, began to bypass the paperwork after 1924 and entered the country illegally.

The Great Depression

During the First World War and into the 1920s, the United States enjoyed a period of great prosperity and economic expansion. The economic boom declined in the mid-1920s and ended abruptly with the 1929 stock market crash. The Great Depression which followed lasted about a decade. The effects of this Depression were disastrous to most of the population, but particularly to the Mexicans and Mexican Americans in the United States.

Many persons whom we now label Mexican Americans were here before there was a United States, and their descendants became citizens when the Southwest was conquered during the Mexican-American War. Many others immigrated to this country from Mexico between 1850 and 1900. Thus, as the Depression began, there were several hundred thousand Mexican Americans as well as Mexican legal residents in the United States.

As the Depression became more severe in the early 1930s, millions of people were jobless and being aided somewhat by the first faltering attempts at public welfare. Throughout the Southwest and such cities as Gary, Indiana; Detroit, Michigan; Toledo, Ohio, where there were large concentrations of Mexicans and Mexican Americans, public officials

Mexican-American farm laborers working in fields near Salinas, California

decided that it would be cheaper to send the Mexican legal aliens back to Mexico than to carry them on the public welfare rolls. Thus, a system of repatriation began.

During the first four years of the 1930s, well over four hundred thousand Mexicans were repatriated to Mexico. Most of those repatriated Mexican citizens were legal residents of the United States; many were American citizens— that is, Mexican Americans. Some had lived in this country thirty or forty years and had established their homes and their roots here. Many families were broken up, for in some cases either the father or mother, or both, were alien, but the children, having been born and raised in this country, were American citizens and allowed to stay while their parents were repatriated. To be sure, some Mexican aliens departed voluntarily, but those who were forcibly removed and those whose families were disrupted suffered enormous hardships during this period.

Needless to say, immigration from Mexico during the 1930s was reduced to a trickle. It did not begin again in any significant number until the 1940s with the advent of the Second World War.

World War II

The United States entered World War II in December 1941. But the country had been preparing for war at least since the European conflict began in 1939. The situation was comparable to that which existed during the First World War. Many men, previously part of a more rudimentary labor force, were absorbed by the armed forces and rapidly expanding defense industry. As a result, the war created a labor shortage, particularly in agriculture. The United States once again turned to Mexico as a supplier of labor. But this time the two nations entered into a formal agreement by which Mexican laborers might be employed.

Even before America's entry into the war and as early as 1940, growers in some southwestern states were petitioning United States agencies for permission to use foreign labor (Craig, 1971: pp. 37–38). A precedent for the importation of foreign labor had already been set in World War I. After the United States entered the Second World War, growers and their spokesmen appealed to the secretaries of agriculture, state, and labor for foreign workers, but now the appeal was not so much on their own behalf but, rather, for the national defense.

> In April, 1942, under pressure from California beet growers, the immigration service formed an Interagency Committee to study the question of agriculture labor. Composed of representatives from the War Manpower Commission and the Departments of Labor, State, Justice and Agriculture, the Committee produced a plan for recruiting Mexican labor. (Craig, 1971: pp. 39–40)

On June 1, 1942, Mexico declared war on the Axis powers and immediately thereafter the Department of State was asked to approach Mexico officially on the question of the importation of foreign labor. During the subsequent discussions it appeared that Mexico doubted that a legitimate labor scarcity existed and viewed these discussions as efforts to obtain cheap labor. Mexican officials remembered and were still concerned about the ignominious deportation and repatriation of Mexicans which occurred in the 1930s and were anxious to prevent another such episode. Moreover, they did not want to permit their workers to be sent to "discrimination-prone" states and felt there might be a danger to Mexico's economic development if many thousands of their workers left for the United States. On the other hand, the Mexican committee was assured that Mexico would have a strong voice in the two-nation agreement. Presumably, Mexico would benefit from the knowledge that the workers would acquire during their visit to the United States. Through such an agreement, Mexico could contribute to the Allied war effort and would benefit economically.

The Bracero Agreement

A government-to-government accord was reached in July 1942. This came to be known as the Bracero agreement. The two nations signed the agreement on August 4, 1942. Under the terms of the agreement, Mexico would permit its nationals to come to work in the United States for temporary periods under stipulated conditions. In a sense, this was part of Mexico's contribution to the war effort. Both nations accepted the agreement in good faith. It was expected to be a temporary effort, lasting presumably for the duration of the war.

Specific conditions governed the manner under which the Mexican nationals were to be brought to the United States. Those conditions stipulated methods of recruitment, means of transportation, standards for health care, wages, housing, food, and the number of working hours. There was also a stipulation that there should be no discrimination against the Mexican nationals.

The agreement which provided temporary wartime labor for American agriculture came to be known as the Bracero program. Although it was meant to be temporary, it lasted much longer than the war itself. Established by executive order in 1942, it was enacted into Public Law 78 in 1951 and was not terminated until December 1964—more than nineteen years after the end of World War II.

Recruitment

Under the original agreement, the recruitment of braceros was to take place in certain centers in Mexico. Once the workers had been approved, they were to be transported to those areas in the United States that had requested them. The recruitment centers themselves became crowded with thousands of Mexicans who were unemployed and who wanted to go to the United States.

Because of the overwhelming numbers of applicants, it became very difficult to obtain permits to enter the program. In many instances a bribery system (a mordida) was set up. Often those who learned the ropes and could bribe the officials were selected as braceros. This procedure left many thousands of Mexicans without an opportunity to join the program. Many of those who were not chosen came to the United States illegally. The number of illegals who entered the United States during the tenure of the Bracero program was equal to or surpassed the number of braceros.

Effect on Domestic Labor

According to the agreement, braceros were not to be brought into areas where domestic labor was available. They were to be paid the prevailing wage for agricultural work in the region, but not less than fifty cents per hour. More often than not, the minimum wage of fifty cents per hour became the maximum wage offered. When domestic laborers refused to accept such low wages, for they could hardly afford to support a family on fifty cents an hour, local officials could claim a shortage of laborers and request braceros. Thus, many domestic laborers who might have worked in agriculture for a decent wage were displaced by Mexican nationals. To the further detriment of both U.S. citizens and braceros, many of the agricultural enterprises of the Southwest hired illegal aliens at wages even lower than fifty cents an hour.

The Bracero program was a great boon to American agriculture. The industry preferred to employ Mexican nationals rather than American citizens, although many of the Americans (whether or not of Mexican descent) were seasonal farm workers or migratory workers.

The advantages of using nationals in agriculture were many. In the first place, the wages were set by the growers, not in a supply-and-demand situation and certainly not in collective bargaining. In addition, seasonal farm workers who were American citizens quite often worked as families. This meant that the growers had to supply housing for a family unit—that is, a man and his wife and several children. But the Mexican nationals were all men and they came in groups. It is much easier to provide transportation and supply barracks or rooms for single men than it is to supply housing for a family unit. The Mexican nationals could be transported from farm to farm, county to county, state to state, without any difficulty. They could be brought in and moved out as they were needed. In contrast, American migratory labor cannot be managed that easily, for it usually involves a crew leader, and people traveling in family groups.

The Bracero program is one of the several instances in which the U.S. government became a supplier of labor in direct competition with the usual supply and demand situation. In a real sense, the government was subsidizing the growers by supplying them with cheap labor. An American citizen wanting to work in agriculture had to compete with the whole Bracero program and, consequently, with the U.S. government. Needless to say, this proved quite advantageous to the American grower. Although the Bracero agreement contained stipulations with regard to health, housing, food, wages, and working hours, most were disregarded by both the U.S. government and the growers. The requirement that Mexican nationals not be discriminated against was also disregarded. In the state of Texas alone, Mexicans were discriminated against to such an extent that the Mexican government forbade the use of its nationals in the fields in Texas.

Texan growers circumvented this ban by hiring "wetbacks" rather than braceros. The wetbacks were more manageable than the braceros because, as illegal aliens, they had absolutely no rights in a foreign country. Therefore, the questions concerning wages, health, housing, food and so forth did not apply.

Prolongation of the Program

When the war ended in 1945, American men began to return from the armed forces. The defense industries began to lay off workers, and, of course, it could no longer be said that a shortage of labor existed. The growers, however, liked the wartime arrangement and persisted in their efforts to keep the Bracero program going. As a result of the growers' powerful influence in Congress, the program survived for nearly twenty years after the end of the war.

TABLE 2

TEMPORARY CONTRACT LABOR FROM MEXICO*

Year	Total	Year	Total
1942	4,203	1955	390,846
1943	52,098	1956	444,581
1944	62,170	1957	450,422
1945	49,454	1958	418,885
1946	32,043	1959	447,535
1947	19,632	1960	427,240
1948	33,288	1961	294,149
1949	143,455	1962	282,556
1950	76,519	1963	195,450
1951	211,098	1964	181,738
1952	187,894	1965	103,563
1953	198,424	1966	18,544
1954	310,476	1967	7,703
		1968	6,127
TOTAL			5,050,093

*Figures correspond to fiscal years. Although the Bracero program ended in December 1964, figures from 1966 to 1968 correspond to aliens admitted and reported under the same category which entitles the table.

Sources: Period from 1942 to 1956 based on figures taken from *Mexican Labor Hearings* (House Committee on Agriculture) 1958, pp. 450–52 as quoted by Hancock 1959:17).

Figures for 1957 and 1958 based on Report of the Select Commission on Western Hemisphere Immigration (1968:98).

Figures from 1959 to 1968 based on data provided by the 1968 Annual Report of the Immigration and Naturalization Service, p. 73.

Braceros stop work for their midday meal.

While it is true that the Bracero program was begun as an emergency measure to help the United States during the war, a legitimate and laudable aim, one cannot help but ask why the program lasted so long when the war itself lasted only from the end of 1941 to the summer of 1945. As a matter of fact, the lowest number of braceros who were hired in the program was hired during the war years and the largest number was hired many years after the war had ended. Table 2 gives an indication of the numbers of Mexican nationals who were brought to the United States for temporary seasonal farm work. During the twenty-two-year period, over five million braceros were employed in the United States.

Commuters

Another category of persons in and from Mexico who had been a source of cheap labor for the United States is the so-called "commuters." Commuters reside in Mexico but work in the United States. These persons, the great majority of whom are citizens of Mexico, at some time have been issued a visa (popularly called a "green card") to come to the United States to live and work, but they have chosen to keep their residence in Mexico.

Some commuters come into the United States to live and work for a month, six months, or a year and then go back to Mexico. They may return to the United States at a later time. The average commuter, however, comes to work in the United States every day, and returns to his home in Mexico in the evening. Early in the morning in Brownsville, Texas, one can stand at the International Bridge and watch the stream of commuters arriving from Matamoros. A similar sight can be seen at El Paso's International Bridge, where thousands of commuters cross the border from Juárez each day. The same daily procession takes place from Mexicali to Calexico, and Tijuana to San Ysidro, California. If one goes back to the same points between six and nine in the evening the same people can be seen returning to their homes in Mexico.

The commuters are legal entrants to this country—but legally, they should also live in the United States. They are generally employed in low-skill jobs or service jobs—as agricultural workers, bus boys, waitresses, elevator operators, store clerks, dishwashers, maintenance men, bartenders, and construction workers. Some, of course, hold skilled jobs. But few would be found in managerial or professional jobs. The number of people thus employed is estimated to be from sixty thousand to four hundred thousand. It is difficult to give an accurate figure because the United States does not keep very accurate records and because the number of commuters fluctuates considerably from day to day.

Most of the people who live in Mexico but who earn their living in the United States tend to spend most of their earnings on the American side of the border. For this reason, the Chamber of Commerce and the business community generally favor the commuter situation. In addition, these people can be hired at wages lower than those demanded by American citizens for the same position.

Opposition to the practice comes from the labor unions and from the people who are displaced by the commuters (that is, American citizens, in many instances Mexican Americans), and other people who see an injustice in the low wages and the exploitation of this labor. It is said by those who oppose the practice that commuters depress the wages in the border area, that they displace the citizen labor (which in many instances becomes migratory and ends up in the northern part of the United States), and that they inter-

fere with organized labor's attempt at unionization of domestic labor. One thing seems very clear: when you have little industry on the American side of the border and when you have a condition of generally low wages, high unemployment, little unionization, and a labor surplus, there is no question that commuters do disturb the local situation with regard to labor and wages.

This is not a new situation nor a recent occurrence in the United States. Commuters have been in this country since the 1920s. By such custom, tradition and the interpretation of the law, those persons have been permitted to live in Mexico and work in the United States, contrary to the letter of the law. And Mexicans are not the only commuters who live in another country and work in the United States. Along the northern border, a number of Canadians come into the United States every day to work in various industries.

Most of the Canadian commuters are concentrated in the Detroit area and farther east. In contrast to the Mexican commuters, most of the Canadians work at skilled and industrial jobs and therefore belong to unions, which means their wages are higher, their jobs more secure, the benefits greater. But American workers do not consider the Canadians as big a threat to labor as they do the commuters from Mexico. One explanation is that the Great Lakes region is an industrialized area and jobs are more plentiful and varied than in much of the Southwest. Another is that Canada is a relatively rich country with a small population while Mexico is considered poor and densely populated. Thus, unemployement in Mexico is higher than in Canada and the need to cross the border into the United States in search of job opportunities is presumably greater.

Illegal Aliens

With the establishment of the Border Patrol in 1924, the "open" border began to disappear. As we indicated earlier, the immigration law of 1921 described the type of person who could enter the United States from any given country and stipulated the conditions of his entrance. This meant that persons entering the United States from any country would be subject to some scrutiny. Consequently, Mexicans could no longer go back and forth freely between the United States and Mexico unless they met certain conditions and obtained the proper legal documents for entry. If a person were apprehended in the United States without papers or documentation, he would be termed an illegal and would be subject to immediate deportation.

The Mexican illegal alien has been popularly called a "wetback." The term originated from the fact that the Rio Grande forms much of the long border between the United States and Mexico, from El Paso to Brownsville, Texas, and many Mexican illegal aliens have crossed into the United States by swimming or wading the river. But the term "wetback" is deceiving because most of the Mexicans who come into the United States without legal documents do not swim or wade across the river.

Factors Involved

In the case of the Mexican illegal alien, one must examine history and the fact that much of the southwestern United States is Mexican territory conquered by the United States. Many Mexicans have had and still have friends and relatives on the U.S. side of the border. In many in-stances what separated these people was merely an imaginary survey line that by chance made some members of a family Mexican and other members American citizens. Even after the border was defined, people crossed back and forth freely for several decades, often working in one country and living in the other. A common economy developed. This changed suddenly with the passage of the nationality acts and the establishment of the Border Patrol. But the habits and attitudes of people do not change easily.

Although there have been no quotas as to the number of Mexicans who can come into the United States legally, the nationality acts do make certain stipulations as to the kinds of people who can enter this country. These stipulations have to do with the moral character of the individual, his educational achievements, the skills he presents to the labor market, and his economic independence. Other requirements suggest that people who are feeble-minded, idiots, lunatics, prostitutes, or persons likely to be public charges, cannot legally enter the United States. The numbers of Mexicans who apply for immigration are so large that the consular offices generally have tremendously long waiting lists for processing applications. Thus, many people who do not care to wait several years before they can become legal immigrants do, in fact, decide to come into the United States without inspection and become illegal aliens.

In looking at the pattern of illegal immigration to the United States from Mexico, one can see that the years when the largest numbers of illegals are apprehended coincide with the periods of economic prosperity in the United States

TABLE 3
MEXICAN ILLEGAL ALIENS REPORTED*

Year	Total	Year	Total	Year	Total
1924	4,614	1941	6,082	1958	37,242
1925	2,961	1942	DNA	1959	30,196
1926	4,047	1943	8,189	1960	29,651
1927	4,495	1944	26,689	1961	29,817
1928	5,529	1945	63,602	1962	30,272
1929	8,538	1946	91,456	1963	39,124
1930	18,319	1947	182,986	1964	43,844
1931	8,409	1948	179,385	1965	55,349
1932	7,116	1949	278,538	1966	89,751
1933	15,865	1950	458,215	1967	108,327
1934	8,910	1951	500,000	1968	151,705
1935	9,139	1952	543,538	1969	201,636
1936	9,534	1953	865,318	1970	277,377
1937	9,535	1954	1,075,168	1971	348,178
1938	8,684	1955	242,608	1972	430,213
1939	9,376	1956	72,442	1973	576,823
1940	8,051	1957	44,451	1974	709,959
				1975	608,335
				TOTAL	8,579,588

*Over the years a variety of categories have been used to report Mexican illegal aliens, with some inconsistency. This table then reflects these inconsistencies. (See Samora, *Los Mojados,* p. 46.)

Sources: From 1924 to 1969: Samora, *Los Mojados,* p. 46. From 1970 to 1975: Annual Report of the Immigration and Naturalization Service.

or periods of depression and high unemployment in Mexico. Such conditions in Mexico are quite often related to natural phenomena such as droughts, tornadoes, or floods.

Numbers Apprehended

It must be noted that we are not talking about the number of illegals from Mexico who come into the United States. No one knows that figure year in and year out. Rather, we must consider the number of illegal aliens apprehended by the authorities—a figure which is fairly accurate. But it must also be borne in mind that some illegals may have entered the United States several times during one year and been deported every time while others have entered repeatedly and not been apprehended. The figures tell us only the number of apprehensions.

The fluctuations in the number of illegals from Mexico who have been apprehended over the years are shown in Table 3. The largest numbers of illegals were apprehended when the Bracero program was in operation. But apprehensions rose sharply in 1954, when the United States government became very concerned about the wetbacks and started what was called "Operation Wetback." Over one million Mexican illegal aliens were apprehended in that year alone. The number of illegal aliens entering in subsequent years declined but began to increase again about the middle of the 1960s and, at the present time, is increasing at a very rapid rate. This movement of illegals is related, of course, to economic conditions in Mexico and the United States.

The Population Explosion

The phenomenon of illegal Mexican aliens in the United States can also be explained largely by the population explosion of this century. The population of Mexico has been increasing rapidly over the past several years due to a high birth rate. Mexico has been industrializing very rapidly in the last twenty years and making great strides in providing jobs, schools, and housing, but its development has not been able to keep abreast of its growing population. It is still a relatively poor country. Moreover the people of Mexico, as in other developing countries, have been moving from the rural areas to the cities in search of an improved standard of living. Mexican urbanization has centered in two geograph-

The U.S. Border Patrol found thirty illegal aliens in the hidden compartment beneath the packing crates of this truck.

Undocumented Workers

"In the late afternoon of September 29, 1968, forty-six Mexican male aliens walked to a designated point about one mile upriver from the international bridge near Piedras Negras, Mexico. They waited until 3:00 a.m. when a Mexican guided them across the river afoot and led them upriver on the American side for about two hours. The man who guided them collected fifty dollars from most of them and told them to wait in the gully until they would be picked up later in the morning. He then departed, presumably returning to Mexico.

"At about 11:00 a.m. on September 30, 1968, another man appeared and told them that they would be picked up in about an hour. When he returned, he collected fifty dollars from each and told them to come out of the gully. They entered a U-Haul truck waiting on the bank. The entire group had the intention of going to Chicago, Illinois, to work. . . .

"After they had entered the truck they were locked in. They never saw the driver of the truck. Upon arrival in Chicago they were to pay another hundred dollars. . . .

"En route some men began to faint for lack of air, others to gasp for breath, others yelled and pounded on the walls of the truck. The driver stopped the truck and told them that he could not open the doors because he did not have a key but that they were only thirty minutes away from San Antonio, Texas.

"Upon arrival at San Antonio at a particular address, one or two of the aliens, in a dazed condition, got out and walked into a neighboring yard. Two or three tried to hide in the alley behind the garage.

"The neighbors called the police about a disturbance at this address, and the police arrived at about 4:30 p.m. . . . Thirteen of the Mexicans were taken to a local hospital. One was dead on arrival and the two others died the following day. Of the forty-six aliens, twenty-three were returned to Mexico, three had died, and twenty were held as witnesses to this case and farmed out for work in San Antonio."—Samora, 1971: pp. 1–2.

This case history is an example of the extremes to which the undocumented worker will go to enter the United States. Born into an area of the world where development cannot keep pace with the increase of population, the Mexican peasant leaves grinding poverty in hopes of finding a livelihood for himself and a future for his family. His hopes quickly turn to disillusionment as he is exploited by smugglers, informants, employers—anyone who knows his status.

Providing he violates no other laws, the undocumented worker who is apprehended for the first time is merely returned to Mexico. Even repeat offenders usually have most of their sentences suspended, otherwise the thousands of illegal immigrants who are caught each year would soon overload federal prisons. Smugglers are now being dealt with more severely.

---

ical areas. One is Mexico City, the capital, and the other, the cities of the northern border.

Because the United States is a rich country, it has acted as a magnet for people from Mexico who are looking for better opportunities. The United States, as we have seen, has always had a demand for cheap labor, and since the 1920s Mexico has been the chief supplier of that labor. Drawn by the available jobs, many Mexicans who have not been able to enter the United States legally have chosen to come in illegally. They have been encouraged by the fact that many employers who want cheap labor are willing to employ wetbacks. It is curious that it is a felony to *be* a wetback, but at the present time it is not a violation of the law to *employ* wetbacks. This was due to Public Law 283 (cf. Samora, 1971: pp. 139–40).

Other Dimensions

Several dimensions of the illegal alien situation are worthy of discussion. As in the case of commuters, American workers have charged that illegals depress wages, displace the domestic labor supply, and retard unionization and collective bargaining. From another viewpoint, humanitarian reformers complain that illegal aliens are defenseless and outside of the law, making them subject to exploitation by some unscrupulous employers.

Most illegal aliens come to this country on their own; in recent years there has been a growing traffic in smuggling. Aliens might contract with a smuggler for a fee of from one hundred to three hundred dollars for transportation as far north as Chicago, well beyond the primary and secondary lines of defense set up by the Border Patrol. The detection and apprehension of smugglers has increased greatly since 1965. But until 1971, the penalties imposed upon captured smugglers were not great enough to deter the smuggling operation. Only after a number of aliens were found dead as a result of the smuggling operation did the Justice Department begin to clamp down a bit more on the fines and jail sentences imposed on smugglers. At the present time, however, smuggling of people into the United States is still on the increase. In 1965, 525 smugglers (who smuggled 1,814 aliens) were apprehended, in contrast to 8,074 smugglers (who smuggled 83,114 aliens) apprehended in 1974.

The smuggling of marijuana and heroin by illegal aliens does not seem to present as large a problem as many people claim. Most illegal aliens are poor people more interested in obtaining a job than in entering into the drug traffic.

Strikebreakers catch farm labor bus at the border near Roma, Texas.

The Visitor's Permit

Still another dimension of the illegal alien situation concerns those persons who have been issued what is called a "visitor's permit" in order to enter the United States. These permits, sometimes called a border crossing card, are issued to persons who wish to come briefly to the United States for business, shopping, or pleasure. Holders of these cards are supposed to return to the country of origin within seventy-two hours, and following a recent adjustment of the law, must not go beyond twenty-five miles of the border unless they have special permission.

What happens in reality, however, is that many persons who have such a permit enter the United States, stay beyond the time allowed, take a job (which is strictly prohibited), and thus violate the law. For example, many women with visitors' cards enter the United States early in the morning, work as a maid for an American housewife during the day, and return to Mexico late in the afternoon, having earned two dollars for the day. This is a direct violation of the is-

suance of the visitor's permit. Other people enter the United States and simply disappear. When they are apprehended several days, weeks, or months later, they can claim they entered without inspection. Thus they become "wetbacks" and are expelled from the country—but they can use their cards to return again. It is impossible to determine how many persons with only a visitor's permit are working in the United States, but it is safe to say that they do augment the pool of cheap labor available.

Some use still another technique in order to gain entrance to the country. Since it usually costs two or three hundred dollars to be smuggled into the northern part of the United States, a person who can raise that amount of money can, in fact, get a tourist card and buy a round-trip airline ticket from Mexico City to Chicago. Upon arrival, he travels to any northern city where he has friends or relatives, who, in fact, may already have found a job for him. The individual then cashes the return-trip portion of the airline ticket, which provides him with money to live on until he receives his first paycheck. How many persons use this method to gain entrance into the United States is, of course, unknown.

Migrant Farm Workers

Many of the Mexicans who enter the United States, legally or illegally, find jobs in seasonal agricultural work. They join an existing farm labor force which is largely Mexican American, but consists also of a few poor whites and blacks from the South, some American Indians from the Southwest, Puerto Ricans, and Filipino immigrants. All these groups follow the crops, moving north as the season advances.

The largest number of migrant Mexican Americans use the lower Rio Grande Valley of Texas as their home base. Others, but not as many, come from California, New Mexico, Colorado, or Arizona. Those who come from Texas, not far from the border region, have been displaced from work in their home communities by the commuters and by the illegal aliens. These Texas migrants are people who have worked in the agricultural fields for very low wages, who are probably the poorest of the poor, the least educated, the least skilled for other types of jobs, and the ones who earn the least money.

The migrants move up from the South or the Southwest early in April to make their rounds in Illinois, Indiana, Michigan, or northern California, Washington, Oregon, and various other places. They work through the summer planting, hoeing, thinning, and harvesting crops and toward fall return home to harvest there in late season. They come as families or as crews in a truck. They may make a large amount of money on the particular day that they work, especially if the whole family is working, but they work comparatively few days of the year. The housing they are given is generally deplorable, the health and the sanitary conditions under which they live and travel are bad, and they seem to be caught in a never-ending cycle of poverty.

In increasing numbers these seasonal farm workers are "dropping off" the migrant stream and beginning to settle down in several areas in the Midwest and the Great Lakes states. As soon as they are able to find work—whether as a dishwasher, a waitress, a janitor, or whatever—they tend to stop the migrant work in favor of the steady job. The steady job means a number of things to them, even if it does not pay high wages. It means that they can settle down and live in one place the year around. It means that the children can go to school for a full year, not just from November to April. Above all, it means that they can stabilize their lives and have access to more opportunities.

In summary, we have suggested that Mexicans, both legal and illegal immigrants as well as Mexican Americans, have in recent years become the main source of cheap labor in the United States. Various factors have contributed to this situation, including the loss of land of the early settlers, the immigration laws, the Great Depression, the boom years of World War II, the Bracero pro-

Migrant housing in rural California

gram, the commuters, wetbacks, and seasonal farm workers. All in all, these are the people who have provided the labor for the agricultural and industrial development of the Southwest. These people have also provided the labor for the railroads and the mines and for the harvesting of crops which provide the food for our daily consumption.

REFERENCES

Craig, Richard B. *The Bracero Program.* Austin and London: University of Texas Press, 1971.

Hancock, Richard H. *The Role of the Bracero in the Economic and Cultural Dynamics of Mexico: A Case Study of Chihuahua.* Stanford: Hispanic American Society, 1959.

Samora, Julian. *Los Mojados: The Wetback Story.* Notre Dame, Ind.: University of Notre Dame Press, 1971.

CHAPTER 16 | The Mexican American in an Industrial Age

In following the history of Mexican Americans in the United States, a number of themes seem to cut across time. One of these themes, of course, is the persistent Indian, Spanish, Mexican and Anglo-American cultural influences in which the Chicano has been formed. Many writers have commented on the heterogeneity, both biological and cultural, of this population—a unique population in American society.

A second theme that flows through time is the Catholicity of the Mexican American. He may not have been an avid churchgoer as in the Irish-American tradition, but there has been a deep sense of religion throughout his history. It is expressed not so much in religious practices—that is, going to church, receiving the sacraments, joining organizations and making monetary contributions to the church—but rather in everyday behavior.

Recently several Protestant denominations have made large-scale proselytizing efforts among Mexican Americans with considerable success. Their success is much more evident in the cities than in the rural areas, although even relatively isolated villages of northern New Mexico now have a Protestant church. However, the great majority of Mexican Americans are at least nominally Catholic.

The third theme is the persistence of the Spanish language. At a time when the United States is essentially a monolingual country and evidently proud of it and at a time when practically every other ethnic minority has lost its mother tongue, the Mexican American has persisted in maintaining his language, his culture and loyalty to his heritage. American Indians and Mexican Americans seem to be the two groups which have retained this cultural pluralism and, to be sure, at great sacrifice and under the pressure of tremendous criticism from the dominant society.

The latest and most concentrated immigration of persons with a Spanish language heritage has reinforced this pluralism. This immigration consists primarily of Puerto Ricans and Cubans, although other Latin Americans have also contributed numbers to the Spanish-speaking community. The majority of the Puerto Rican and Cuban immigrants reside in large eastern cities or in Dade

151

Rural housing in New Mexico

County, Florida. But sufficiently large numbers have moved to other parts of the U.S. to make an impact in those centers where Mexican Americans are in larger proportion.

The fourth theme that has run through the history is the fact of rural residence. Although most Mexican Americans in the United States are urban dwellers today, it can safely be said that the great majority of them had their origin in rural areas, either in Mexico or the United States. Throughout their history, beginning in the 1600s and up until 1960, Mexican Americans have been a predominately rural population.

The differences between rural and urban life can be examined from many points of view. One method of assessing the impact of the rural or urban experience on people is to consider visible differences in the geographical setting. Environment is a very important measure of the differences that exist.

Housing differs visibly in rural and urban areas. As an example, many people in urban settings live in apartment buildings, a type of dwelling almost unknown outside the cities. Furthermore, the space available for living is significantly larger in rural areas, where there are fewer roads and highways, few if any sidewalks, and an abundance of trees, grass, and open fields. Available facilities differ considerably as well. Consider, for instance, the small country school versus the city's large educational system, or the urban supermarket compared to a general store in a small rural community. Consider also the availability of public transportation—buses, streetcars, taxis, railroads—servicing the cities. Access to such services is limited in rural areas, if it exists at all, as is the availability of electrical power, gas, and appliances.

Equally important, the numbers and types of people with whom one comes in contact varies radically from urban to rural areas. Urban areas tend to be highly congested, with an abundance of entertainment facilities and a general anonymity of the populace. In contrast, there is greater familiarity among rural dwellers, a greater sense of comradeship among the people of a community. As we have seen, similarities developed between people who lived in the isolated atmosphere of the colonial borderlands.

The variety of occupations and the division of labor also differ considerably from rural to urban settings. Many urban jobs are related to the production of goods and services, while few rural jobs fall into this catergory. Rather, many rural jobs are related to farming. As a consequence of these visible differences, growing up and living in a rural area leads to the development of one type of lifestyle while the urban setting creates another.

Migration to the Cities

The point is that Mexican Americans, for the most part, have grown up and lived in rural areas. It was not until the 1960s that they began to leave their rural homes in large numbers and migrate to the cities. Like any other rural people, these Mexican Americans faced a number of problems in adjusting to the urban way of life. In the familiar rural situation, it was highly likely that the relatives and people around an individual would share the same culture. Moving into an urban setting often meant moving into an environment with a diversity of people and cultures and having to contend with new ways of life. As an example, the work environment provided a new experience. Working, even for others, in villages and small towns requires a different kind of behavior than does working in cities. In the city the worker must contend with time and punctuality, transportation, machines, office buildings, crowds of people of different backgrounds, unions, bureaucracies and a whole host of other factors that might be quite strange and different.

Not all rural people have been able to adjust well to an urban setting. This has led to an upsurge of a series of social problems, including delinquency, alcoholism and drug abuse, prostitution, broken families, and many other psychological maladjustments. Many of these problems have plagued the Mexican Americans who have moved to the city as well as other migrants from rural areas.

Of course, some Mexican Americans have always lived in cities. Among the first dwellers were those who migrated to

Urban housing in Sante Fe, New Mexico

Many Mexican Americans find semiskilled jobs in urban industries.

Los Angeles and San Antonio generations ago. Significant numbers of Mexican Americans have trickled into the cities during the past century. Many who worked on building and later running the transcontinental railroad networks have ended up in the urban centers in Pennsylvania, Illinois, Kansas, and other states. Migratory agricultural workers often found seasonal work on the fringe of the cities and some have opted to remain there.

Although the migration of Mexican Americans to the cities had already begun, it intensified during the second decade of this century. This phenomenon was directly related to the recruiting practices of many industries. An acute shortage of cheap labor in the Midwest led many industries to recruit actively in the Southwest and in Mexico. The existing labor shortage was further complicated by the growing militancy of the unions and increased strike activity. Many companies, such as Inland Steel of East Chicago, Indiana, imported thousands of Mexicans and Mexican Americans as strikebreakers during labor disputes. Additional numbers migrated to

the cities to seek jobs in the defense industries that sprang up throughout the country during World War I. More often than not, these people remained in the cities even when the jobs were no longer available.

The Great Depression had a catastrophic effect on urban workers. As industries cut back production or closed completely, thousands of workers were left without jobs. But at least in the cities the unemployed and destitute could find some relief in the breadlines and soup kitchens and could find occasional odd jobs which brought in a few pennies. On the other hand, conditions in rural areas were often intolerable. Nature conspired with man-made economic turmoil to increase the hardships of the rural dwellers when long-lasting drought turned much of the South and Southwest into a huge, useless dust bowl. During this period, many people were compelled to leave the farms and rural communities in their fight for survival. For the most part, they ended up on the relief rolls in the cities. Many of the Mexicans among their numbers were repatriated to Mexico by the U.S. government.

Mexican Americans and World War II

The Second World War served as a catalyst which brought the United States out of the Depression. Furthermore, it served as the most important single event in changing the lifestyle of the Mexican-American population. Mexican Americans were either drafted in large proportions into the armed services or volunteered to serve. For the first time they dispersed in large numbers throughout the United States and many parts of the world. While in the armed services, their horizons expanded and many learned new skills not available in the rural areas. Mexican Americans conducted themselves well in the Second World War and they had the highest proportion of Congressional Medal of Honor winners of any minority in the United States. They also saw the world outside and when they returned many became dissatisfied with their previous condition of subordination, low paying jobs, and discrimination. Many decided to change the system in which they were reared.

The termination of the war also brought into being the "G.I. Bill of Rights." This act provided veterans with opportunities for employment, high school and college education, job training, and resources for purchasing homes and life insurance. Many Mexican Americans took advantage of the G.I. Bill. For the first time, they entered college in large numbers. Within a few years after the war, their slightly higher educational achievements would lead to expanding opportunities in employment.

The war also created intense labor shortages as defense industries grew. Many Mexican Americans who did not serve in the armed forces found new employment opportunities open to them. New facilities had to be built such as training camps and air bases, concentration camps for the Japanese Americans and prisoner of war camps. Basic supplies and war materials had to be produced and delivered to distant places. The production of food and fiber had to be accelerated. Even the establishment of the Bracero program required many Mexican Americans as administrators, office workers and interpreters.

While in military service many Mexican Americans were trained in usable work skills.

Since most war-related job opportunities existed in urban centers, there was considerable migration of Mexican Americans to the cities in the decades of the 1940s and 1950s. The impact on rural areas was frequently tremendous. For instance, the smaller towns and cities in the southern part of Colorado lost many residents who moved to Pueblo and Denver for employment. In New Mexico, Texas, and Arizona there was a large exodus of the population to the urban centers. Perhaps the state which received the most migrants during this period was California, giving it a Mexican-American population equal to that of Texas. Most of California's recent Mexican-American migrants have come from other parts of the Southwest. In contrast, most of the recent migrants to Texas have come from Mexico.

Many of the people who made a move either for employment or because of the armed services during and after World War II never returned permanently to their home residences. A general redistribution of the Mexican-American population had taken place and the majority eventually took residence in urban areas.

Thus, a generation of Mexican Americans with new experiences, wider horizons, different goals and values and greater expectations began to appear. These were persons who wanted an education and/or had achieved it, who wanted more than the usual menial jobs, and who also wanted to be treated as first-class citizens. They considered themselves as Americans and wanted their full civil rights. They also wanted an end to prejudice and discrimination. They were no longer content with the old way of life as they sought equality and justice.

The changes that occurred, however, did not come easily or without penalties. The larger society does not always accept changes gracefully and Mexican Americans had to suffer the scourge of discrimination in jobs, housing, public accommodations, and civil rights. Some of this discrimination is still evident today in spite of the laws and in spite of the affirmative action that local, state, and federal governments sometimes attempt.

One of the most serious incidents of discrimination occurred during World War II in the Zoot-Suit Riots of Los Angeles. The incident received its name from the type of clothing, known as a Zoot Suit, worn by many young Mexican Americans of the early 1940s. In the summer of 1943, a private quarrel between a Mexican American and an Anglo erupted into widespread rioting. Anglo members of the armed forces were soon joined by civilians in a spree of attacking and beating Mexican Americans wherever they were found. The Zoot-Suit Riots created a heritage of bitterness and fear that is still remembered among the Mexican Americans of Los Angeles. The riots represented a blatant example of discrimination and violation of civil rights in U.S. history. It compares with acts of violence perpetrated by Americans on Indians and blacks.

An Urban Population

Although encountering problems of discrimination, Mexican Americans continued to settle in the urban areas. By the 1960s they were a significant element in

The Zoot Suit Riots

In the early 1940s many Mexican-American teenagers wore "drapes." This popular style of clothing resembled the zoot suits worn in Harlem. It was designed to be comfortable to dance in, and was sometimes used as a signal that the wearer belonged to a club or gang. Most Anglos called the outfit a zoot suit and assumed that only hoodlums wore them.

In 1942, in the name of national security, all the Japanese Americans on the west coast had been taken from their homes and interred in camps. With this group of scapegoats safely out of the way, Los Angeles newspapers began to blame crime in the city on the Mexican Americans. They began to give prominence to incidents involving Mexican Americans, or as they called them "zoot suiters."

On the evening of June 3, 1943, eleven sailors on shore leave walked into one of Los Angeles's worst Mexican-American slums and became involved in a fight with persons unknown, but who were thought to be Mexican Americans. This incident stirred up the anger of the citizenry, as well as that of the many members of the armed forces who were stationed in Los Angeles.

The next evening two hundred sailors hired a fleet of taxicabs and drove through the heart of the city to the Mexican-American communities on the east side. Everytime they saw a Mexican-American boy in a zoot suit they would stop and beat him up. The city police did nothing to stop them.

The following two nights the sailors were joined by other servicemen as they wandered freely through the city harassing Mexican Americans. Los Angeles police arrested several severely beaten Mexican-American boys on charges of rioting, even though no resistance had been offered by the Mexican Americans. The newspapers featured headlines such as "44 Zooters Jailed in Attacks on Sailors."

On June seventh, thousands of civilians joined in the riot. Filipinos and Negroes as well as Mexican Americans were attacked. At midnight military authorities decided the local police could not handle the situation and declared downtown Los Angeles off limits to military personnel. The rioting spread to the suburbs for two more days before it finally subsided.

The Los Angeles zoot suit riots touched off similar disturbances across the country in the summer of 1943: in San Diego; Beaumont, Texas; Chicago; Detroit; Evansville, Indiana; Philadelphia and Harlem.

A restaurant in a Los Angeles barrio features foods familiar to the people of the area.

the industrial and urban setting of American society.

Many of those who went to college became teachers. Others continued on to professional schools in the fields of medicine, dentistry, law, and social work. Only a few entered graduate school to obtain their doctorates and become university professors, researchers, or writers.

Others chose to work in industry and in factories. Some became technicians, some engaged in unskilled work and some entered services as clerks, waiters, secretaries, truck-drivers and salesmen. A few became proprietors, mostly owners of small businesses. Coming from a rural background, a considerable number continued working in agriculture and many became seasonal farm workers.

Regardless of their occupation, it soon became evident that urban centers had acquired large concentrations of the Mexican-American population which became more and more visible. In California, the Mexican-American population had grown in Los Angeles, San Francisco, and San Diego. In Arizona, the major concentrations settled in Phoenix and Tucson. The Mexican-American population grew in New Mexico in Albuquerque, Las Cruces, and Santa Fe. In Colorado, Denver, Pueblo, and Colorado Springs attracted much of the Mexican-American population from the rural areas. The border cities of Texas such as El Paso, McAllen, Laredo, and Brownsville have always had high concentrations of Mexican Americans, but now the large cities of San Antonio, Dallas, and Houston attracted many.

Chicago, Kansas City, Detroit, Toledo, Gary, and East Chicago, Indiana attracted many Mexican Americans. In 1940, the Census Bureau reported that the majority of people with Spanish surnames in the Southwest were rural residents. In the census of 1960 it was reported that the majority of Mexican Americans were urban residents. Thus, the transition from rural to urban residence occurred over a twenty-year period. The 1970 census shows the continued trend in urban residence, but not at the same accelerated rate.

PART FOUR

The New Awareness

CHAPTER 17 | Search for Equality

The American educational system was established as a free, public, and compulsory system. Its basic premise was that all children should have an equal opportunity for education. The school system not only provided the academic education but further served the national interest. It provided a means of "Americanizing" the children of hundreds of thousands of immigrants who came to these shores.

Among the basic premises of American education as it has developed over the years, at least two are highly significant. The first is that the child should be accepted as he is. Education should be based on the talents, the heritage, and sociocultural attributes which the student possesses. We interpret this to mean that if a child does not know English, his native language presumably should be used in order to teach him English or special efforts should be made in his behalf. A recent Supreme Court decision (Lau V. Nichols, 414 U.S. 563, 1974) confirmed this interpretation. Another, later, decision, however, determined that only English would be allowed.

The second premise of American education is that it should serve the total community. Public education was estab-

lished so that it would be in the hands of the local community through small school districts and school boards, the members being elected by their peers. This provided a means of administering the schools in the best interests of the community.

The two premises are basic to American education. Had they been adhered to, the public educational system would be a strong one and the needs of children in any community would have been served.

What actually happened, however, was that the American public schools developed a system of Americanization. In so doing, they neglected the particular needs of many children and focused on teaching American middle-class values and mores. The American Southwest offers a graphic example of the consequences of this trend. American Indians as well as Spanish-speaking children were stripped by the school systems of their language, their culture, their traditions and customs. The burden of conforming to an American middle-class mold was placed on the minorities. The results of these actions and policies on the part of the schools have been that, at least among

161

these two populations, many individuals who have attended school have not been adequately educated and they have either dropped out or been pushed out of the educational system.

As to the second premise of serving the total community, a curious but predictable situation has developed in most school districts, where the control of the school through a school board tends to be in the hands of the dominant society—indeed, in the hands of the more affluent members of that society. Certain segments of the community, in particular the poor and the ethnic groups, are not well represented either in the governing of the school through the school board, in the administration of the school (that is, superintendents and principals), or among the teaching staff. Studies by the United States Commission on Civil Rights support the above statement.

Mexican Americans and the Schools

The educational history of Mexican Americans in this country has been, unfortunately, one of neglect and misunderstanding. The Treaty of Guadalupe-Hidalgo guaranteed the rights of this population after Mexico was conquered and the people of the Southwest became American citizens. Among the rights guaranteed by citizenship is the right to equal opportunity in education. But schools were not immediately established after the conquest, and when they were established they quite often did not take into account the special needs of the students. Among those needs would be a recognition of their language and their culture and the use of both the language and the culture in the educational process.

Spanish Language

In an effort to insure that Mexican Americans learn the English language, some states passed laws prohibiting the use of Spanish in instruction. Furthermore, many children who could not speak English were punished, sometimes physically, for speaking Spanish in the classroom or on the school grounds. This reprehensible practice persisted up to the 1970s.

Some schools of the Southwest placed children with a distinguishable Spanish surname in classrooms separate from children with non-Spanish names. These were often called "Mexican" rooms. The schools justified this action by claiming that if one placed children who did not speak English together in the same classroom, they would somehow learn the new language more quickly than if they were placed in a room with English-speaking children. One thing the educators overlooked was the fact that many children with Spanish surnames did not speak Spanish at all.

By and large, the instruction for children in the "Mexican" room was inferior to the instruction given the other children. Even language training was inadequate and many children with Spanish surnames remained in separate "Mexican" rooms up through the sixth, seventh, or eighth grade. Obviously, this kind of separatism created attitudes of inferiority within the Mexican-American child and of superiority within the Anglo children.

Gerrymandering

The failure of the school system can be illustrated in other ways. In large school districts in cities such as San Antonio and Los Angeles, much gerrymandering took place in order to separate the Mexican-American population from the dominant society through changes in the political boundaries defining the school district. This manipulation of school district boundaries assured the poor and the ethnics who remained in one district that their schools would be inferior to those of the more well-to-do population. The difference in quality is quite simply a matter of the difference in funds available for the operation of the respective schools. The funds to run a school depend on the value of the property in which the school district is located and the property taxes collected. Thus, the Anglo schools generally had more money for materials, equipment, school buildings, and teachers' salaries than schools in poorer neighborhoods.

Intelligence Tests

The use of intelligence tests in placing students also has had a discriminatory effect upon children with different linguistic and cultural backgrounds. Since the tests are usually standardized and validated among the dominant English-speaking middle-class population, people who do not fall into this group often score poorly. Since the poor and the ethnics tend to receive lower test scores, they are often considered either retarded or not quite up to the level of high-scoring, middle-class students. Consequently, Mexican-American students have frequently been relegated to a non-academic education curriculum—that is to vocational, business, or industrial studies rather than to an educational curriculum geared to academic achievement and preparation for college. In many schools this type of discrimination carried over into extra-curricular activities. Few Mexican Americans found opportunity to play basketball or football, be cheerleaders, play in the band, or join the social clubs.

The Parent Teacher Association (PTA) is intended to be the link between the community and the school. But its policies and procedures have generally made it difficult for Mexican Americans to participate. If they were poor and could not speak English well, they were excluded

Education will play an important part in the advancement of Mexican Americans.

from this one organization in which they might learn something about the school and the education of their children.

All in all, we think it is reasonable to state that the school systems in the five southwestern states served to create an attitude of superiority among students of the dominant society and an attitude of inferiority among minority groups and poor people. It is also fair to state that the children of the dominant society received an education which was superior to that of the children of minority groups and the poor.

In California, the community college system does not prepare minority students well enough for them to go on to enter a four-year school. The Mexican American Legal Defense and Education Fund (M.A.L.D.E.F.) revealed that about 10 percent of Mexican Americans and about 70 percent of white students go on to attend a four-year college or university. For this reason, M.A.L.D.E.F. has sued the state and the appropriate boards of education in order to determine what lies behind this dramatic difference in statistics. The suit is still pending.

Moves for Equal Opportunity

Many Mexican-American educators, such as the late Dr. George I. Sánchez, devoted their lives to the elimination of discrimination in the school system. They did so through teaching, research, and publication. They also spent much of their energy trying to establish programs which would foster equal opportunity for the Mexican-American minority. Organizations such as the League of United Latin American Citizens (LULAC) fostered school attendance, scholarships, and programs to teach Spanish-speaking children a basic 400-word vocabulary in English before they entered grade school. One of the most important organizations to be heard on the question of discrimination in education, particularly in Texas, was the American G.I. Forum, founded by Dr. Hector García of Corpus Christi. The American G.I. Forum successfully led court battles which brought an end to official and legal discrimination against Mexican Americans in the schools.

Although the goal of equality of educational opportunity has not yet been achieved throughout the nation, a number of important events have occurred which suggest that it might yet be realized. Significant changes are being made in the curricula of the school systems, not only at the elementary level but also at the secondary level and in the universities. New courses are being directed toward the history and culture of Mexican Americans. And many existing courses are being modified to include this content. Sometimes a series of courses comprises a program in Chicano or Mexican-American Studies. In support of this trend, a number of persons throughout the United States, including some individuals in public and private agencies, have begun to develop educational materials which can be used in teaching Mexican Americans. Furthermore, the federal government in recent years has funded bilingual education programs aimed primarily at elementary schools with high concentrations of Mexican Americans. Some of these programs have also become bicultural. They have not yet, however, been evaluated.

Many colleges and universities have developed Chicano studies. The programs range from providing meeting places (La Casa Latina, where minority students can gather for mutual support) to academic

TABLE 4

MEDIAN SCHOOL YEARS COMPLETED

(by Spanish surname, total white, and non-white populations for five southwestern states, 1950 and 1960,*
and for male and female Spanish surname 1970**)

| | 1950 | | | 1960 | | | 1970*** Spanish | |
	Spanish	Total White	Non-White	Spanish	Total White	Non-White	Male	Female
Arizona	6.1	10.6	5.5	7.9	11.7	7.0	9.8	9.5
California	7.6	11.8	8.9	9.0	12.1	10.5	10.5	10.4
Colorado	6.4	10.9	9.8	8.6	12.1	11.2	10.3	10.4
New Mexico	7.4	9.5	5.8	8.4	11.5	7.1	10.3	10.3
Texas	3.6	9.7	7.0	6.1	10.8	8.1	8.4	8.1

*For both sexes, 14 years and over. (Source: Donald N. Barrett in Samora, p. 179, Table 9A.).

**1970 Census of Population—subject reports—Persons of Spanish Surname, June, 1973, Table 8,
pp. 32–41.

***Comparable statistics were not available.

TABLE 4A

MEDIAN SCHOOL YEARS COMPLETED OF THE HISPANIC
AND NON-HISPANIC POPULATION AS OF MARCH 1987

Total Population	Total Population, Hispanic	Mexican	Puerto Rican	Cuban	Central and South American	Other Hispanic	Non-Hispanic
12.7	12.0	10.8	12.1	12.4	12.3	12.4	12.7

Source: *The Hispanic Population in the United States: March 1986 and 1987 (Advance Report). Series P-20,
No. 416, Issued August 1987*, p. 6.

classes, programs, departments, and graduate studies.

A person can take a course, or pursue a minor or a major in the subject, or receive a degree in the field. Some professors and others criticize such degree-granting programs as being "soft" or as not being "real" academic disciplines. Chicano studies are, however, just as legitimate as programs in Russian studies, women studies, Latin American studies, American studies, or any other such course of study. How are undergraduate or graduate degree programs in, for example, business, agriculture, nursing, or engineering any less proper academic disciplines than Chicano studies?

Teacher-training institutions have become aware of the fact that teachers are not generally educated in the history and culture of ethnic groups. Many teachers are ignorant of the culture and traditions and language of the children in their classrooms who come from various minority groups. Efforts are being made to correct this situation either by changing the curriculum of the university classes or by offering summer workshops or in-service training programs for teachers of minority children.

The federal government has also taken some steps to train teachers, sponsoring a variety of programs in the field of migrant education. Since the majority of migrant workers are Mexican American, the government programs quite often have been oriented toward this particular ethnic group. Migrant educational programs vary from state to state and county to county. Some are innovative and quite good. Others, such as those in the state of Indiana, have yet to accept bicultural, bilingual education or even to use bilingual teachers.

The deficiencies in the education available to Mexican-American children can be graphically demonstrated, as can the trend toward improvement, by comparing the educational level of Mexican Americans with that of other groups in 1950, 1960, and 1970. We will limit the comparison of educational achievement to the southwestern states, because this is the only region for which we have comparable statistics. A look at these statistics in Table 4 will make readily apparent the failure of the system with regard to the education of the Mexican-American population.

Starring actor Olmos, the movie *Stand and Deliver* shows the true documentary of a teacher from Bolivia. Mr. E. Calante teaches a class of Mexican American students calculus. The students, in turn, take the national standard test in mathematics, and fourteen pass the test with high marks. The school—Garfield High in Los Angeles—had never qualified before for its students to take the test, and, of course, the students are accused of cheating because they did so well. The students are made to retake the test; they pass it; and today Garfield is well known for its excellent instruction in mathematics and for the great number of its students who pass the national tests.

Struggle against Discrimination

Discrimination against Mexican Americans in the United States has not been as overt as it has in the case of blacks, with the exception of the state of Texas.

Mexican-American lawyers are active in defending the rights of their people.

Discrimination against blacks in this country up until the civil rights acts in the 1950s and the 1960s was institutionalized because it was built into the fabric of the society and the laws of the nation. If one can believe that in a democracy it was lawful to discriminate officially and overtly against a certain segment of the society in the areas of housing, public accommodations, education, voting, and employment, one can understand the presence of separate drinking fountains, separate toilet facilities, separate parks, separate schools, separate housing, and separate churches. Under this system, a large group of Americans were being denied their basic constitutional rights.

Discrimination against Mexican Americans was not institutionalized to this extent. It was not supported by the vast body of legislation that made discrimination against blacks official. On the one hand, Mexican Americans were considered to be Caucasians (white) and, therefore, laws which were aimed at blacks did not necessarily apply. On the other hand, middle-class Anglos have generally considered themselves superior to everyone else. And this fact opened the door to discrimination against Mexican Americans and other Caucasian ethnic groups. The discrimination was often subtle, because it usually had no legal basis. But legal or not, subtle or overt, discrimination leaves its mark on the entire society. It specifically affects the persons who are subjected to discriminatory action. But the people who discriminate are also changed by their behavior.

Housing

Discrimination in housing has provided one of the most painful experiences for Mexican Americans. In most areas of the Southwest and the Midwest, the commu-

Mexican Americans are today serving the cause of justice as judges.

nity, town, or city is invariably divided into clearly defined sections. It is rarely difficult to locate the "Mexican section" in most communities. It may be found on the other side of a main highway, across the tracks, or across the river. If there is no natural geographical division, the Mexican-American population may congregate in one particular area.

Discrimination against Mexican Americans with regard to housing was never official, as we have indicated, yet it is curious that in most communities this population lives in a particular section of town. One underlying factor may be that they are frequently poor and cannot afford housing in other parts of the community. But we cannot ignore the fact that in many communities real estate agencies do not show houses in certain sections of town, let alone sell them, to Mexican Americans. This does not happen because the prospective buyer does not appear to be "white" but because of an accent or a Spanish surname. Many incidents have been recorded in which Mexican Americans attempted to buy homes in certain neighborhoods and, although they were not overtly refused, the property was suddenly no longer for sale. Thus, discrimination in housing has been as effective as if laws existed which would prohibit Mexican Americans from buying or renting housing in certain neighborhoods.

Jury Selection

Jury service offers another example of discrimination against Mexican Americans. A basic tenet of American law is that people should be judged by their peers. In

More opportunity to join police forces is needed by Mexican Americans.

other words, in all trials requiring a jury or all investigations conducted by a grand jury, every segment of the population should have an equal chance of being represented.

But most studies reveal that minorities and poor people are not well represented on juries. When a jury without minority representation convicts a person with a minority background, then that person has been denied the right of being judged by his peers. The history of convictions through court cases is replete with such examples—as when an all-white jury convicts a black defendant. Similarly, if an all-male jury tries a female defendant or a jury composed entirely of older people tries a young man or woman, the defendant is not given the opportunity of a trial by his peers.

The implication seems to be that the jury selection process is selective in itself. In some cases, this has been a matter of overt discrimination. The individuals charged with jury selection passed over or eliminated the names of potential minority jurors—a matter which was simplified in the case of Mexican Americans by the fact that a Spanish surname is easily recognized. If minority individuals were called for jury duty, it was still possible to make sure by failing to select them from the larger body of jurors.

Frequently, such overt tactics have proven unnecessary, because jury selection in many areas is tied to voter registration. The names of potential jurors are taken from among the county's registered voters. Traditionally, minority populations were disenfranchised. In some cases, they were legally prevented from registering to vote, as with some blacks in the South prior to the civil rights movement. Even when minorities could register, a variety of tactics, including physical violence,

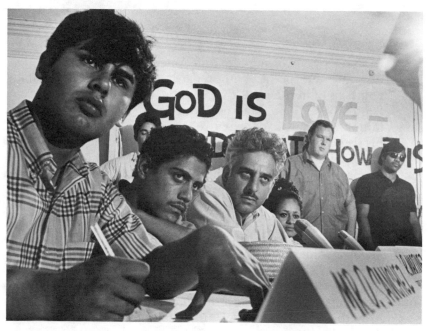

Answers are sought in a conference with a police chief in East Los Angeles.

discouraged them from doing so. Commonly, they were kept ignorant of the political system because no effort was made to solicit minority registration and this effectively kept minorities off the juries. Although the situation is changing, due partly to active minority voter registration drives in recent years, large numbers of minority citizens do not register to vote. Consequently, their names are not available for jury selection.

With the establishment of the Southwest Voter Registration Office in San Antonio, Texas, Willie Velasquez was able to bring about many much-needed changes to the voting process. A newsletter published by the Southwest Voter Registration Office is available.

Law Enforcement

Still another area in which an element of discrimination appears may be found in the relationship of police departments to minority groups. Numerous studies have shown that, historically, the police have been more apt to stop, search, and arrest members of minority groups than they have members of the dominant society. The records of arrest in most cities with large minority populations will indicate that minorities are arrested in greater proportion to their numbers in the community than are members of the dominant group. Again, the studies will show that of those who are arrested, a greater proportion of minority members of the community will be brought to trial than non-minorities. Furthermore, of those who are brought to trial, a greater proportion of minorities are convicted than non-minorities, and of those who are convicted, minorities are likely to get harsher sentences than non-minorities for the same offenses. If the studies are objective, it becomes clear that a general pattern of discrimination by the police and the courts against the minorities has existed for a very long time.

When considering police brutality, similar statements can be made about the behavior of the police toward members of minority groups. In the racial riots of the late 1960s and early 1970s, such behavior was well documented in the mass media.

Two cases involving Mexican Americans illustrate our point. With regard to the courts, a rather famous case came to light September 2, 1969. The case, concerning a minor who had had sexual relations with his sister, was brought before Judge Gerald S. Chargin in the Superior Court of California, San Jose, California. The case is presented verbatim in Appendix I. The judge made a number of derogatory, inflammatory and pejorative statements. These remarks were interpreted by many Mexican Americans across the country as prejudicial statements directed at all Mexican Americans. Thousands of statements of protest were sent to government officials from the president of the United States on down. Most statements asked for an investigation of the judge and his immediate removal from office. But Judge Chargin was not removed from office.

Another case began on August 29, 1970, during the National Chicano Moratorium March in East Los Angeles. Ruben Salazar, Los Angeles Times columnist and news director for the Spanish language television station KMEX, was shot and killed at the Silver Dollar Cafe on Whittier Boulevard. He was shot by a member of the Los Angeles County Sheriff's Department. Two other people were killed—Angel Gilberto Díaz and Lynn Ward. Hundreds of people were beaten and injured by the police and over four hundred were arrested. Five hundred police and sheriff's deputies were active in what Chicanos believe was an unprovoked police riot. The sheriff's department claimed that forty officers were injured and twenty-five radio cars damaged (Morales, 1972: p: 101).

We will not go into the details concerning the circumstances of the riot. These have been reported by Dr. Armando Morales in *Ando Sangrando: A Study of Mexican American–Police Conflict* and in

the journal *La Raza,* Vol. no. 3, Special Issue (no date, pagination, or volume number).

The testimony at the inquest was most conflicting and it pitted the sheriff's department against the witnesses from the Chicano Moratorium. Suffice it to say that despite the logical flaws in the officers' testimony and the evidence to the contrary no charges were brought against the officers and the case was closed.

The article from *La Raza* is reprinted in Appendix II. We feel that this article best expressed the Chicanos' attitude toward the judicial system. Mexican Americans have been discriminated against in all areas of life, systematically, though perhaps not officially. One such area of discrimination is in the use of public facilities and public accommodations.

Public Accommodations

While the actions on the part of the majority group toward Mexican Americans has not been as overt as toward blacks in the South, there have been few cities or towns in the Southwest or in other parts of the country that have not denied Mexican Americans access to public accommodations. For example, in many communities, Roman Catholic churches have traditionally seated Mexican Americans on one side of the church and members of the Anglo community on the other side. The same practice has been followed in theaters. Access to swimming pools has been difficult for Mexican Americans in many communities. Many restaurants and hotels have traditionally discriminated against Mexican Americans. The use of toilet facilities in filling stations has been denied Mexican Americans in the migratory labor stream as they move from Texas to points north. And some communities have even

Through education and training, Mexican Americans have gained better work positions.

denied Chicanos burial plots in cemeteries.

Employment Opportunity

Even more serious discrimination has occurred in employment. Mexican Americans like blacks and Indians have usually been employed in low-status positions, and in many instances have been denied access to white-collar jobs. Labor unions have discriminated against minority groups, including Mexican Americans. This has been particularly true of the craft unions which organize trades such as plumbing, carpentry, masonry, and the like. Major unions have admitted Mexican Americans to membership, but again if we look at the statistics as to the type of employment of Mexican-American union members, we find that they generally occupy low-status jobs. The same pattern has been true, too, of major educational systems. That is, in large educational systems one commonly finds many Mexican Americans at the janitorial and custodial level, fewer at the clerical, fewer still at the teacher level, and very few indeed at the administrative level. Major industries would have similar records. Even state governments and employment in federal agencies reveal the same trend.

Jack Otero, a Cubano, is president of the Labor Counsel for Latin American Advancement (LACLAA). Mr. Montoya has been the executive director for many years. LACLAA attempts to organize Hispanics in the labor movement have been very successful. Recently at the University of Notre Dame, many young Hispanics were brought in for a workshop on labor, which was sponsored by the LACLAA with the help of Otero and Patrick Sullivan (a professor in the sociology department at Notre Dame) and other professors at the university.

Pursuing Civil Rights

A great deal of energy has been expended in efforts to end discrimination. Although discrimination still exists and its opponents are frequently discouraged, attempts to eliminate it have not been totally without success.

Some of the most effective tools for fighting discrimination have been provided by the federal government through the promulgation of anti-discriminatory legislation. Although the laws came into being as a result of the demands of pressure groups and do not necessarily reflect the values and beliefs of the senators and congressmen who passed them, they serve a useful purpose. Civil rights acts have made discrimination illegal throughout the country. Many efforts to end discriminatory practices were initiated following passage of the Civil Rights Act of 1964 and the publication of evidence of discrimination collected by the United States Commission on Civil Rights. The establishment of the U.S. Equal Employment Opportunity Commission was a milestone in attempts by the federal government to end discrimination in employment.

State and local governments have followed the example of the federal government. Most states have established civil rights commissions which are empowered to investigate discrimination in housing, employment, public accommodations, and education. The commissions generally work very effectively in their attempts to investigate discrimination or to bring redress for discriminatory practices. Many communities attempt the same thing at the local level. They have established committees or commissions on human rights or human relations, charged with investigation and correction of acts of discrimination.

The minority groups themselves have provided impetus for the movement to end discrimination. This is the real grass roots movement and it is essential to the ultimate success of all efforts to end discrimination. It is the source of much of the pressure which has resulted in action at the federal, state, and local levels.

Much of the early action by minorities was spontaneous and disorganized. It began to gain cohesion during the civil rights protest of the 1950s and 1960s. Eventually, members of minority groups began to organize into constructive working units, with considerable success. The establishment of legal aid societies for the poor and the Mexican American Legal Defense and Education Fund have brought acts of discrimination against Mexican Americans into the courts and to the attention of the nation. Of course, a great deal remains to be done. The efforts we have described treat the symptoms. The cure is possible only if Americans change their attitudes toward race.

REFERENCES

Morales, Armando. *Ando Sangrando: A Study of Mexican American-Police Conflict.* La Puente, California: Perspectiva Publication, 1972.

Samora, Julian, ed. *La Raza: Forgotten Americans.* Notre Dame, Ind.: University of Notre Dame Press, 1966.

CHAPTER 18 | Striving for Self-Determination

Social and fraternal organizations have always played an important role in the Mexican-American community. This is perhaps one reason why Mexican Americans have been able to organize more effectively than other minority groups in their fight against discrimination. But the importance of organization is far greater than the banding together of people to overcome discriminatory practices against them. It is one of the very bases of the Mexican American's search for self-determination.

The organizations created by Chicanos served a variety of purposes, as did the organizations created by European immigrants who came to America. They helped perpetuate and reinforce the customs, language and traditions of their members' forefathers. They also helped cushion the jolt of cultural shock which immigrants often experience when they leave their homeland and settle in another country. These organizations also performed a limited service by helping newcomers in time of need. The Mexican American in the Southwest—whether he was a newly arrived immigrant from Mexico or a long-term resident who had become a U.S. citizen following the Treaty of Guadlupe-Hidalgo—established and joined organizations intended to help him cope with the new society and the hardships which he encountered within it.

Generally speaking, the organizations of Mexican Americans can be placed in one of five categories, though at times the functions and purposes of some organizations overlapped. The categories can be broadly described as fraternal, labor, religious, service and political organizations. The last of these did not become prominent until after World War II.

Two organizations have been particularly active and successful in the academic world: the National Association of Chicano Studies (NACS) and the Society for the Advancement of Chicanos and Native Americans in Science (SACNAS). Each group holds a very worthwhile annual meeting.

173

times of need, and to give social and psychological support in crisis situations. For instance, the mutual aid societies provided very limited insurance as well as death benefits for members and thus assured families that the deceased would receive a proper burial.

These organizations were supported by membership dues. Each member was required to contribute a small amount of money or whatever he could afford to the treasury of the mutual aid society. Since cash income was generally low in many of the rural areas, the resources of many mutualistas were seldom able to provide long-term assistance for any members.

In spite of hardships and handicaps, the mutualistas were a financial resource that would help a family with immediate needs before, during or after a birth, a wedding or a death. In most cases the mutualistas were concerned with the total family, but memberships were usually restricted to the breadwinner or to males over a specified age.

Perhaps even more important, the mutual societies offered families social and psychological support in times of crisis. In addition, they served to bring all of the members of a community together for funerals, feast days, weddings, or baptisms. This helped to maintain the allegiance of the individual to his group as well as to his culture. To further assure the loyalty of each member, persons seeking membership were required to swear allegiance to the society. For the most part, these societies did not encourage assimilation. This was the case in the border towns as well as in some northern cities such as Chicago, Illinois and East Chicago, Indiana, where the mutualistas sought to maintain close cultural ties with Mexico.

The foundation and growth of many mutual aid societies such as La Alianza Hispano Americana (1894); La Camara de Comercio Mexicana (1918); La Sociedad Progresista Mexicana y Recreativa (1918); La Sociedad Mutualista Mexicana (1918); La Sociedad Union Cultural Mexicana (1924), and countless others was spontaneous, their establishment usually undertaken in response to certain local issues (Grebler, 1966: pp. 542–43). Thus, the mutual aid societies were almost always local or regional in character, whether in rural or urban areas. For the most part, the mutualistas concerned themselves with either social or labor issues, rather than political issues.

As we have said, many of the early mutualistas made strong efforts to imbue their members with an intense nationalism toward Mexico and discouraged assimilation into the large society. These efforts continued to be successful in those communities and barrios that remained isolated from the Anglo society. However, the story was different in those few areas where Mexican Americans began to experience some social and economic success. In such cases, strong identification with Mexico soon declined, with the end result that Mexican-American organizations began to concern themselves with the status of their membership in the United States. This was especially true of the smaller number of middle-class Mexican Americans who, as with most socially mobile immigrant groups, felt that they had to demonstrate their "Americanness" to others.

The earliest expression of this kind of spirit among the Mexican Americans occurred in San Antonio, Texas, in 1921, with the formation of the order of the Sons of America. According to its constitution, the central purpose of the Sons was that the members "use their influ-

Mexican Americans play an important role in many national and international fraternal organizations.

ence in all fields of social, economic, and political action in order to realize the greatest enjoyment possible of all the rights and privileges and prerogatives extended by the American Constitution" (Weeks, 1929: p. 260).

The Sons of America appealed to similar elements of the Mexican-American community in the southern part of Texas so much that on August 24, 1927, the Mexican Americans of the Rio Grande Valley held a convention in Harlingen, Texas, in the hope of forming a new organization based upon a union with the Sons. Following the refusal of the Sons of America to partake in such a union, the valley group formed a League of United

Latin American Citizens (LULAC) in 1928.

LULAC's constitution reflects the integrationist tendencies in its stipulation that English would be the official language of the organization. In addition to working toward assimilation, LULAC also attempted to call attention to the contributions which Mexicans had made to the United States in the social, economic, and cultural realms. For the most part, members of LULAC were middle-class Mexican Americans who held a strong identification with the United States and its culture. LULAC established the Four Hundred Clubs, which sought to teach English to Mexican-American youngsters by having them learn a basic vocabulary of 400 words in English before entering formal schooling. The English language was important to LULAC for "the enjoyment of our rights and privileges" (Weeks, 1929: p. 265).

It is important to point out that LULAC also strove to end discrimination against Mexican Americans and "to maintain a sincere and respectful reverence for our social origins of which we are proud" (ibid.). In essence, LULAC represented the first general attempt by Mexican Americans to organize for the purpose of giving voice to their aspirations and needs as citizens of the United States. It was both a fraternal and a service organization, yet differed significantly from the mutualista societies.

The mutualista societies and the assimilation-oriented groups failed to elicit any type of response, either negative or positive, from the dominant society, primarily because they posed no threat to the society. However, the myth of the docile Mexican began to explode in the wake of his organizing efforts in the labor field.

Early Labor Organizations

Mexican-American efforts to organize labor began in the late nineteenth century. Such efforts usually grew out of an attempt to join together for self-protection (McWilliams, 1949: p. 190). One of the earliest events of this type on record involved several hundred cowboys, including a handful of Mexican vaqueros, who went on strike in 1883 against a large number of cattle companies. One of the signatures that appeared on the strike declaration was that of Juan Gomez, a Mexican American. The striking vaqueros won their demands for better wages.

The Chicano had long provided the labor for the development of the Southwest. He had helped build the railroads in the Southwest and had maintained them throughout the nation. His labor cleared the land and planted and harvested the crops in the developing agricultural industry. His skills and labor were essential for the growing mining industry. He was the original cowboy of the nation. He also herded sheep, cut timber, and worked in lumber yards and sawmills. During the last decades of the nineteenth century, the Chicano fought for equal wages and better working conditions. He was by no means passive, and in many instances his efforts led to violence.

By the latter part of the nineteenth century, the Southwest had witnessed considerable organizing activity among labor, most successfully in the mining industry (Acuña, 1972: p. 95). The 1880s saw the rise of the Caballeros of Labor, a group of men who concentrated on fighting Anglo land-grabbing schemes. In the mid-1890s the Western Federation of Miners was established. Chicanos made up an important segment of the mining population in the Southwest and they provided the union's leadership (Meier and Rivera, 1972: p. 170). Significantly, that leadership usually emanated from the mutualistas, which for some time continued to provide many of the organizers and leaders in the turbulent labor history of the Southwest (Acuña, 1972: p. 96).

In the first decade of the twentieth century union activity among Mexican Americans increased. The move to organize coincided with the rise of large commercial farm and mining operations in the Southwest which created a pressing demand for cheap Mexican labor.

In response to overt discrimination and to rampant exploitation practiced by their employers, the Mexican laborers began organizing themselves in order to secure some means of protection. As in the case of the mutual aid societies, many of these labor organizations were created for the purpose of dealing with a specific and often isolated labor issue. Once that issue or conflict in agriculture or industry was resolved, the organization ceased to exist. Of course, the demise of such unions. was quite often helped along by the violent and repressive measures taken by the employers and their vigilante groups.

SPMDTU

As stated earlier, many of the organizations formed by Mexican Americans had their roots in the mutualistas. A significant example was the Sociedad Protección Mutua de Trabajadores Unidos (SPMDTU), founded on November 26,

1900, in Antonito, Colorado. The express purpose of the SPMDTU was to combat discrimination against the Mexican American (José López, 1958: p. 11). Like the mutualistas, the SPMDTU provided aid and support for the individual as well as guidance and advice through which it hoped to encourage the progress and prosperity of its membership. All members of the Mexican-American community over eighteen years old could join. The SPMDTU established lodges in the states of Colorado, New Mexico, and Utah (ibid., p. 28).

Organizing Mine Workers

The Mexican Revolution of 1910 not only brought an increased supply of cheap labor to the United States; it also brought activists and social reformers who had been forced to flee Mexico because of their opposition to Porfirio Díaz. One of the most notable was Ricardo Flores Magón, who had relentlessly attacked Díaz and his regime through his newspaper entitled *Regeneración*.

Flores Magón came to the United States in 1904, hoping to continue his work without the threat of imprisonment. However, he found little peace. He was constantly harassed by American officials, who for the most part supported Díaz, and in time he realized that the struggle he had been waging for the Mexican could not be confined to Mexico. Organization of the Mexican worker was needed in the United States as well. In response to this need, Flores Magón founded the Unión Liberal Humanidad, a labor union that was to bring violence and death to some of its members during the Cananea mine strike of 1906.

Mexican and Anglo authorities ruthlessly suppressed the strike at Cananea, Mexico. Flores Magón and his followers fled in order to avoid incarceration and to keep the union movement alive. The governments of the United States and Mexico worked together in an all-out effort to capture him. After serving eighteen months in prison beginning in 1909, and three years beginning in 1911 for his organizational activities, Flores Magón was once again arrested in 1918. He was charged with violating United States neutrality laws and sentenced to twenty years in prison. In 1922, after President Obregón had arranged for his return to Mexico, Flores Magón was found dead in his cell. His friends charged that he had been murdered, but the authorities resisted all efforts to investigate and prove that claim (Cockcroft, 1969: p. 124).

Ricardo Flores Magón was among the first to recognize and attempt to change the conditions under which Mexican-American laborers worked. But the problem facing Mexican-American laborers was far greater than merely poor working conditions. It concerned the differential wage paid to them and to Anglos for the same work. For example, in the mines at Clifton and Morenci, Arizona, Mexican workers received $2.39 for a seven-and-a-half hour shift while their American counterparts were paid $2.89 for the same shift and the same work (Kluger, 1970: p. 23).

In September 1915, Mexican and Anglo mine workers at Clifton and Morenci went out on strike. The issues in this strike, which lasted nineteen weeks, involved the lower Mexican pay scale, the tyrannical conduct of foremen who sold jobs to Mexicans, and the low salaries paid during prosperous periods (ibid., p. 25). At one point, the strikers invited the Western Federation of Miners to Clifton-Morenci, a somewhat ironic move, since this organization had been a leading advocate of the so-called "80 Percent Law." This law stated that 80 percent of all workers employed by companies in Arizona must be Americans; only 20 percent could be aliens—a stipulation which would have deprived most of the Mexican workers of their jobs. The law was declared unconstitutional by the United States Supreme Court in December 1915, but it seems strange that an organization which had been a staunch supporter of this law should be invited to assist striking Mexican miners. The Western Federation of Miners proposed to organize the miners of Clifton and Morenci (ibid., p. 26).

The strike itself was not marred by the bloodshed and property destruction that characterized many other strikes of the era. This was largely due to the efforts of the Mexican organizers and the actions of Governor G.W.P. Hunt and Sheriff James G. Cash, who prevented the importation of strikebreakers by calling the National Guard. After four and a half months the strike came to an end when the company agreed to guarantee equal wage rates for Anglo and Mexican workers.

Strikes were called again in the Clifton-Morenci mining region in 1917 and 1918, with quite different results.

Both strikes were broken by vigilante action and the wholesale deportation of hundreds of Mexicans. In fact, the so-called "Bisbee Deportations" occurred during the 1917 strike. In all the mines 1,876 strikers were arrested and shipped to Columbus, New Mexico. Columbus officials refused to take charge of the prisoners and the Mexican-American strikers were taken out to the desert where they were released and left to make their own way back home. In an investigation of this incident some months later, Felix Frankfurter reported for the federal government that "too often there is a glaring inconsistency between our democratic purposes in this war abroad and the autocratic conduct of some at home" (McWilliams, 1949: p. 197).

The labor movement gained momentum in the second decade of this century. Strikes spread from the mines of Arizona to Los Angeles, California, where street railway workers went on strike for better wages and to oppose job discrimination. The Mexican Americans received support from the metal trades, leather and brewery industries. However, this support soon ended when the building of the strongly anti-union Los Angeles Times was dynamited. Twenty-one employees were killed; although no proof was presented that the strikers were involved, many supporters of the Mexican Americans dropped out. Soon after, the strike failed.

Organizing Agricultural Workers

Labor unrest quickly spread from mining to agriculture, where improvements in the workers' situation were desperately needed. Efforts to unionize Mexican and

Mexican-American agricultural workers occurred repeatedly during the 1920s and 1930s (Meier and Rivera, 1972: p. 184).

Agricultural workers were among the

most difficult to organize, for "the workers were dispersed, they were on the move, and above all, agriculture ruled the southwest" (Acuña, 1972: p. 154). Yet this is where organization was most necessary. The migrant worker was ruthlessly exploited by the growers, forced to live in substandard housing, and paid meager wages. In addition to this, the Mexican-American worker had to compete with the large waves of Mexican illegals, whose entry was encouraged by agribusiness. Yet as was the case with the Mexican Americans who worked in the mines, organization had to come mainly from their own ranks because the Mexican Americans were considered foreigners and therefore not entitled to the protection the United States gave Anglo workers (ibid., p. 154).

In 1903, a strike by sugar beet workers in Ventura, California—mainly Mexicans and Japanese—began two months of violence between growers and strikers. The settlement favored the strikers, who won the right to negotiate directly with the grower rather than with the Western Agriculture Contracting Company, a labor contractor (Meier and Rivera, 1972: pp. 170–71).

The Wheatland Riot

A period of inactivity followed the Ventura strike. But ten years later, in August 1913, Mexican-American agricultural workers called a strike against the Durst Ranch, in Wheatland, California. The owners of the ranch had provided filthy, inadequate housing for the laborers (ibid., p. 172). And the main issues in the strike were substandard housing and low wages.

The Industrial Workers of the World sent two organizers, Herman Suhr and Blackie Ford, to Wheatland to lead the laborers in their protest. During one of many subsequent tense confrontations between strikers and police officials, called in by growers, a deputy sheriff fired a warning shot into the air. His goal was to break up the protesters. But a wholesale riot ensued, leaving four strikers dead. The National Guard was called in and 100 migrant workers were arrested. This action effectively ended the strike and Suhr and Ford later received life sentences for their part in the riot (ibid.).

The Wheatland Riot became a milestone in the history of agricultural conflict. First of all, it attracted national attention, which helped to reveal the ugly facts about the condition of farm labor in California. Secondly, it led to the creation of the California Commission on Immigration and Housing which substantiated and articulated the plight of the agricultural worker. (However, even though this commission made recommendations that led to state regulation of California's farm labor camps, only negligible improvements occurred.) And, finally, two important documents bearing on the subject of farm labor were published. One, Carleton H. Parker's *The Casual Laborer* (1920), was the first serious study of migratory labor. The second document was "The Seasonal Labor Problem in Agriculture" published in volume 5 of the Report of the United States Commission on Industrial Relations (McWilliams, 1939: p. 154).

The Wheatland Riot was only one of many agricultural strikes that occurred in California. It appears that Mexican leaders in that state made a great effort to organize the farm workers, while union activity elsewhere in the Southwest was largely restricted to non-agricultural laborers. In fact, "Unionism played a less important role in New Mexico, Arizona, and Texas;

and its activities, usually led by Anglos, were often directed against Mexicans as a source of cheap, strike-breaking labor'' (Meier and Rivera, 1972: p. 182).

The establishment of labor unions among Mexican Americans in California met with somewhat greater success during the 1920s and the results were more encouraging. For example, in 1928 a strike was called by the cantaloupe workers in the Imperial Valley. This strike was important because it represented another attempt at a major work stoppage by Mexican workers in California (Wollenberg, 1969: p. 45).

MMAS

During the Imperial Valley strike, a new union—La Unión de Trabajadores del Valle Imperial—was formed on the foundations of two mutual aid societies, La Sociedad Mutualista Benito Juárez El Centro (1919) and La Sociedad Mutualista Hidalgo El Brawley (1921). From these two mutualistas would come the leadership of the Unión de Trabajadores (ibid., p. 50). By April, this union had changed its name to the Mexican Mutual Aid Society (MMAS) of the Imperial Valley and was given further organizational support by the Mexican Counsel at Calexico.

One of the chief demands of the MMAS was that they, rather than the *contratista* (labor broker), be recognized as the spokesmen for the worker. This demand had long been a goal of farm laborers, mainly because the contratista was the one who most exploited the laborer (Meier and Rivera, 1972: p. 175). Other MMAS demands were a minimum wage of seventy-five cents an hour and requirements that picking sacks and crates, iced drinking water, and better housing be provided. The growers were reluctant to meet all the demands because they feared an agreement would be mistaken for weakness. They, therefore, offered a compromise proposal which the melon pickers quickly refused. The subsequent strike was marred by the actions of vigilante groups and the importation of strikebreakers.

In spite of the fact that their strike was broken, the efforts of the MMAS increased unionization efforts in the Imperial Valley. Furthermore, the strike resulted in the formulation of the harvest contract form. This form, though largely an unforeseen result of the melon strike, proved to be a significant victory for MMAS. Drawn up by the California Department of Industrial Relations, the harvest contract form recommended the abolition of deeply entrenched abusive practices on the part of the growers and made the growers rather than the labor contractors responsible for wages. It also eliminated the common practice of withholding 25 percent of the workers' wages until the end of the season. A bonus replaced the withholding amount as an incentive to workers to stay until the completion of the harvest.

The form was not mandatory but gained widespread use. In the summer of 1972, in Marshall County, Indiana, the "bonus" system was still in use—more than forty years after the Imperial Valley melon strike. The "bonus," however, was actually part of the wage. The growers used it as "incentive" for workers to remain until the end of the harvest. The workers generally interpreted it as a form of "coercion," since they were told that if they left before the harvest was over they would not be paid the "bonus." In many instances, under pressure, growers did pay the "bonus" for workers who left early, thus recognizing it as part of the wage.

National Farm Workers Association rally near Fresno, California

CUOM

In November 1927, the Federation of American Societies in Los Angeles brought about the organization of a number of local unions. This new federation was named the Confederación de Uniones Obreras Mexicanas (CUOM), and was modeled after the chief Mexican labor union, the Confederación Regional Obrera Mexicana (CROM).

CUOM was the first really stable organization of Mexican workers and the first that included both rural and urban workers in its rank and file membership. It resembled La Liga Protectiva Mexicana, which had been formed in 1921, in Kansas City, in that the primary purpose of CUOM was to protect the Mexican-American laborer against unfair deportation practices. However, CUOM went one step further. It sought to protect Mexican-American labor by asking that the federal government further restrict immigration from Mexico. It also extended its efforts to get the Mexican government to restrict the flow of Mexican immigrant labor to the United States. CUOM was well aware of the fact that as long as corporate growers had an almost unlimited pool of cheap labor from Mexico, the chances for successful union activity would remain slim.

For various reasons, CUOM, after a very promising start, declined in membership from three thousand workers representing twenty locals, to only two hundred workers and only ten locals. Yet its efforts to organize Mexican-American laborers in order to improve their economic welfare remain important in the history of labor organizing because it served as a training ground for future leaders of more successful labor organizations.

Mexican Labor and the Great Depression

The Great Depression had a tremendous effect on agricultural labor—in fact on all phases of American life. For a number of years, particularly during the harsh decade of the 1930s, Americans fought hunger, deprivation, and unemployment in the land of plenty. The desperate need to survive, and perhaps a desire to search for a new start, turned many Anglo-Americans into migrant agricultural workers. Among those hardest hit were small farmers from the Midwest and South. The general economic depression was compounded by forces of nature that turned their fertile farms into a useless dust bowl. Bankrupt and destitute, these men joined the swelling stream of migratory workers, just as the Mexican Americans had been forced to do at an earlier date (1850–1920), when they were deprived of their lands in the years after the Mexican-American War. This situation only increased agricultural unrest as competiton for jobs intensified. The scarcity of jobs made it easier for ruthless growers to further exploit the agricultural worker. As a result, workers now had to fight even harder against low wages, substandard housing, poor sanitation facilities and increased exploitation by the contratista.

The Great Depression placed a strain on the American people and made them less tolerant of actual or perceived aliens and foreigners. Old memories of the efforts of militant Mexicans to organize unions between 1900 and 1930 were revived. Cheap labor was no longer a blessing, not even to the large corporate farmer who had continually supported the large importation of workers from Mexico. By the early 1930s, the Mexican was viewed in a different light. He was seen as an albatross who represented one more burden on growing welfare rolls. As a result Mexican-American citizens, Mexican legal residents, and Mexican illegals all emerged as scapegoats of the Depression. As had occurred in previous times of national stress and economic depression, American nationalists sought to renew capitalist prosperity by deporting and repatriating the foreign elements. Over four hundred thousand Mexican immigrants and "undesirable" aliens were thus returned to Mexico.

Such repressive actions, however, did not deter the Mexican American in his efforts to organize (Acuña, 1972: p. 159). In fact, these efforts became more intense in the face of repression, and by 1930 the myth of the docility of the Mexican laborer had been thoroughly exploded (McWilliams, 1949: p. 193). Increased labor unrest has been attributed to two sources—the Mexican-American workers themselves and the Trade Union Unity League (TUUL), one of the most active radical labor groups in the West and one which showed a great deal of interest in organizing the Mexican-American workers (Meier and Rivera, 1972: p. 176). The number of strikes increased and the strikers became more unrelenting in their demands.

The El Monte Strike

The berry strike at El Monte in the San Gabriel Valley began in June 1933 and was the largest strike that had taken place in California up to that time. The strike was sparked by the wage rate, which had dropped as low as nine cents an hour by May 1933. It began with several thousand Mexican-American workers walking off the strawberry fields. The impact was tremendous. "It was this strike," writes Carey McWilliams, "which first aroused acute apprehensions on the part of the growers that the Mexicans might not be as docile as they had imagined" (McWilliams, 1949: p. 191).

The El Monte strike was organized by the Cannery and Agricultural Workers Industrial Union (C&AWIU). This union would prove to be the predominant force in California labor in 1933 through its involvement in thirty-seven recorded strikes, twenty-four for which it provided leadership (Ronald López, 1970: p. 102). The Mexican Consul, Alejandro Martínez, constituted a second prominent force during the strike by offering aid and advice to the workers. Such aid was not unusual. The government of Mexico supported Mexican-American unions in the 1930s and its representatives in American communities frequently helped organize such unions (Acuña, 1972: p. 167). The aid form these and other sources was monetary as well as psychological. The El Monte strikers received contributions from Mexico amounting to about four thousand dollars. They also received help from CROM (the Mexican labor union) and from former Mexican President Plutarco Elias Calles and Vice-Consul Ricardo Hill (ibid., p. 106).

The growers attempted to break the El Monte strike and their effort inevitably led to violence. Yet in spite of intimidation, vigilante action, and the awesome task of picketing along a 100-mile front, the strike continued. As its effects spread, the Los Angeles Chamber of Commerce became concerned and pressed the growers for a compromise settlement.

On June 26, 1933, the growers agreed to the demands of the strikers and offered them between twenty cents and twenty-five cents an hour for a ten-hour day (Acuña, 1972: p. 162). The mediators were stunned when the strikers refused to accept this offer. The reason for the rejection was quite simple. The strikers were aware that the Chamber of Commerce was anxious for a settlement, fearing that the restrictionists would exploit the strike to limit immigration. The strikers were also aware of growing fear among those

pushing for mediation that the strike might spread. Thus, the strikers believed that the situation favored them and decided to press for more demands.

Settlement of the strike came on July 6, 1933. The settlement called for a wage of $1.50 for a nine-hour day, or twenty cents an hour where the employment was not steady (Ronald López, 1970: p. 109). Some viewed the strike as unsuccessful. After all, the wage increase had been negligible and settlement had come at the end of the berry season, so that the workers would not enjoy immediate benefit from increased wages. However, organizers enjoyed a taste of success and were encouraged by the settlement.

First and most important, the union had been recognized as a result of the strike. Secondly, the strike had resolved a power struggle within the union which had developed between local Mexican-American leaders and outside representatives of the radical C&AWIU. This struggle was finally resolved when Mexican-American workers were persuaded by Alejandro Martínez, the Mexican consul, to abandon the Communist-inspired C&AWIU and form their own union. The resulting Confederación de Uniones Campesinos y Obreros Mexicanos (CUCOM) would prove to be the most successful of the Mexican-American unions. According to Ronald López, "the El Monte Union was probably a direct descendant of the Confederación de Uniones Obreras Mexicanas (CUOM)," that had been formed in 1928 (Ronald López, 1970: p. 105). In fact, much of the experienced leadership that organized El Monte strikers came from the ranks of CUOM (ibid.). Another outcome of the El Monte strike was that many of the strikers became politicized and carried the *Huelga* idea with them to other parts of California.

This helps to account for the rash of strikes by agricultural workers that hit California in 1933, placing that state at the front of the Chicano Huelga activity.

San Joaquin Valley Strike

The San Joaquin Valley strike followed close on the heels of the El Monte strike. This time the walkout was staged by the cotton-pickers under the leadership of the C&AWIU. Again, the grievances concerned wages and exploitation on the part of the contratistas. While the labor bureau offered only sixty cents per hundred pounds of cotton, the organizers demanded a dollar per hundred pounds. When the growers responded by evicting strikers from camps and company property, the organizers intensified the efforts to achieve their demands.

From Corcoran the strike spread. It soon encompassed the entire southern part of the San Joaquin Valley and the ranks of the strikers swelled to 18,000. The growers, frightened by this mass demonstration on the part of the workers, once again resorted to violence and repressive measures to break the strike. The most notable incident occurred on October 12, 1933, when the Union Hall at Pixley was riddled by rifle fire. Two strikers were killed and several others wounded. The same day another striker was shot to death at Arvin, a town farther south. Little was done to stem the violence following the so-called "Pixley riots." Such negligence by law enforcement officials resulted in the wounding of 42 more strikers and the arrest of 113 by the time the strike ended (London and Anderson, 1970: p. 2).

In an effort to restore some semblance of order to the San Joaquin Valley, Governor James Rolf mobilized the National Guard. He also appointed a fact-finding committee which recommended that the State Mediation Board be established to handle labor disputes. This board, headed by Archbishop Edward J. Hannah, worked out a compromise that gave the workers seventy-five cents per hundred pounds of cotton (Meier and Rivera, 1972: pp. 178–79).

Grower Resistance

The growers became increasingly upset over the organizing abilities and persistence of the Mexican Americans. By the end of 1933, California had experienced a series of thirty-seven agricultural strikes affecting practically all of the major crops in the state (Ronald López, 1970: p. 101). In an effort to stem the swelling tide of resistance, the growers gathered in November 1933 and formed the Associated Farmers of California under the auspices of the Agricultural Labor Subcommittee of the California Chamber of Commerce.

This organization opposed unions in general as communistic movements and devoted itself to combating unionism through education, persuasion, and a permanent lobby at Sacramento. By 1934, the Associated Farmers, well financed and supported by law enforcement agencies, turned to more overt means of suppressing labor union activity. According to Meier and Rivera, "the Associated Farmers contributed substantially to the demoralization and decline of Mexican-American labor in the 1930s; it was also responsible for much of the labor violence which occurred during this period" (Meier and Rivera, 1972: p. 179).

The record itself reflects the truth of the above statement. In January 1936, the Federation of Agricultural Workers'

Mexican Americans have learned to organize to speak out for their rights and liberties.

Union of America (FAWUA) came into existence. Behind this federation was CUCOM, since it provided the necessary leadership for this organization. In April 1936, the FAWUA called a strike in the celery fields. The strike, led by Guillermo Velarde of CUCOM, was finally settled in August 1936 after a great deal of resistance on the part of the Japanese growers. The benefits to the strikers again were negligible.

In June 1936, the Orange County citrus groves were hit by a strike. There followed a great deal of repression, property destruction, bloodshed, and a mass arrest of 115 Mexican-American strikers on the charge of trespassing on a public highway. By July the morale of the strikers had declined to such a low point that many of the workers returned to the groves with only a slight wage increase.

Other strikes met with even less success. A strike in September 1936 by the Vegetable Packers Association, an AFL affiliate, was crushed by the Associated Farmers. A similar fate befell the cannery workers in Stockton in April 1937. The strong-arm tactics of the Associated Farmers proved so successful that by 1936 and 1937 there were few strikes among field workers in California.

Spread of the Movement

Strikes and unionization drives were, of course, not confined solely to California during the Depression years. Similar events occurred wherever Mexicans were employed in agriculture. "Mexican field workers struck in Arizona; in Idaho and Washington; in Colorado; in Michigan; and in the lower Rio Grande Valley in Texas" (McWilliams, 1949: pp. 193–94). In fact, Dr. Stuart Jamison has stated that "the most effective agricultural labor unions during 1935 and 1936 were those organized among Mexicans" (ibid. p. 193).

It should be pointed out here that Mexicans also continued to organize in the mines. For example, in 1934, Mexican coal miners went on strike against the Gallup American Company in New Mexico. The strike, which saw the arrest of one hundred miners, was led by Jesús Pallares, who founded the Liga Obrera de Habla Español. La Liga, whose influence spread throughout northern New Mexico and southern Colorado, claimed a membership of 8,000. It worked to protect the jobs of its members and to provide some guarantee for relief payments to members in case of injury. The efforts of the league were successful in that it forced the authorities to abandon criminal proceedings against those arrested during the strike and in that it won relief rights for the strikers. However, Pallares, who was considered an agitator, was arrested and deported. Deprived of its leader, La Liga soon declined.

As the Depression deepened, unscrupulous employers took advantage of the desperate plight of the unemployed to exploit them further. This was the case in the pecan industry in Texas where the Depression insured an overabundance of cheap labor. By 1938, the situation had worsened and wages were reduced from six and seven cents per pound of shelled pecans, to the old scale of five and six cents per pound. Many of the shellers walked off their jobs in disgust and anger.

The pecan shellers' strike was also characterized by vigilante action and mass arrests. Police Chief Owen Kilday had little sympathy for the strikers and reverted to every repressive tactic he could think of to break their resistance. He even revived an obscure city ordinance that allowed the arrest of anyone carrying an advertising sign unless a permit had been issued by the city marshal (a post that no longer existed in 1938).

The strikers, lacking a formal union, organized their own under the leadership of the fiery Mrs. Emma Tenayuca Brooks, who at the time of the strike was only twenty years old. Under her guidance the strikers protested the harsh treatment of prisoners by the police chief. They claimed that many of those arrested were crowded into jails where they suffered from unhealthy sanitary conditions. Their charges resulted in public hearings held by the Texas State Industrial Commission. According to its report, the commission found that the interference by police authorities under the leadership of Chief Kilday had been unjustified (Walker, 1965: p. 53).

On October 24, 1938, the Fair Labor Standards Act went into effect. This law required employers to pay their workers a minimum wage of twenty-five cents per hour. Prior to this, the striking pecan workers had been persuaded to return to work pending the decision of an arbitration board. The decision, rendered on April 13, 1938, favored the operators, though it did recognize Local 172 as the sole bargaining agent of the workers. However, all of this went for naught, for with a failure of the employers to overturn the minimum wage rate imposed by the Fair Labor Standards Act, many of the operators either closed their doors or mechanized their operations. In the end, the efforts of the union and the National Recovery Administration (NRA) had failed. In the case of the NRA this situation reflected the enforcement problems that had plagued it since its inception in 1933. As for the union, membership soon declined because of the widespread layoffs. By 1948, the union had dissolved.

The last of the important pre–World War II farmworker strikes took place in Ventura County, California in January 1941. The strike involved 1,500 lemon pickers, most of whom were Mexican Americans. During the strike, they organized the Agricultural and Citrus Workers' Union and affiliated themselves with the AFL. After four months the strike collapsed due to the importation of strikebreakers. Few of those involved in the strike returned to work since their jobs had been taken by dust-bowl refugees.

World War II brought an abrupt end to the labor organization among Mexican-American workers. The history of their organizational efforts had been marked by violence, harsh repression, racism, and militant protest. In addition to those obstacles created by the growers and operators against the efforts of the Mexican American to organize, there had been the added burden of attempting to organize the migrant worker, perhaps the most difficult to organize because of his mobility. Yet the Mexican Americans and the Mexicans had shown themselves to be militant, active, and determined during the strike-ridden years. They had destroyed the popular stereotype, prevalent among their employers, of the docile, submissive, inarticulate peon. They would continue to fight for equality despite the fact that World War II decimated the ranks of their leaders, many of whom were drafted. In the words of Dr. R.W. Rosskelly, their determination for equal status was bound to persist since they would not "willingly relegate themselves to the status of second-class citizens in a country where equal opportunity, regardless of race, is a symbol of freedom" (McWilliams, 1949: p. 194).

Common themes running through Mexican-American agricultural workers' efforts to unionize have been concern over:

1. Lack of federal and state legislation protecting farm workers' rights to collective bargaining on a level with other workers.

2. Repressive legislation aimed at agriculture labor, prohibiting strikes and denying minimum wages and benefits from Social Security and Workmen's Compensation.

3. The collusion of local and state law enforcement organizations (police, sheriffs, Texas Rangers) with the growers in efforts to suppress unionization and strike activities, and their nonenforcement of child labor laws and sanitation, transportation, and health codes.

4. The collusion of federal agencies and state employment agencies with the employers to provide an overly large cheap labor pool to serve as direct and unfair competition with farm workers. The Bracero program, the "green carders," and the use of illegal Mexican aliens are cases in point.

REFERENCES

Acuña, Rodolfo. *Occupied America: The Chicano's Struggle Toward Liberation*. San Francisco: Canfield Press, 1972.

Cockcroft, James D. *Intellectual Precursors of the Mexican Revolution*. Latin American Monograph Series, No 14. Austin: University of Texas Press, 1969.

Grebler, Leo. *Mexican Immigration to the United States*. Los Angeles: University of California Press, 1966.

Kluger, James R. *The Clifton-Morenci Strike: Labor Difficulty in Arizona 1915–1916.* Tucson: University of Arizona Press, 1970.

London, Joan, and Anderson, Henry. *So Shall Ye Reap.* New York: Thomas Y. Crowell, 1970.

López, José. *La Historia de la Sociedad Protección Mutua de Trabajadores Unidos.* New York: Comet Press Book, 1958.

López, Ronald W. "The El Monte Berry Strike of 1933." *Aztlan: Chicano Journal of the Social Sciences and the Arts,* vol. 1, no. 1 (Spring 1970), pp. 101–14.

McWilliams, Carey. *Factories in the Field.* Boston: Little, Brown, 1939.

———. *North from Mexico.* Philadelphia: J. B. Lippincott, 1949.

Meier, Matt S., and Rivera, Feliciano. *The Chicanos: A History of Mexican Americans.* New York: Hill and Wang, 1972.

Walker, Kenneth. "The Pecan Shellers of San Antonio and Mechanization," *Southwestern Historical Quarterly,* July 1965.

Weeks, Douglas O. "The League of United Latin American Citizens: A Texas Mexican Civic Organization," *Southwestern Political and Social Science Quarterly,* December, 1929.

Wollenberg, Charles. "Huelga, 1928 Style: The Imperial Valley Cantaloupe Workers' Strike," *Pacific Historical Review,* February, 1969.

CHAPTER 19 | Organizing for Survival

The involvement of the United States in World War II interrupted many of the organizing activities of the Mexican Americans. This was partly due to the fact that many Chicanos were drafted into the armed services and many others volunteered. Indeed, the number of Chicanos serving in World War II was considerably out of proportion to their representation in American society. They served well and earned many honors and distinctions for valor (Acuña, p. 198), including the largest number of Congressional Medal of Honor awards. But while they were in the armed forces, Chicano males were not available for the labor market.

As was the case during World War I, American industry expanded to produce for the war effort. Many job opportunities in a variety of industries became available to some Chicanos for the first time. The jobs paid well. And when union membership was necessary for employment, the unions accepted Chicanos, since a labor shortage existed. It was a time of national crisis and wages and salaries were extremely good, jobs were plentiful and there was little labor strife.

In the agricultural industry it soon became apparent that few people would harvest the fields at the low wages offered when other opportunities for employment existed. Male seasonal farm workers joined the armed forces in large numbers and both men and women left the fields to work in defense and other industries.

To take care of the harvest the United States and Mexico entered into the Bracero agreement, discussed in chapter 15. After the war, however, defense industries began to slow down and lay off workers and the GIs were discharged, creating an abundance of labor but not of jobs. Those who chose to enter the farm labor market encountered direct competition for jobs with the Braceros and the United States government. The Bracero program directly affected the organizing activities of Mexican Americans as we shall see. Obviously, seasonal farm workers disliked the Bracero program since it competed directly with them in terms of jobs and pay scale.

The DiGiorgio Strike

Refugees from the dust bowl of the 1930s and 40s as well as Mexican Americans worked as seasonal farm laborers in California before and after World War II. In 1947, some of these people as well as Mexican Braceros were working on the DiGiorgio farms in Kern County. Many of the workers talked about collective bargaining and creating an organization of farm workers. Among the more active was Bob Whatley, who wrote to the President of the National Farm Workers Union, H.L. Mitchell. Mitchell sent Henry Hasiwar and Ernesto Galarza to help organize Local 218, chartered by the National Farm Labor Union.

By September 1947 the Local had 858 signed members who worked for the DiGiorgio corporation. After many unsuccessful attempts to meet with the corporation officials for a recognition of the union, the local decided to strike on October 1, 1947. The strike ended in failure in 1949 and Local 218 was crushed by a collusion between the DiGiorgio Fruit Corporation and the members of a House investigating subcommittee led by Representatives Richard M. Nixon, Tom Steed, Thurston B. Morton, and Thomas H. Werdel. A "report" under the name of Nixon, Steed, and Morton (but not necessarily prepared by them nor signed by them) was placed in the *Congressional Record* under the Extension of Remarks by the Honorable T.H. Werdel. This "report" was then resuscitated as evidence of congressional debate and action. After years of litigation, fading memories, and lost evidence, the goal of preventing unionization among farm workers was finally achieved. A detailed account of what transpired can be found in Dr. Ernesto Galarza's *Spiders in the House and Workers in the Field*, 1970.

César Chávez and the Farm Workers

Although the organizing activities among seasonal farm workers (mostly Mexican Americans) in the late 1940s and 50s were crushed, the 1960s produced continuing activity through the efforts of César Chávez. For the first time, farm labor found a broad base of support and organizing efforts eventually met with considerable success.

César Chávez was born in 1927, the son of migrant workers. He followed the occupation of his parents and settled in San Jose, California. There, in 1952, he met Fred Ross of the Community Service Organization (CSO). Chávez went to work for the CSO as a local organizer. But he was so effective that he was soon named state-wide organizer for the CSO. He remained with the organization until 1962, when he quit over the refusal of the CSO to implement a rural-oriented program. César Chávez then moved to Delano, California, where he formed the Farm Workers Association, later the National Farm Workers Association (NFW). Chávez elected to move the union along slowly in order to gain a solid base before taking any action against the growers. But in 1965, his membership voted to join Larry Itliong's Filipino Agricultural Workers Organizing Committee (AWOC) grape strike, long before Chávez felt the

César Chávez leading strikers at Delano, California

union would be ready for strike activity.

The grape strike proved to be a catalyst. In December 1965, the union began a boycott of grapes grown by Schenley farms. Anxious to strengthen their postion, Chávez's NFW and Itliong's AWOC merged to form the United Farm Workers Organizing Committee (UFWOC). Chávez became the director and Itliong the assistant director of the new union.

César Chávez, a man of vision, realized the union needed more widespread support than could be offered by its own membership. The cause of the farm worker needed to be brought to national attention and public wrath against the growers aroused. He planned and led a march of farm workers from Delano to the state capitol at Sacramento and in the process stirred millions of Americans. The grape boycott spread across the nation and was soon expanded to include all table grapes.

Chávez abhorred violence and tried to keep his strikes peaceful, using the tactic of hunger strikes to publicize his peaceful intentions. He experienced some success.

In 1970, two of the largest grape growers had come to terms with the union. But this proved to be just one battle in a long war.

In 1974, the union was fighting for its life in an attempt to sign new contracts with the grape and lettuce growers. It was threatened not only by the growers but by the more powerful unions. The Teamsters Union had muscled its way into the fields and began to sign "sweetheart" contracts with growers who had not signed with the United Farm Workers. Since the sweetheart contracts were advantageous to the growers, many of the growers whose contracts terminated with the United Farm Workers signed up with the Teamsters Union rather than with the Chávez organization. The future of the United Farm Workers as a genuinely "grass roots" organization representing seasonal farmworkers was in serious jeopardy given the great political power and wealth which the growers' organizations and the Teamsters had arrayed in their efforts to crush the union. The United Farm Workers survived the threat, however, and are today continuing the struggle.

López Tijerina and the Alianza

Another organizing effort emerged in the 1960s. This occurred among Hispanos of northern New Mexico attempting to regain the lands granted to their ancestors by the Spanish kings and, later, the Mexican government. After 1848, much of this land was lost. The idea was not a new one. Earlier organizations (such as Gorras Blancas and Mano Negra) had been formed for the same purpose. But like the early unionization efforts, they had failed.

A charismatic leader, Reies López Tijerina, drew attention to the land problem. Born in Fall City, Texas, on September 21, 1926, Reies was the son of seasonal farm workers. Like César Chávez, he worked in the fields as a boy. As a young man, he received aid to study and became an ordained minister. Later, Reies gathered a group of families together and purchased land in Arizona (called the Valley of Peace) to begin their own community. They were eventually forced out by hostile Anglo neighbors and Reies move to New Mexico.

López Tijerina soon became familiar with the land grant problem and was appalled. He felt compelled to take some action and, in 1963, founded the Alianza Federal de Mercedes (alliance of land grants). In October 1966, the Alianza took its first action by occupying Echo Amphitheater, part of a national forest and a piece of an old land grant. The Alianza set up a government and declared the area a free and autonomous state. Two forest rangers were arrested for trespassing on this new state. They were tried and convicted by the people and given suspended sentences.

Federal attorneys pressed charges against López Tijerina and on November 6, 1967, he was convicted of two counts of assault stemming from the Echo Amphitheater incident and was sentenced to two years in prison and five years probation. He was released on bail, pending appeal. This was overshadowed, however, by events of the previous summer. After the Echo Amphitheater clash, the court had ordered the Alianza to produce a list of its membership. To avoid doing so, the Alianza formally disbanded

Reies Tijerina with his wife Patsy after acquittal in the first Tierra Amarilla trial in December, 1968

and reorganized under the name of La Confederación de Pueblos Libres. But on June 5, 1967, a raid was carried out on the Tierra Amarilla Courthouse to free jailed members of the Alianza. Whether Reies López Tijerina knew of the raid or not is open to speculation. In any event, he was arrested and tried for crimes committed. He defended himself and won an acquittal.

This and other episodes received national attention because of reaction on the part of the New Mexico state government. The National Guard was called out, as well as the forest rangers and the state police. Suspected members of the Alianza were taken prisoner at a barbecue and held in a corral for over twenty-four hours. Reies eventually served concurrent sentences for assault in the Amphitheater incident and destruction of federal property, and assault on a federal officer during the occupation of the Kit Carson National Forest at the Coyote Campsite (Acuña, 1972: pp. 237–40). He was released in 1971 with the provision he make no contacts with the former Alianza. Through legal restrictions, questionable judicial procedures and threats of terrorism, the established powers have stalled, at least temporarily, the efforts of Mexican Americans to regain lands once theirs. The precursors to this movement, like their counterparts among the Indian Land Claims organizations, began many years ago in northern New Mexico and the movement will probably survive this setback.

Good Neighbors at Home

The period from World War II to the present has also produced activity in the urban areas and among professionals. During the war, Franklin Roosevelt's Good Neighbor policy sought to expand the diplomatic effort to the domestic scene by establishing a Spanish-speaking Peoples' Division under the Office of Inter-American Affairs. The stated purpose of this Division was to "stimulate and organize public and private rehabilitation programs aimed at preparing the Spanish-speaking to participate more actively in American life and to educate the English-speaking to the necessity of eliminating discriminatory practices injurious to the war effort and to our relations with Spanish America" (McWilliams, 1949: p. 276).

While the Good Neighbor policy was primarily aimed at building good relations with Latin American allies, it also led to some organizing activity in the Southwest. A large conference was held in Denver, Colorado, in June and July 1943, followed by similar ones in August 1943 in Santa Fe, New Mexico, and at Arizona Teachers College. These conferences consisted of workshops and meetings on the understanding needed between the two cultures.

With funds from the Office of Inter-American Affairs, the National Catholic Welfare Conference held its first seminar on the Spanish-speaking in San Antonio, Texas, in July 1943. This was later followed by similar conferences in Denver, Santa Fe, and Los Angeles. Funds provided by the office also helped begin the Colorado Inter-American Field Service Commission in the fall of 1944. The first service club was founded in Rocky Ford, Colorado. Subsequently, clubs were established throughout Colorado—in Pueblo, Walsenburg, Trinidad, San Luis, Alamosa, Monte Vista, and Greeley. A club was also founded in Taos, New Mexico. The individual clubs formed the Community Service Clubs, Inc., which published the *Pan American News* with offices based in Denver, Colorado. The purposes of these clubs were to register voters, provide scholarships, make health surveys, promote better recreational facilities, and to end discrimination and secure rights for Spanish-speaking Americans.

The Mexican-Americans did not need the push from the federal government to fight for their rights. Toward the end of World War II, the fight against segregation was carried into the courts by individuals. In 1945, Gonzalo Mendez of Westminister, California, filed a suit against segregation in local schools. And on March 21, Judge Paul J. McCormick ruled this segregation illegal—an early victory for equal rights in education (McWilliams, 1949: pp. 280–82). Another suit concerned the segregation of Mexican-Americans and blacks in the schools of Bell Town, California, near Riverside. Guidance was provided by Fred Ross of the Community Service Organization, which later recruited César Chávez to its ranks. The defense claimed integration would depreciate property values, but the plaintiffs finally won a decision for desegregation. These suits were important factors leading to the 1954 Supreme Court decision banning school segregation.

The American G.I. Forum, founded in Corpus Christi, Texas, in 1948, continued the fight for equal rights. The immediate cause for establishing the organization was the refusal in Three Rivers, Texas, to permit the burial of a Mexican-American veteran in the local cemetery. The G.I. Forum, founded and led by Dr. Hector García, had for its goals the attainment of first-class citizenship for Mexican Americans through education and the elimination of discrimination and has devoted considerable time to raising money for scholarships for Chicano students. The main emphasis of the organization, however, has been in the area of fair employment practices and the effort to eliminate discrimination in public facilities. The Forum has played a major role in opening public facilities such as schools, swimming pools, theaters, etc., to the Mexican American. And the Forum has established active chapters throughout the United States.

Stimulating Political Action

Political organizations have become increasingly important to Mexican American survival. The first postwar organization for political purposes was the Unity Leagues founded by Ignacio López. These leagues appealed to veterans and blue-collar workers among others. They organized voter registration drives and supported the campaigns of Mexican Americans running for positions on boards of education and city councils. The Unity Leagues were established primarily in California and they were different from previous organizations in two aspects. First, they were not aimed at the middle class, and second, they were not trade unionist in orientation. Their main objective was to stimulate political action.

Following the Unity Leagues and par-

These marchers bear witness to a minority's constant search for justice and equality.

tially building on the base of the Leagues were the Community Service Organizations (CSO) founded in 1947. Technically non-political and non-partisan, these organizations grew out of a group formed to elect Edward Roybal to the Los Angeles City Council. A prime mover behind the CSO was Fred Ross, who was influenced by Saul Alinsky. The CSO urged the Mexican Americans to unite with other concerned groups to push for social reforms. To this end, they organized voter registration drives among Mexican Americans so they could vote for social legislation needed by all minority groups. They began English language and citizenship classes. They also began new projects in consumer education with money obtained from the Office of Economic Opportunity.

The decade beginning in 1950 was one in which Mexican-American organizations suffered several setbacks. The McCarran-Walter Acts of 1950 and 1952 set up machinery for the deportation and investigation of so-called subversive groups. These laws were used to drive Mexican-American leaders from the scene or silence them in their fight for equality. Several prominent leaders were deported under this act.

Another factor disrupting Mexican-American unity at this time was Operation Wetback. This was an organized effort by the federal government to locate and deport all illegal Mexican aliens then in the United States. Little effort was made to distinguish between American citizens of Mexican descent and an illegal alien. Thus, as in the 1930s, the Mexican American waged a fight to defend his right to live in the United States. In 1953, the year the program was put into action, 865,318 people of Mexican descent were deported. The next three years also saw large numbers being deported: 1954—1,075,168; 1955—242,608; and 1956—72,442 (Samora, 1971: p. 46).

One organization, however, did manage to begin and function without being silenced by repressive measures. This was the Council of Mexican American Affairs (CMAA), founded in 1953 in Los Angeles. The focus of the group was on social aspects and it stressed cooperation with and coordination of other groups as well as the development of effective leadership. The CMAA was mainly a middle-class organization and one of its main concerns was to change the images members of the larger society held of Mexican Americans. It defined itself as non-profit, non-partisan and non-sectarian. It was organized at first to aid Mexican-

American claims to full citizenship and to influence government. It wanted to show that the Mexican American exemplified the best of each culture and could enrich the whole community. Unfortunately, the council encountered financial problems, which forced it to curtail its programs, and thus lost its effectiveness.

Educational Organizations

It may be obvious to the reader at this point that many of the organizing efforts of Mexican Americans since World War II have stressed education. The Latin American Educational Foundation of Denver, Colorado, is a case in point. It has supplied hundreds of scholarships and loans to college-bound students. In this respect, several organizations have been established by and for students and teachers and administrators. These organizations are found at both the high school and college levels. One of the student groups is the United Mexican-American Students (UMAS). It has stressed that the Mexican American need not be ashamed of his heritage and that he can be a benefit to society and still be proud of being Mexican. Its purpose is to give a voice to the Mexican American at the college level. In May 1969, an attempt was made to unify all the student groups into one; the Movimiento Estudiantil Chicano de Aztlán (MECHA) emerged from this effort. This organization united UMAS, the Mexican American Student Association (MASA), the Mexican-American Student Confederation (MASC), the Mexican-American Youth Organization (MAYO), and the Committee for the Advancement of the Mexican American

(CAMA). MECHA still has no central statewide organization to represent it, but the group does mark a change from intergrationist methods to ones that stress pride in being Mexican.

Teachers and administrators have also banded together to work for the benefit of the Mexican American. One such group is the Association of Mexican-American Educators, founded in 1965. It acts as an advisor to state and local boards of education, administrators, and faculties in relation to the educational needs of Mexican-American youth. It also serves as a pressure group and was organized partially to aid the campaign of a Mexican American running for the Los Angeles School Board. In addition to stressing education, especially higher education, it acts as a clearing house for current research on Mexican-American education.

Another group along this line has been the California Association of Educators of Mexican Descent. It is open to all teachers, administrators, and superintendents. This organization has suffered a major difficulty in the differing philosophies of its members (as we have seen, Mexican Americans form a very heterogeneous group).

Crusade for Justice

We cannot mention all the organizations which have been founded, but one which has had considerable impact is La Crusada Para la Justicia (Crusade for Justice), founded at Denver, Colorado, by Rodolfo Gonzales in 1965. Gonzales was active in politics and business throughout a good part of his life. He was the first Mexican-American district captain for the Democratic Party in Denver and in 1960 was the Colorado coordinator of "Viva Kennedy!" clubs. He then became a leader in the poverty programs including the War on Poverty. During this time, Gonzales was also a successful insurance salesman and author, writing a play, *A Cross for Maclovio*, and a poem, *I Am Joaquín.*

Rodolfo Gonzales became disillusioned with the establishment and in particular with the Democratic Party. In establishing the Crusade for Justice, his goal is appeal to the cultural nationalism and

Tenants meet to discuss common problems in El Paso, Texas.

the establishment of communities controlled by Chicanos. The Crusade for Justice organization includes a school teaching "liberation classes," a nursery, gym, Mayan ballroom, art gallery, shops, library, dining room, community center, legal aid service, "skill bank," Barrio Police Board, health and housing social workers, athletic leagues, newspaper (*El Gallo*), bail bond service, and "Revolutionary Theater." A "Plan of the Barrio" has been issued calling for housing, education, economic opportunities, agricultural reforms including land reform, and the redistribution of wealth.

On Palm Sunday, 1969, the Crusade convened the Chicano Youth Liberation Front, a national convention of barrio youth. Here the "Spiritual Plan of Aztlán" was issued calling for separate Chicano communities and control of their own political, social, economic, and educational destinies. The Crusade also helped to organize La Raza Unida Party in Colorado, led by Gonzales. The Crusade participated in the Poor People's March of 1968 and the school walkouts at West Denver High School which attempted to end discrimination against Chicano children.

Some Chicanos have been extremely active politically for many years—in particular those persons who lived in small towns and villages of southern Colorado and northern New Mexico. In those instances when they have been in the majority, they have dominated the politics of the county or community. In the rural areas and towns of Texas, however, even when Mexican Americans have been in the majority, they have seldom been able to control local governments. In the urban areas of the Southwest and Midwest, they have not been particularly successful in the political arena until recent years.

Political Action of the 60s and 70s

During the decade of the 1960s and the early 1970s, a number of political organizations were formed for the express purposes of seeking recognition, justice, and better opportunities for Chicanos— to endorse candidates; to take stands on issues; to register voters, and to increase political activity among the Chicano population. Other more specific purposes were proposed in certain regions, states or localities. Among the organizations which were formed are The Mexican American Political Association (MAPA) of California, The Political Association of Spanish Speaking Organizations (PASSO) of Texas, the American Coordinating Council on Political Education (ACCPE) of Arizona, and El Partido La Raza Unida of Texas, Colorado, and California.

Traditionally, Chicanos have voted in the majority for candidates of the Democratic Party. The party invariably made promises to Mexican Americans, but seldom did any noticeable benefits accrue to the Chicano community. To be sure, some Chicano candidates, particularly at the local levels of government, have held elective or appointed positions. Some have held positions in state legislatures and a few have been in Congress. The perception of Chicanos that political activity has seldom benefited the community in large measure is probably correct. Seldom have Chicanos been in decision-making positions in sufficient numbers to bring about any substantial reforms even if they attempted to initiate legislation or programs. Chicanos who have attained such positions have not been inclined to "rock the system" or go against the status quo.

Having been disillusioned with both the Democratic and Republican Parties, many Chicanos have flocked to MAPA, PASSO, and La Raza Unida in their efforts to influence the political process. In areas where Chicanos have numerical strength and the organizations have worked hard, there have been phenomenal results in the election of Chicano candidates. In situations where their proportionate numbers are low (for example a state-wide or congressional election) the tactics of the organizations have been that of a third party or a swing vote in the direction which most benefits the community.

Since Chicanos are not a homogeneous population, there is not universal agreement on the philosophies and ideologies of political organizations. Even within the organizations there are obviously varying points of views. Nevertheless, these political organizations are important. For many, these groups are seen as the hope for the future in righting the wrongs and severe injustices thrust upon them by the established parties. They will no longer tolerate false promises, benign neglect, and chicanery.*

A more militant phase of the Mexican-American movement is provided by the Brown Berets. The organization began in 1967 as the Young Citizens for Community Action. It was founded by Ralph Ramírez, Carlos Monten, and David Sánchez. It centered around a coffee house, "La Peranya," which served as an office

*For more detailed analysis see Richard Santillan, *La Raza Unida* (Los Angeles: Tlaquilo Publications, 1973) and John Shockley, *Chicano Revolt in a Texas Town* (Notre Dame, Ind.: University of Notre Dame Press, 1974).

Boycotting Mexican-American students standing outside of Crystal City High School

La Raza Unida

In Crystal City, Texas, Mexican Americans twice in the past decade revolted against the political domination of Anglos. Located in the heart of the Winter Garden Area of Texas not too far from the Mexican border, Crystal City is made up of 80 percent Mexican Americans, many of them poor migrant laborers. Since the town's inception this majority had been controlled by the Anglo community.

Backed by the Teamsters Union and the Political Association of Spanish-speaking Organizations, poor, undereducated Chicanos won all five city council seats in the election of 1963. However, political inexperience, Anglo resistance to reform, and internal dissension led to their downfall two years later. Anglos working with middle-class Mexican Americans regained control of the town, leaving the poorer Chicanos leaderless and demoralized.

In 1969 a second revolt hit Crystal City, more radical and more successful than the first. The school board had always remained in control of the Anglos. But Mexican Americans were dissatisfied with conditions in the schools—they resented teachers who were bigoted against them; they desired a democratic election of cheerleaders, the homecoming football queen, and other recipients of honors; they wanted more Mexican-American teachers in the schools and a bilingual education program.

The immediate occasion of the second revolt was the selection of two Anglo cheerleaders by faculty judges to replace vacancies, when Chicano students felt one of their group was as good as any of the Anglos. The students protested to school officials, and found their demands finally rebuffed by the school board.

At this point José Angel Gutiérrez came on the scene. He was a native of Crystal City who had been educated in San Antonio and been active in a Mexican-American youth organization.

Gutiérrez found some outside, foundation support as a means to fund a small organization, and he immediately went to work to direct the students in their campaign against the school board in the fall of 1969. A school boycott by Mexican Americans was called, and was successfully carried out. Gutiérrez reached the adult Mexican Americans through their children.

The next step was the formation of the La Raza Unida party, whose candidates won both the school board and city council elections in the spring of 1970. Gutiérrez was elected to the school board, and at the reorganization meeting of the board was elected its president.

The schools then underwent a minor revolution. A great number of Mexican Americans were hired in administrative, teaching, and staff positions in the school system. Bilingual education was begun in the early grades, and courses in Mexican-American history and culture were started. Also topics of concern to Chicanos were introduced in history, literature, and other subject areas, while Chicano literature was purchased for the library.

In less than a decade an apathetic, powerless Mexican-American community had been mobilized into a majority fully in control of the political institutions of the town. La Raza Unida candidates also won elections in two nearby towns.

As a result of these victories, La Raza Unida has organized branches in many other Texas counties with large Chicano populations and in Colorado, New Mexico, Arizona, and California. The political apathy that formerly marked the Southwest is disappearing as Mexican Americans have challenged the system to achieve representative government.

Brown Berets of Fresno, California

and meeting hall. The group shortly changed its name to Young Chicanos for Community Action and finally to the Brown Berets. Despite the changes in the name and the closing of the coffee house in March 1968, the principal stress has remained the same—ethnic nationalism. The Brown Berets played a major role in the confrontation of students and police in the school walkouts in East Los Angeles in 1968.

> The Brown Berets, in effect, panicked police officials and exposed their basic undemocratic attitudes toward Mexicans or groups attempting to achieve liberation. This is especially true in Los Angeles, where the Berets were founded. The police and sheriff's departments there abandoned reason in harassing, intimidating, and persecuting the Brown Berets in a way that no other Chicano organization has experienced in recent times. Police and sheriff's deputies raided the Berets, infiltrated them, libeled and slandered them, and even encouraged countergroups to attack the members. The objective was to destroy the Berets and to invalidate the membership in the eyes

of both the Anglo and the Chicano communities. (Acuña, 1972: p. 231)

The effectiveness of the Brown Berets in *La Causa* is difficult to assess at this time. Professor Acuña states:

> A basic weakness in the Brown Berets is that it does not have the strong family structure that has heretofore marked survival and success for most Chicano organizations. It has not been accepted as the "Army of the Brown People." Most poeple have been puzzled by the failure of the group to define what it considers to be its role in society.... Nonetheless, despite the failures the Brown Berets are important, because they are one of the few Chicano groups that have not attempted to work entirely within the civil rights framework of the present reform movement. They are the bridge between the groups of the past and those of liberation, which shall become more offensive. (Acuña, 1972: p. 233)

In conclusion, several things can be noted about Chicano organizations since World War II. The first is the movement into the barrio: efforts are now being

The National Chicano Moratorium

On August 29, 1970, Rosalio Muñoz and other Chicano leaders organized a demonstration in East Los Angeles against the Vietnam War, citing moral grounds and the casualty rate for Mexican Americans in the War (19% for Mexican-Americans compared to 12% for *all* Americans). Among the speakers scheduled for the anti-war rally were Cesar Chavez, Corky Gonzales, Mario Compean (national chairman of the Mexican American Youth Organization), and David Sanchez (prime minister of the Brown Berets).

The demonstrators paraded peacefully to Laguna Park where the speakers and entertainment were scheduled. A crowd of 15–20,000, including many families, gathered at the park, peacefully waiting for the proceedings to begin.

Early in the afternoon, before the speeches began, a fight broke out at a nearby liquor store between some of the demonstrators and deputy sheriffs. Tear gas was used to quell the disturbance. The deputies then called for reinforcements, lined up, and advanced toward the park. When they began firing tear gas into the crowd, rioting erupted. In the melee people were injured, stores were damaged and looted, and a number of Chicanos were arrested, including Corky Gonzales. Ruben Salazar, prominent newspaper and television reporter, died after being struck in the head by a tear gas capsule. Two other Mexican Americans lost their lives as a result of the riot.

Organizers of the moratorium blamed the violence on overreaction by law enforcement officials, while Mayor Yorty and the sheriff's department contended that militant radicals had infiltrated the assembly.

---

made, and with success, to mobilize the urban Chicano. Secondly, a rather close relationship has developed between the student organizations—both high school and university—and the local community. The relationship between the "Ivory Tower" and the town appears to be a most significant development not found among other groups. Thirdly, the mutual aid, fraternal, and social emphasis of the organizations has given way to a more political, self-determination, and self-development focus. The realization is clear that basic changes must occur in the society in the economic, political, educational, and civil rights realms before the general goals of equality and justice can be reached. Finally, the emergence of national leadership potential is quite evident. The next few years should see the crystallization of national organizations, with national goals and programs, and with a constituency served by their leaders.

REFERENCES

Acuña, Rodolfo. *Occupied America: The Chicano's Struggle Toward Liberation*. San Francisco: Canfield Press, 1972.

Galaraza, Ernesto. *Spiders in the House and Workers in the Field*. Notre Dame, Ind.: University of Notre Dame Press, 1970.

McWilliams, Carey. *North from Mexico*. Philadelphia: J. B. Lippincott, 1949.

Samora, Julian. *Los Mojados: The Wetback Story*. Notre Dame, Ind.: University of Notre Dame Press, 1971.

Santillan, Richard. *La Raza Unida*. Los Angeles: Tlaquilo Publications, 1973.

Shockley, John S. *Chicano Revolt in a Texas Town*. Notre Dame, Ind.: University of Notre Dame Press, 1974.

CHAPTER **20** | # A Rich Tradition Continues

The roots of Chicano/a art are ancient. In fact, we can appropriately describe it as the second oldest artistic tradition in North America, after the Native American. The antiquity of Chicano/a art—literature, drama, music, the visual arts, cinema—can be explained in part by the intermingling of Spanish and Indian cultures after the conquest of Mexico. As we have seen in earlier chapters, New World and European artistic and folkloric customs blended from the earliest days of Spanish settlement in the fifteenth century. This meeting of cultures evolved over centuries and resulted in an inextricable mingling of traditions.

As with other numerical minorities in the United States, however, the pressure toward acculturation to the dominant society greatly modified artistic expression among Mexican Americans in the nineteenth and early twentieth centuries. Artistic production did not altogether cease developing, but it encountered the multiple hardships of oppression and marginalization typical of conquered populations. That the arts and literature survived and later flourished despite the hardships of prejudice against Mexicans, the Spanish language, and mestizo culture indicates the resilience of the creative imagination, as well as the people's endurance.

The form "Chicano/a" is used to avoid sexism and to designate gender inclusiveness. Contemporary Chicago/a art thus may be characterized as born of an ancient tradition but slowed in its progress by external pressures after the Treaty of Guadalupe Hidalgo.

This chapter describes the development of Mexican American creativity in drama, literature, music, the visual arts, and cinema. Readers are encouraged to consult the reading lists and guides at the end of the chapter for further exploration of the treasures of Chicano/a aesthetics.

Drama

Modern Chicano/a drama has arisen directly from the people—whether of the barrios, the migrant stream, or the outgrowths of ancient settlements in New Mexico and Colorado. The origins of this drama, as scholar Jorge Huerta has shown, lie in earlier dramatic forms. For example, at the time of the conquest of Mexico, two types of drama were popular—one Indian, the other Spanish.

The Indian religious rituals, called *mitotes*, and the reenactments of Christian rites by the Spaniards, called *pastores*, were not compatible because of the differences in their underlying beliefs. Nevertheless, over time the two forms blended to produce a new form, the Mexican *mascaradas*. The mascaradas were dramatic allegories that flourished throughout the sixteenth century. Indeed, the first non-native Indian New World play, *The Last Judgment*, written by Friar Olmos in 1533, was an extended mascarada.

The early settlers of post-conquest Mexico took these dramatic practices with them as they moved northward to the Borderlands. Like language and other forms of human expression, art changes with use and time. The mascaradas also evolved into new forms. They became the *posadas* and *pastorales* still performed and popular in the Southwest. These dramas celebrate religious beliefs and holy days in grassroots community settings (like church, school, and/or neighborhood).

Another form that emerged in the isolation of the border frontier was the traveling roadshow. Called *carpas* and *maromeras*, they were performed by road companies similar to the modern vaudeville and summer-stock theater. These traveling performers provided entertainment to towns and villages distant from urban theatrical centers.

This early, popular theatrical base has contributed in a variety of ways to twentieth-century Chicano/a drama. Mexican American dramatists borrowed techniques and customs from them in creating their contemporary plays. Earlier in this century, these dramatists focused primarily on broad religious and historical themes familiar to audiences who understood the cultural traditions from which they evolved. These themes are evident in such works as Arthur Campa's *Spanish Religious Folk Theatre in the Spanish Southwest* published in 1934.

In more recent times, however, Chicano/a playwrights have worked into their plays more visibly social and political themes. These more recent works combine sophisticated dramatic techniques with ideas from their grassroots origins to make bold thematic statements. The work of El Teatro Campesino and other *teatros* (i.e., community theater groups), along with the plays of Estela Portillo Trambley, Jorge Huerta, and Carlos Mortón offer fine examples of this development.

Perhaps the most popular of these examples is El Teatro Campesino (ETC), an internationally acclaimed repertory company that grew out of the 1960s' activism in support of farmworkers and the United Farm Workers' Union (UFW). During the UFW grape strike of 1965, farm workers under the direction of Luís Váldez began entertaining UFW strikers and supporters on their picket lines in order to keep up their morale. Váldez and his amateur performers entertained the strikers with music and improvised skits called *actos*. The purpose of the *actos*, according to Váldez, was to "inspire the audience to social action. Illuminate specific points about social problems. Satirize the opposition. Show or hint at a solution. Express what people are feeling" (Váldez, 1971: p. 6). These political themes inspired the founding of ETC and defined its development into a professional theatrical company. Its success led to worldwide tours, numerous awards, and publication of the scripts of some of the *actos*. Among its most acclaimed productions were *Los Vendídos, La Carpa de los*

Los Vendídos

As the Revolucionario (played by José Delgade at left) stands at attention, Honest Sancho (center and played by Felix Alvarez) offers a sales pitch for this "used Mexican" to Miss Jiminez (on right, played by Socorro Valdez) of the Governor's office in the film version of the play *Los Vendidos*, distributed by the Pixan Film Center of the El Centro Campesino Cultural.

Los Vendidos (The Sellouts) by Luis Valdez is one of the best plays of El Teatro Campesino to portray the Chicano struggle for survival against social injustice. Through the use of satire and humor the author shows the prejudice faced by Chicanos as he depicts a secretary from the Governor's office who has come to buy a Mexican American from Honest Sancho's Used Mexican Shop for token integration of his administration. Several "types" are interviewed and rejected, including the Revolucionario depicted above. "Made in Mexico," he is passed over since only American-made models are acceptable for the position available.

Rasquáchis, and *The Shrunken Head of Pancho Villa.*

Váldez and his group eventually expanded their work to motion pictures and produced some of the most memorable of the Chicano/a-identified films of the 1980s. Besides adapting to the screen the famous 1967 poem, *I Am Joaquín* by Rudolfo "Corky" Gónzales, ETC also produced the movies *Zoot Suit* and *Corridos.* In 1988 Váldez directed *La Bamba,* a commercially successful movie that included in its production some members of the original El Teatro Campesino. As scholar Jorge Huerta states, "any serious study of Chicano theatre must begin with Luís Váldez" (Huerta, 1984: p. 403).

Mexican American contributions to motion pictures are varied. They include the work of actors Anthony Quinn, Rita Hayworth, and, more recently, Martin Sheen and Edward James Olmos. Chicano/a film producers and directors include Móctezuma Esparza, Jésus Treviño, Sylvia Castillo, José Luís Rúiz, Paul Espinoza, brothers Daniel and Juan Salazar of Denver, and others. (See Gary Keller's *Chicano Cinema: Research, Reviews, and Resources* for further information).

This brief discussion reveals that Chicano/a drama spans a rich heritage of accomplishment. That heritage spans a vast time frame—from ancient origins to twentieth-century film technology.

Alurista, a Chicano poet who juxtaposes Spanish and English, and who is publisher of the literary magazine *Maize.*

Courtesy of *Los Angeles Times*, photo by Patrick Downs.

Pre-Columbian statue

Folklore

American literature before the 1960s traditionally referred to written material grounded in a British-centered New England culture. One flaw of this view is its neglect of a significant body of literary production that traces its origins to ancient Mesoamerican art and ritual. Another problem is the neglect of important writers (like Miguel de Cervantes, author of *Don Quixote*, and Nobel laureate Gábriel García Márquez) who write in Spanish, the actual or historical mother tongue of Mexican Americans. Further, the Anglocentric view ignores the folklore of Mexican America that constitutes a central source of its artistic achievement.

A full appreciation of Chicano/a literature requires knowledge of its folklore. Myths, legends, *cuentos* (tales), *chistes* (jokes), and other types of grassroots expression form a basic part of the culture. This is true for all people, of course. Public schools introduce U.S. American children of all ethnic backgrounds to the stories of Cinderella, Robin Hood, Paul Bunyan,

Daniel Boone, and Brer Rabbit. In contrast, Mexican American folklore is usually learned informally in the home and neighborhoods, often passed down by *abuelos* (grandparents) to the younger generations.

Most Mexican Americans can recount stories learned in childhood about *la llorona* (the weeping woman) and *el coyote* (the deceitful agent). Many can relate embellished accounts of such historical heroes as Benito Juárez, Emiliano Zapáta, and Pancho Villa, like those told of George Washington and Abraham Lincoln. A few Chicanos/as learn the legends surrounding figures like La Malinche/Doña Marina, the Aztec guide who assisted Hernán Cortéz, and Joaquín Muriéta, the nineteenth-century Californio accused by Anglos of being a bandit. Another turn-of-the-century folk hero was Gregório Cortéz, a Texan about whom many *corridos* (ballads) were written, both during and after his lifetime. The film, *The True Story of Gregório Cortéz*, based on the book by folklorist

Américo Paredes, presents another version of the legend.

Folklore relating to heroes like Villa or Zapáta have inspired countless artists and writers. Similarly, folklore originating from among the common people appears throughout Mexican American art and literature.

Poetry

One way of looking at Chicano/a poetry is to see it as part of the tradition of *flor y canto* (flower and song) which extends back to the pre-Columbian poems of Mesoamerica. To the Nahuas (Aztec Indians), *flor y canto* was a form of prayer-poem to the divine Giver of Life Ométéotl, a male/female deity. Playwright Luís Váldez and poet Alurísta were among the first to link Chicano/a literature to its ancient roots in *flor y canto*, but the idea quickly took firm hold among writers. The phrase is often used as a synonym for Chicano/a poetry.

Another way of understanding this poetry is suggested in *Chicano Poetry: A Critical Introduction*. In it, scholar Cordelia Chávez Candelaria, presents the subject in three ways. First, she discusses the contexts of cultural and literary history from which Chicano poetry emerged. Second, she proposes an approach to the analysis of the poetry based on phases of style and theme. Third, she examines individual authors and poems from 1967 through the mid-1980s.

Phase I poetry by Mexican Americans refers to political protest writing linked closely to the Chicano movement. The principal energy of the movement, which emerged in the 1960s, was directed to the political and socioeconomic empowerment of Mexican Americans. Phase I poetry appeared roughly between 1967 and 1974, but it is important to stress that protest poetry cannot be confined to one time period alone, for it is still being composed.

Examples of writing that display Phase I features especially clearly include the epic poem *I Am Joaquín* by Rudolfo "Corky" Gónzales; the early work of Alurísta; and *Pérros y ántiperros* by Sérgio Élizondo. Much of the work of Abelardo Delgado, Ángela De Hoyos, Ricardo Sánchez, and Carmen Tafolla also fits within this category.

The later phases show a shift away from blunt political statement and social message. Phase II poetry describes the work that helped define and expand a distinct and unique Chicano/a poetics—poetics shaped from three sources:

1. its multilingualism (primarily English, Spanish, and Aztec and Mayan terms);
2. its *mestizo/a* symbols drawn from Mexican history and Chicano/a culture; and
3. its concern with ritual, both in its emphasis on the poem/performance as a communal rite and in its respect for the ritual traditions of the primitive past.

Alurísta is one master of Phase II poetry, particularly in his *Flóricanto en Aztlán* and *Nationchild Plúmaroja*. Also contributing to this verse are poets Luís Omar Salínas, Bernice Zámora, Ernest Padilla, José Montoya, Rául Salínas, and others, including some of the original movement protest poets.

Phase III poetry contains many of these traits as well as a degree of political protest. The phase is distinguished by greater sophistication of literary form and greater use of a private, subjective narrative voice.

The work of Gary Soto, Lorna Dee Cervantes, Alberto Ríos, Luís Omar Salínas, Yolanda Lúera, and others exemplify this group. Their finely crafted poems are read and appreciated by ever-wider audiences.

Since 1977 and the publication of the first edition of *A History of the Mexican American People*, the production of Chicano/a poetry has increased and expanded greatly. Throughout its growth, however, one major theme has defined the field: identity. The nature, essence, and development of Chicano/a identity recur throughout the poetry as image, symbol, motif, and theme. To understand the cultural identity of Mexican America, therefore, requires the appreciation of its poetry.

Fiction

During the flourishing of the Chicano movement, very few prose fiction writers were identified with Mexican America. Among the few were José Antonio Villareal, whose *Pocho* captured the struggles of a first-generation immigrant family in California, and Rudólfo Anaya, whose *Bless Me, Ultima* portrayed the sensitivities of a New Mexican boy growing up within a U.S. culture older than the Declaration of Independence. Also published were the depictions of migrant farmworkers by Raymond Barrio in *The Plum Plum Pickers* and Tomás Rivera in "*. . . y no se lo trago la tierra.*" The autobiographical fiction of Oscar Zeta Acosta, the urban novels of Floyd Sálas, and the regional fictions of Miguel Méndez, Sabíne Úlibarri, and Rolando Hínojosa also appeared in this first generation of Chicano/a literary production.

In the late 1970s and throughout the 1980s, the landscape of fiction has changed considerably. Writers like Anaya, Hínojosa, and Méndez continued to publish and to solidify their place in Chicano/a letters, while some of their contemporaries are no longer writing. Other writers have entered the scene with fresh material and skillful styles. Some of these include Estela Portillo Trambley, Cherrie Morága, Ana Castillo, Denise Chávez, Ron Arias, Sandra Cisneros, and Nash Candelaria.

The landscape has also changed because literary scholars have uncovered the work of Mexican American fiction writers from earlier decades of the century. The narratives of Josefina Niggli, Fray Angélico Chávez, and Fabióla Cabéza de Vaca are studied for their insight into the pre-Chicano/a experience of the Indohispanic United States. Research in archival sources continues to reveal a wealth of nineteenth- and early twentieth-century fiction long hidden from an active readership.

As this summary suggests and as scholar Vernon Lattin has declared, "the growth in both the quantity and quality of the Chicano novel since the publication of *Pocho* in 1959 has been phenomenal" (Lattin, 1986: p. 9). If we expand his comment to include short fiction as well, then the growth has been virtually astronomical. Two collections of short stories published in the early 1980s make this point effectively. They are *Cuentos: Stories by Latinas* (edited by Alma Gómez, Cherrie Morága, and Mariána Rómo-Carmona) and *Cuentos Chicanos: A Short Story Anthology* (edited by Rudólfo Anaya and Antonío Márquez).

In the 1977 edition of *A History of the Mexican American People*, this section concluded with a brief complaint about the lack of a "complete interpretation of Chicano literature" and the need for a stronger literary criticism (Samora and Simon, 1977: p. 208). Since then there have been some fine gains in this area. The excellent bibliographies by Catherine Loeb, Francísco Lomelí and Donaldo Urióste, Ernestina Éger, and Lillian Castillo-Speed attest to the improvement. Similarly, the following key reference tools made literary research easier in the eighties: Bruce-Novoa's *Chicano Authors, Inquiry by Interview* (1980), Meier and Rivera's *Dictionary of Mexican American History* (1981), Martínez and Lomelí's *Chicano Literature, A Reference Guide* (1984), and Lomelí and Shirley's *Dictionary of Literary Biography, Chicano/a Volume* (1989).

Despite these and other advances in criticism, large gaps still remain. The most noticeable is a need for the critical study of literature by Chicanas, as well as of feminist theory and gender issues in literature. Scholars like Márta E. Sánchez, Cordelia Chávez Candelaria, Maria Herrera-Sobek, Norma Alarcón, and others are contributing greatly to this important area. Finally, as in 1977, the overwhelming immediate need persists for active, responsive readers among the general public and greater space in major national publications.

The Visual Arts

As with the other art forms, productivity among Mexican American painters and sculptors has expanded phenomenally in the past decade. More and more artists are showing their work in galleries, traveling exhibits, museums, and other institutions, and reproductions of their artwork appear in more and more journals and magazines. In addition, a greater number of published studies of Chicano/a art have appeared.

Chicano/a art bears at least three distinct characteristics. First, there is the distinction of Mexican origins and/or ethnic background, including the foreign birth and bilingualism of many artsits. Second, these artists enjoy the rich heritages of ancient cultures from both the eastern and western hemispheres. The pre-Columbian Indian cultural sources join the Jewish-Christian and Greco-Roman sources as creative inspiration for the aesthetics of Chicano/a artists. Third, many more Mexican American artists now express their *chicanismo* (Chicano/a values and philosophy) forcefully and self-consciously in their creations.

Besides being shaped by the ancient heritages of Europe, Chicanos/as have been influenced by pre-Columbian and Mexican artistic traditions. Mexico and parts of the U.S. Southwest contain many effects, both visible and hidden, of indigenous mythology and of Toltec, Mayan, and Aztec arts, crafts, and architecture (Shearer, 1971: pp. 33–51). The temples of Oaxáca, the pyramids of Yucatán, the jewelry and tapestries of the Mixtecs, and the mammoth Toltec sculptures reflect the fine artistry that attained a "golden age" long before Columbus and other Europeans landed in the hemisphere. These early societies have played a significant role in shaping modern Mexican society and culture, and this influence in turn has helped create twentieth-century Mexican America.

Another important historical source of Chicano/a art occurs in the religious crafts of the Southwest. The mission architecture developed from the sixteenth to

Artist in El Paso, Texas

eighteenth centuries represents a successful blend of function and beauty. The designers of these churches used native materials of the region to construct buildings of simple elegance (Quirárte, 1973: p. 18). The other influential religious art form of the Southwest is *santo* making, the crafting of "carved or painted representation[s] of holy persons, not exclusively restricted to saints" (Quirárte, 1973: p. 26). This form flourished in the late seventeenth and eighteenth centuries and continues today, primarily in the greater Santa Fe area of New Mexico.

Perhaps the most direct influence on Mexican American art in the twentieth century has been the work of internationally renowned Mexican muralists Diégo Rivera, Juan Orózco, and Davíd Alfáro Siquíeros. Their murals synthesized European and Indian heritages into uniquely "Mexican" styles, forms, and themes. Although it is difficult to prove artistic influence, the worldwide acclaim of these painters have had inescapable effect on Chicano/a art. The same is true for the inspiration of Mexican painter Frida Káhlo—especially on Chicana and other feminist artists.

The late 1960s witnessed the emergence of artists' organizations identified as Chicano/a in perspective. Two of the more well known of these groups were MALAF (the Mexican American Liberation Art Front), based in San Francisco, and C/S (Con Safo), located in San Antonio. These and similar associations sought to present in visual form an artistic record of Mexican American experience and of the Chicano/a movement. By collective organizing and promotion of their goals, they have helped many aspiring artists in their training and also in gaining public exposure for their work.

The 1980s has seen the emergence of galleries and exhibits focusing on Latino/a art, and many of these have showcased the work of Mexican Americans. San Francisco's Mexican Museum and the city's Gallery Imago, Austin's Galería Sin Frontéras, and Denver's CHAC (Chicano Humanities and Arts Council) are but four of a number of galleries actively showing the work of Chicanos/as across the nation. Similarly, traveling exhibits sponsored by private corporations have brought increased national attention to Chicano/a and other Latino/a artists.

Although it is impossible adequately to cover all artists of merit in these few pages, some important names must be noted. Two sculptors of established reputation are Medellín (born 1907) and Luís Jiménez (born 1940). Working primarily in wood, Medellín's sculptures convey the timeless strength of pre-Columbian symbols. Quite a different style appears in Jiménez's creations, which are built primarily from such contemporary materials as epoxy and fiberglass. Jiménez favors mammoth size, bold colors, and modernistic themes to express his views of the failures and beauties of America's machine-based, pollution-producing culture.

Painters working and showing prior to the Sixties include António García (born 1901), primarily a muralist; Porfirio Salínas (b. 1912), famous for his Texas landscape paintings; Edward Chávez (b. 1917), who works in mural, easel, and sculpture; and Melesío Cásas (b. 1929), creator of mural-size canvases and also a movie scriptwriter. Among the most commercially successful post-Sixties artists are Amádo Peña and Alejándro Roméro. Emphasizing his American Indian origins, Peña's work features elaborately stylized images of Indian figures and motifs. Now based in Chicago, Mexican-born Roméro paints a brilliantly colored canvas charged with dynamic energy, busy crowd scenes, and musical imagery.

Other important painters of this period include Peter Rodríguez, Melaquías Montoya, Judith Baca, and Max Martínez. Tireless advocates of the social equity issues advanced by the Chicano movement, Montoya, Baca, and Martinez employ many clearly Chicano/a images in their work, while Rodriguez, founder of the Mexican Museum of San Francisco, is decidedly non-representational. One of the founders of MALAF, Montoya is eclectic in creating both representational images and highly abstract forms. Artistic director of SPARC (the Social and Public Art Resource Center), Baca is perhaps best known for her design and coordination of "The Great Wall of Los Angeles" mural project painted from 1976 to 1983, and currently for her "World Wall: A Vision of the Future without Fear," which explores "the material and spiritual transformation of an international society seeking peace" (Pohl, 1990: p. 34). Recognized for his portraits of barrio figures, especially *pachuco* subjects, Martínez uses pastels and watercolors in often unexpected colors to convey the private side of Chicano/a experience.

One of the most exciting developments of the visual arts today is the productivity by Mexican American women. Painters Carmen Lómas Garza, Yolanda López, and Esther Hernández have produced increasingly popular artwork of great skill and originality. Along with the individuals discussed above, they and other fine artists (like Manuél Joél, Orlando Roméro, Carmen Samora, Pedro Roméro, and many others) assure the quality and integrity of a distinctly Chicano/a aesthetics and artistic production.

Music

The same roots that sprouted Mexican American literature and the visual arts also underlie Mexican American music—with one major difference, however. "The music brought over by the Spaniards and Portuguese practically obliterated

Traditional Mexican dances are being taught these youth.

indigenous music, and we have no guarantee that the latter has survived anywhere in its primitive form.... Examples of indigenous melody that has not undergone some European influence are very rare in Latin America'' (Chase, 1959: p. 263).

The absence of a word for music among many pre-Columbian Mesoamerican tribes has led to the assumption that these societies restricted music to ceremonial function. That many pre-Columbian musical instruments have sacred markings reinforces that assumption. Further research indicates otherwise, however, and reveals that music was actually an integral part of their daily life. Scholars have shown that ''the teaching of music existed and special musical instruction was required in all religious and military schools'' (Chávez, 1933: p. 170). Music was also the center of various public celebrations, and many early emperors (notably Nézahualcoyótl, a favored model for Chicano/a writers) devoted much time to musical composition (Boroff, 1971: p. 250).

With Mexico's colonization came

the development of Spanish music in the New World. Nearly a century before the English settled in North America, the Spaniards had established music schools (Chase, 1959: p. 259). Although the New England *Bay Psalm Book* of 1640 is usually touted in U.S. textbooks as the first music book published in the New World, the first such publication, the *Ordinarium*, was actually printed in Mexico City in 1556, and it was followed by six other books of music published in Mexico before 1600 (Chase, 1959: p. 259).

Twentieth-century classical Mexican composers and musicians have increasingly worked the strains of folk music into their compositions. They follow the path of Manuel de Fálla, one of the most important Spanish composers, who used folk themes and motifs in his classical music. Mexico's Silvestre Revuéltas and Carlos Chávez are particularly notable for their synthesis of folk song into their classical work. Chávez in particular is ''one of the few American musicians [who] ... is more than a reflection of Europe ... his work

[is] . . . one of the first authentic signs of a new world with its own new music" (Copland, 1933: p. 106). These examples (and others, like singer Plácido Domingo) of Mexican music and musicians form an important part of America's contribution to the world's classical repertoire.

In the popular music category, Mexicans and Chicanos/as are also well represented. Top-forty stars include singers like Ritchie Valens, Linda Ronstadt, Vicki Carr, and Johnny Rodríguez, as well as groups like Los Lobos.

Chicano/a art, in all its forms, reflects the complex history and vigorous experience of Mexican American culture. Whether music, literature, or visual arts, Chicano/a aesthetics grows from many roots. It is Mesoamerican Indian. It is Spanish. It is Southwest American Indian. It is Anglo American. It is *mestizo*—it is Chicano/Chicana.

The music and dance of festival times are a part of the Mexican-American heritage.

REFERENCES

Alarcón, Norma. "Chicana's Feminist Literature: A Re-Vision through Malintzin/Malinche: Putting Flesh Back on the Object." In *This Bridge Called My Back*, ed. by Cherrie Moraga and Gloria Anzaldua. 2nd ed. New York: Kitchen Table Press, 1983.

———. "Chicana Writers and Critics in a Social Context: Towards a Contemporary Bibliography." *Third Woman*, vol. 4, 1989.

———. "The Sardonic Powers of the Erotic in the Work of Ana Castillo." In *Breaking Boundaries: Latina Writings and Critical Readings*, ed. by Asuncion Horno-Delgado, Eliana Ortega, Nina M. Scott, and Nancy Saporta Sternbach, pp. 94–107. Amherst: University of Massachusetts Press, 1989.

Arroyo, Ronald D. "La Raza Influence in Jazz." *El Grito*, vol. 4, no. 4 (summer 1972), pp. 80–84.

Popular dance music reflects the Mexican-American culture in its beat and rhythm.

Borroff, Edith. *Music in Europe and the United States: A History*. Englewood Cliffs, Prentice-Hall, 1971.

Bruce-Novoa, Juan. *Chicano Authors: Inquiry by Interview*. Austin: University of Texas Press, 1980.

———. *Chicano Poetry: A Response to Chaos*. Austin: University of Texas Press, 1982.

Candelaria, Cordelia Chávez. "Anáhuac Again and the Influence of Chicano Writers." *American Book Review*, vol. 4, no. 5, 1982.

———. "Bibliography." In *Chicano Poetry: A Critical Introduction*. Westport, Conn.: Greenwood Press, 1986.

———. "Chicano Focus." *American Book Review*, vol. 11, no. 6 (January–February), 1989.

———. *Chicano Poetry: A Critical Introduction*. Westport, Conn.: Greenwood Press, 1986.

———. "Code-Switching as Metaphor in Chicano Poetry." In *European Perspectives on Hispanic Literature in the United States*, ed. by Geneviève Fabre. Houston: Arte Publico Press, 1988.

———. "Hang-Up of Memory: Another View of Growing Up Chicano." *American Book Review*, vol. 5, no. 2, 1983.

———. "La Malinche: Feminist Precursor." *Frontiers: A Journal of Women Studies*, vol. 5, no. 2, 1980, pp. 1–16.

———. "*Los Ancianos* in Chicano Literature." *Agenda: A Journal of Hispanic Issues*, vol. 10, no. 5, 1979.

————. "The Multicultural 'Wild Zone' of Ethnic-Identified American Literatures." In *Multiethnic Literatures of the United States: Critical Introductions and Classroom Resources*, pp. i–xiv. Boulder: University of Colorado Press, 1989.

————. "The 'Wild Zone' in Chicana Literary Study." *Journal of Chicana Studies*, vol. 1, no. 1, 1992.

Candelaria, Cordelia Chávez, and Mary Romero, eds. "Las Chicanas." *Frontiers: A Journal of Women Studies*, vol. 11, no. 1 (special issue), 1990.

Castillo-Speed, Lillian. "Chicano Studies: A Selected List of Materials since 1980." *Frontiers: A Journal of Women Studies*, ed. by Cordelia Chávez Candelaria and Mary Romero, vol. 11, no. 1, 1990.

Chase, Gilbert. *The Music of Spain*. Rev. ed. New York: Dover Publications, 1959.

Chávez, Carlos. "The Music of Mexico." In *American Composers on American Music*, ed. by Henry Cowell, pp. 167–72. New York: Frederick Ungar, 1933.

Copland, Aaron. "Carlos Chávez—Mexican Composer." In *American Composers on American Music*, ed. by Henry Cowell, pp. 102–6. New York: Frederick Ungar, 1933.

Éger, Ernestina N. *A Bibliography of Criticism of Contemporary Chicano Literature*. Berkeley, Cal.: Chicano Studies Library Publications, 1982.

Herrera-Sobek, María, ed. *Beyond Stereotypes: The Critical Analysis of Chicana Literature*. Binghamton, N.Y.: Bilingual Press / Editorial Bilingue, 1985.

Herrera-Sobek, María, and Helena María Viramontes, eds. "Chicana Creativity and Criticism: Charting New Frontiers in American Literature." *The American Review*, vol. 15 (fall-winter; special issue), 1987.

Huerta, Jorge, ed. *Necessary Theater: Six Plays about the Chicano Experience*. Houston: Arte Publico Press, 1989.

Limon, José E. "La Llorona: The Third Legend of Greater Mexico: Cultural Symbols, Women, and the Political Unconscious." In *Between Borders: Essays on Mexicana/Chicana History*, ed. by Adelaida R. Del Castillo, pp. 399–432. Encino, Cal.: Floricanto Press, 1990.

Lattin, Vernon E. *Contemporary Chicano Fiction: A Critical Survey*. Binghamton, N.Y.: Bilingual Press / Editorial Bilingue, 1986.

Lomelí, Francísco, and Carl Shirley, eds. *Dictionary of Literary Biography*. Vol. 82: *Chicano Writers*. Detroit: Gale Research Tower, 1989.

Lomelí, Francísco, and Donaldo Urióste. *Chicano Perspectives in Literature: A Critical and Annotated Bibliography*. Albuquerque: Pajarito Publications, 1976.

Lomelí, Francísco, and Júlio A. Martínez, eds. *Chicano Literature: A Reference Guide.* Westport, Conn.: Greenwood Press, 1984.

Nicholson, Irene. *Mexican and Central American Mythology.* London: Paul Hamlyn, 1967.

Ortego, Philip D., ed. *We Are Chicanos: An Anthology of Mexican-American Literature.* New York: Washington Square, 1973.

Pohl, Frances F. "The World Wall, a Vision of the Future without Fear: An Interview with Judith F. Baca." *Frontiers: A Journal of Women Studies,* vol. 11, no.1, 1990, ed. by Cordelia Chávez Candelaria and Mary Romero.

Quirárte, Jacinto. *Mexican American Artists.* Austin: University of Texas Press, 1973.

Romano-V., Octávio I., ed. *Voices: Readings from El Grito.* Berkeley, Cal.: Quinto Sol, 1971.

Sabloski, Irving. *American Music.* Chicago: University of Chicago Press, 1969.

Shearer, Tony. *Lord of the Dawn: Quetzalcoatl.* Healdburg, Cal.: Naturegraph Publishers, 1971.

Swan, Howard. *Music in the Southwest.* San Marino, Cal.: Huntington Library, 1952.

Váldez, Luís. *Actos.* Fresno, Cal.: Cucaracha Press, 1971.

GUIDE TO THE WORKS OF ARTISTS, MUSICIANS, WRITERS

Alurísta. *Floricanto en Aztlan.* Los Angeles: UCLA Chicano Studies Center, 1971 (poetry).

——. *Nationchild Plumaroja.* San Diego: Tolecas de Aztlan Press, 1972 (poetry).

Anaya, Rudólfo. *Bless Me, Última.* Berkeley, Cal.: Tonatiuh, 1972 (novel).

Anaya, Rudólfo, and António Márquez, eds. *Cuentos Chicanos: A Short Story Anthology.* Rev. ed. Albuquerque: New America / University of New Mexico Press, 1984 (short stories).

Anzaldua, Gloria. *Borderlands / La Frontera: The New Mestiza.* San Francisco: Spinsters Press / Aunt Lute Foundation, 1987.

——. *Making Face, Making Soul: Haciendo caras: Creative and Critical Perspectives by Women of Color.* San Francisco: Aunt Lute Foundation, 1990.

Barrio, Raymond. *The Plum Pickers.* Sunnyvale, Cal.: Ventura Press, 1969 (novel).

Cabeza de Baca, Fabiola. *We Fed Them Cactus.* Albuquerque: University of New Mexico Press, 1954.

Casas, Mel. "Chicano Artists C/S." San Antonio, unpublished typescript, n.d. (art).

———. *Mel Casas Paintings.* Mexican American Institute of Cultural Exchange. San Antonio: Mexican Art Gallery, April 1968 (art).

Campa, Arthur L. *Spanish Religious Folk Theatre in the Spanish Southwest.* Albuquerque, 1934 (drama).

Candelaria, Cordelia. *Ojo de la Cueva / Cave Springs.* Colorado Springs: Maize Press, 1984.

Castillo, Ana. *I Close My Eyes (To See).* Pullman: Washington State University Press, 1976.

———. *The Mixquiahuala Letters.* Binghamton, N.Y.: Bilingual Press / Editorial Bilingue, 1986.

———. *My Father Was a Toltec.* Albuquerque: West End, 1988.

———. *Otro Canto.* Cahicago, unpublished, 1977.

———. *Sapogonia.* Tempe, Ariz.: Bilingual Review Press / Editorial Bilingue, 1990.

———. *Women Are Not Roses.* Houston: Arte Publico Press, 1984.

———. *Zero Make Me Happy.* Greenview, Ill.: Scott-Foresman, 1975.

Cervantes, Lorna Dee. *Cable of Genocide: Poems of Love and Hunger.* 1991.

Chávez, Carlos. *The Four Suns.* Ballet with orchestra, 1926 (music).

———. *H. P., Dance of Men and Machines.* Ballet with orchestra, 1931 (music).

Chávez, Denise. *The Last of the Menu Girls.* Houston: Arte Publico Press, 1986.

Cisneros, Sandra. *The House on Mango Street.* Houston: Arte Publico Press, 1985.

———. *My Wicked Ways.* Bloomington, Ind.: Third Woman Press, 1987.

———. *Woman Hollering Creek and Other Stories.* New York: Random House, 1991.

Corpi, Lucha. "The Marina Poems." In *The Other Voice: Twentieth-Century Women's Poetry in Translation,* ed. by Lucha Corpi and trans. by Catherine Rodriguez-Nieto, pp. 154–56. New York: W. W. Norton, 1976.

Cowell, Henry, ed. *American Composers on American Music.* Rev. ed. New York: Frederick Ungar, 1961 (music).

Cota-Cardenas, Margarita. *Noches despertando inconsciences.* Tuscon: Scorpion Press, 1977.

———. *Puppet: A Chicano Novella.* Austin: Relampago Books Press, 1985.

De Hoyos, Angela. *Arise Chicano and Other Poems.* San Antonio: M and A Editions, 1975.

———. *Woman, Woman.* Houston: Arte Publico Press, 1985.

De Fálla, Manuel. *El Amor Brujo.* Ballet, 1915 (music).

———. *El Sombrero de Tres Picos.* Ballet, 1917 (music).

Delgado, Abelardo. Excerpted in *Aztlan: An Anthology of Mexican American Literature,* ed. by Váldez and Steiner. New York: Vintage Press, 1972 (poetry).

———. *It's Cold: 52 Cold Thought–Poems of Abelardo.* Salt Lake City: Barrio Publications, 1974 (poetry).

Galarza, Ernesto. *Barrio Boy.* Notre Dame, Ind.: University of Notre Dame Press, 1971 (novel).

Gómez, Alma, Cherrie Moraga, and Mariana Romo-Carmona, eds. *Cuentos: Stories by Latinas.* New York: Kitchen Table Press, 1983 (short stories).

Gónzales, Rudólfo Corky. *I Am Joaquín.* Denver: Crusade for Justice, 1967; New York: Bantam, 1972 (poetry).

Guzmán, Martín L. *The Eagle and the Serpent.* Glouchester, Mass.: Peter Smith Publications, 1930 (novel).

Huerta, Jorge, ed. *Necessary Theatre: Six Plays about the Chicano Experience.* Houston: Arte Publico Press, 1989.

Medellín, Octavio. *Xtol: Dance of the Ancient Mayan People.* Dallas: Dallas Museum of Fine Arts, 1947 (linoleum block prints, limited edition).

Moraga, Cherrie. *Loving in the War Years: Lo que nunca paso por sus labios.* Boston: South End Press, 1983.

Moraga, Cherrie, ed. *This Bridge Called My Back: Writings by Radical Women of Color.* Persephone Press, 1981.

Murieta, Joaquín. (*See below:* Ridge, John R.).

Niggli, Josephina. *Mexican Village.* Chapel Hill, N.C.: University of North Carolina Press, 1945.

———. *Step Down Elder Brother.* New York: Rinehart, 1947.

Ortiz, Ralph. *Destructions—Past and Present.* Fordham University, 10–28 Nov. 1967 (exhibition catalogue; art).

————. "Destruction Theatre Manifesto." *Studio International* 172, no. 884 (December 1966) (art).

Padilla, Ernie. Excerpted in *El Grito*, vol. 3 (fall 1969) (poetry).

Paredes, Américo. *With His Pistol in His Hand: A Border Ballad and Its Hero.* Austin: University of Texas Press, 1958 (folklore).

Pérez, Luis. *El Coyote the Rebel.* New York, 1947 (novel).

Portillo Trambley, Estela. *The Day of the Swallows.* In *Contemporary Chicano Theatre*, ed. by Roberto Garza, pp. 204–45. Notre Dame, Ind.: University of Notre Dame Press, 1976.

————. Excerpted in *El Grito*, vol. 7 (September 1973) (drama).

————. *Rain of Scorpions and Other Writings.* Berkeley, Cal.: Tonatiuh International, 1975.

————. *Sor Juana and Other Plays.* Ypsilanti, Mich.: Bilingual Press / Editorial Bilingue, 1983.

————. *Trini.* Binghamton, N.Y.: Bilingual Press / Editorial Bilingue, 1986.

Ridge, John R. *The Life and Adventures of Joaquín Murieta.* Norman: University of Oklahoma Press, 1955 (folklore).

Rios, Isabella [Diana Lopez]. *Victuum.* Ventura, Cal.: Diana-Etna, 1976.

Rivera, Tomás. Excerpted in *El Grito*, vol. 2 and 3 (1969) (poetry).

Salinas, Omar. *Crazy Gypsy.* Fresno, Cal.: Origenes, 1970 (poetry).

Salinas, Paul. Excerpted in Ortego's *We Are Chicanos: An Anthology of Mexican-American Literature.* New York: Washington Square, 1973 (poetry).

Sánchez, George I., and Eleanor Delaney. *Spanish Gold.* New York: Macmillan, 1946 (novel).

Shedd, Margaret. *Malinche and Cortés.* New York: Doubleday, 1971 (novel).

Steinbeck, John. *Tortilla Flat.* New York: Grosset and Dunlap, 1935 (novel).

Tafolla, Carmen. *Curandera.* San Antonio: M and A Editions, 1983.

————. "La Malinche." In *Encuentro Artistico Femenil*, pp. 41–42. Austin: Casa Tejidos Publications, 1978.

Tafolla, Carmen, et al. *Get Your Tortillas Together.* San Antonio: Caracol Press, 1976.

Taylor, Sheila Ortiz. *Faultline.* Tallahassee, Fla.: Naiad Press, 1982.

El Teatro del Piojo, El Teatro Bilingüe, El Teatro del Barrio-Chicano (drama groups).

Váldez, Luís. *Actos.* Fresno, Cal.: Cucaracha Press, 1971 (drama).

Villanueva, Alma Luz. *Bloodroot.* Austin: Place of Herons Press, 1977.

———. *Lifespan.* Austin: Place of Herons Press, 1984.

———. *Mother, May I.* Pittsburgh, Pa.: Motheroot Publications, 1978. Reprint in *Contemporary Chicana Poetry*, ed. Marta E. Sanchez, 1985.

———. *The Ultraviolet Sky.* Tempe, Ariz.: Bilingual Press / Editorial Bilingue, 1988.

Villarreal, José António. *Pocho.* New York: Doubleday, 1959 (novel).

Viramontes, Anna. *The Moths and Other Stories.* Houston: Arte Publico Press, 1985.

21 | # The Religious Dimension of Mexican Americans

Mexican American Catholicism

An examination of the Mexican American religious experience in contemporary North American society reveals a deeply religious group that is predominantly Roman Catholic. As a group, Mexican American Catholics have remained religiously devout throughout the history and transformation of the Southwest. But only recently, with persuasion from bold women and men who coalesced around the Chicano movement during the 1960s have we witnessed any formal recognition of the Mexican American Catholic presence by the American Catholic church. In 1970, Patricio Flores, from Ganado, Texas, was ordained as the first Mexican American bishop in the history of the American Catholic church. Since then, twenty more Latino bishops have been appointed to the American Catholic hierarchy. In addition, the hierarchy has acknowledged the importance of Latinos by drafting the U.S. Catholic Bishops pastoral letter, "The Hispanic Presence: Challenge and Commitment," in January of 1984. No longer are Latino Catholics portrayed as a large pastoral problem; they are now recognized as a unique pastoral opportunity—one to which the hierarchy is committed. According to this document, Latino Catholicism is a diverse religious expression and provides a challenge to an institution that should be guided by the vision of cultural pluralism, not assimilation.

Popular and Institutional Religion

From this, one could conclude that a process of reconciliation between Mexican American Catholics and the American Catholic church has begun. Nonetheless, this new-found friendship continues to be strained with problems of cultural conflict and misunderstanding that must be overcome if a long-lasting relationship of mutual affection and respect is to evolve. Some problems apply to all members of the Roman Catholic church, but some are unique to the Mexican American Catholic experience. Consider, for example, that the growth of the Mexican American laity is not reflected by an equivalent growth of Mexican American clergy. Current estimates place the Latino population, the majority of which is Mexican American, at one-quarter of the total Roman Catholic population in the United States, a figure that is estimated to increase to one-third by the year 2000. Projections place Latinos at thirty million by the year 2010, making them the single largest Roman Catholic ethnic group in the United States. By the year 2010, Latino bishops will only comprise 10 percent of the four hundred Roman Catholic bishops and of the fifty-three thousand priests. This demographic reality is a concern for the entire church, which is experiencing a severe shortage of clergy in general.

Photo by Rev. Jaime Rasura.

The decorations at Our Lady of Guadalupe Church (San Diego, 1922–1930) show a true sense of Mexican American nationalism. Mexican flags and American flags fly side by side, flanking a picture of Our Lady of Guadalupe.

An equally difficult problem is posed by the fact that Mexican and Mexican American religiosity is characterized by a style and approach of worshiping the sacred that clashes directly with the vision of the institutional American Catholic church. Mexican and Mexican American religious expression is a type of worship that is closely interwoven with the everyday life experiences and historical struggles of the Mexican American community and that is deeply influenced by cultural, political, and economic realities.

A religious tradition has nevertheless survived in the absence of strong ecclesiastical support and has evolved as a noninstitutional type of religion influenced heavily by popular religion and piety—what Moises Sandoval so accurately refers to as a "self-reliant" religious tradition. Recent polls indicate that only 57 percent of Latinos are church members, compared to 67 percent of the general population. Nonetheless, the majority of Latinos are extremely pious. In this tension between popular and institutional religion strains the most serious conflict between Mexican American Catholics and the rest of the American Catholic church.

Mexican American Catholics experience an ubiquitous religious tradition that is difficult to contain within the institutionalized boundaries of American Catholicism. Church leaders have interpreted the tradition as unadaptable and therefore inferior; they think change is necessitated in order to fit the tradition into the canons of American Catholicism. Historically, the Catholic hierarchy has consistently depicted Mexican Americans as deficient Catholics who neglect regular Mass attendance.

Emergence of Popular Piety

Historically, the Mexican American religious experience emerges from the history of the American Southwest. From 1821 to 1846 the Mexican Catholic church period was formed along with the establishment of the Mexican frontier. The Mexican Catholic church is best described as a laity focused tradition with neither the support nor the direction of a religious clergy. By 1830, close to half of the 4,229 prelates, the majority of whom were Spanish, had departed from the Mexican frontier.

Perceived as isolated and dangerous with few, if any, rewards, the region was avoided by Catholic priests. Mexican Catholics in Texas and present-day Arizona never saw a Catholic bishop in their communities during this period. Consequently, they developed a self-reliant form of religion that was preserved by beliefs and traditions within the Mexican/Mexican American context and more commonly known as "popular religion."

This pilgrimage attests to the centrality of popular piety in the religious expression of Mexican Americans.

Photo by M. Sandoval.

The popular and informal characteristics of Mexican/Mexican American Catholicism were reinforced without the imprint of the official Catholic hierarchy. Consider that since the eighteenth century, Los Hermanos Penitentes (the Confraternity of Our Father, Jesus the Nazarene) were vital for the maintenance of community and unity in northern New Mexico. Los Penitentes flourished in the early nineteenth century as a result of the spiritual neglect of Mexican/Mexican American Catholics by the Catholic clergy. As a mutual aid society, Los Penitentes functioned as a civil and ecclesiastical organization and led the community in prayer, worship, and catechism, while at the same time they made sure that everyone had the basics for a decent quality of life. The members of the confraternity included an official rezador (prayer leader) and cantor (who led song and prayer at rosaries and wakes). They spiritually consoled and offered material aid for the dying and their families. This form of popular religion expressed the lifestyle, beliefs, and values that were interwoven with Mexican culture throughout the northern frontier and largely created a Catholic atmosphere that lacked the bearing of a religious clergy.

Sensitive to the unique political, economic, and cultural dimensions out of which religion emerges, popular religion recognizes the presence of the divine in the world as it embraces the everyday life experiences and beliefs of a people. For this ethnic group, it reflected a rural and communal existence that we define as Mexican or Mexican American. What follows is a brief overview of Mexican American popular piety.

Characteristics of Popular Piety

The Mexican American Cultural Center, a national center for pastoral education and language studies, has identified popular piety in terms of events or periods; based on a liturgical calendar; and as "sacramental," "devotional," and "protective" constellations. Each facet offers a unique aspect of popular religion.

The Liturgical Calendar of Popular Piety

Determining the feasts and celebrations of Mexican/Mexican American popular piety, the liturgical calendar begins during the winter season with the period of Advent and the preparation for Christmas. The focal point of the pre-Christmas celebrations center around the feast of Nuestra Señora de Guadalupe on 12 December that honor her as empress of the Americas. As a brown-skinned apparition who spoke Nahuatl to the Indian Juan Diego on the hill of Tepeyac, Our Lady of Guadalupe gave order and meaning to an indigenous culture that had been shaken into chaos as a result of the Spanish conquest in 1521. Her apparition occurred outside the structures of the institutional church, during a unique political climate of racial strife and conflict, and her image and identity was sustained by the indigenous people of the Americas separate from the Roman Catholic hierarchy.

Las Posadas is another important pre-Christmas procession and ceremony that reenacts the pilgrimage of Mary and Joseph to Bethlehem and their search for lodging. This ceremony is based on the biblical passage of Luke 2:1–7 and was introduced by early Augustinian missionaries.

Very frequently Mexican American Catholics celebrate Christmas at the midnight mass on Christmas day, popularly known as La Misa de Gallo. The service traditionally begins with a procession in which two padrinos (godparents) carry a statue of El Niño Jesus, (the baby Jesus) that is placed in the manger—a ceremony known as *la acostada del Niño*. Another important tradition during this season is the performance of *La Pastorela*, a mystery play of Spanish origin that dates back to the Middle Ages and is performed any time between Christmas and the feast of the baptism of the Lord that marks the end of the Christmas season. This form of theater provides through drama a popular interpretation of the prophecies preceding the coming of Christ and the probable reaction of the shepherds to the announcement of the birth of the Christ child. With the use of devils and angels and comical improvisation, the real tension of good and evil in the play contributes to the convivial atmosphere of the celebration.

Additional celebrations during winter that are observed by Mexican Americans include an end of the year Mass that occurs on 31 December and the feast of the Epiphany, El Dia de Los Reyes, on 6 January. The last day of December is observed by Mexican Americans as a time to give thanks to God for all God's grace during the past year and to implore God's blessing in the coming new year; this is an important family event in which all members actively participate. El Dia de Los Reyes is symbolic for children, for they are taught to be mindful of animals and to experience the joy of gratitude; these ideals are reinforced as children are taught to shine one of their shoes, put some straw in it, and, together with a small bowl of water, place it on the window sill or at the door to feed the animals of the passing Magi. In certain areas of the American Southwest, gifts are given to the children, as this marks the end of the Christmas season.

The spring season introduces the Easter cycle marked by El Miercoles de Ceniza. Considered the most important feast for Mexican Americans as they reflect on their ties to the earth as a mestizo people, Ash Wednesday is a moment when people profess publicly their Christian faith with an awareness of their human sinfulness and limitations. The images of a suffering Christ and a sorrowful mother are historically two important elements of Mexican American popular piety and are intensified during the Easter season. The observance of Holy Thursday focuses on the agony of Christ in the garden and is popularly known as El Santo Dolor del Huerto. On Good Friday, the faithful customarily reenact the pain and suffering of the three falls of Christ in the service La Procesión de las Tres Caidas. Certain communities still hold the service of Las Siete Palabras (The Seven Last Words), which usually consists of a lengthy sermon interrupted by readings, prayers, and penitential songs. In Texas, some communities will attend an evening service on this day to express their condolences to the Virgin who has lost her son in a tradition known as El Pésame a la Virgen. In northern New Mexico, Los Hermanos Penitentes are especially active during Holy Week as they commemorate the sufferings of Jesus at the hour of his death.

The observance of Holy Saturday and Easter Sunday are days of joy and expectation to celebrate the resurrection of Jesus Christ. Easter Sunday is a procession that highlights the sacred encounter of the risen Christ and his mother, and that reaches a crescendo with the burning of an effigy of Judas. Additional celebrations during the spring season are the Feast of the Cross (El Cinco de Mayo), Mother's Day, and the feast of San Isidro. The feast of San Isidro is celebrated on 15 May with great vigor by the people of New Mexico, as he has traditionally been regarded as the patron saint of farmers and those who work the land. Certain communities choose this date to bless their farm animals and pets. This feast exemplifies how popular religion emerges out of a social and economic context which is reflective of a rural Mexican/Mexican American experience.

The seasons of summer and fall are marked by numerous feast days for saints. The feast of St. John the Baptist, the patron saint of San Juan, is celebrated in particular by Puerto Ricans in the United States. In New Mexico numerous saint days are observed, such as the feasts of St. James (Señor Santiago) and of San Lorenzo, who offer historical significance to the region. Señor Santiago is considered the apostle entrusted with the evangelization of the Spanish and his spirit is said to have accompanied the Spanish soldiers into the villages of New Mexico. San Lorenzo is a Spanish martyr whose feastday marks the reconquest of northern New Spain by the Spaniards, who entered through El Paso in 1692. Another very important observance during this season is El Día de Los Muertos (the Feast of All Souls) where food is brought to the dead for their journey. This practice predates Christianity in the Americas and is very popular throughout Texas.

Constellations of Popular Piety

Additional dimensions of Mexican American popular piety have been placed into the three constellations mentioned above-sacramental, devotional, and protective. I proceed here with a brief discussion of each.

Sacramental Constellation

According to the Mexican American Cultural Center, the sacramental constellation of popular piety embraces sacraments and rites that are important to the Mexican American family. Sacraments such as baptism, first communion, and matrimony strengthen kinship and ties in the extended family. In all three, godparents (padrinos, or compadres) share in the ceremony, and now make up part of a special bond or friendship with the family. Another sacrament-like celebration that also has important meaning to the family is the quinceañera. In honor of a young woman's fifteenth birthday, a Mass is celebrated to give thanks to God and to mark her passage from youth to adulthood. This celebration is said to have its roots in Mayan and Toltec cultures of pre-Columbian Mexico.

Devotional Constellation

A second constellation focuses on devotional acts through religious acts or prayers to Jesus Christ, the Virgin Mary, and the saints, acts carried out with some regularity and often with the help of some image, book, or object, such as a rosary. The devotion to Jesus Christ has been honored throughout the American Southwest as El Nazareno since the Mexican people were first evangelized. He is depicted as a

Courtesy of *Los Angeles Times*, photo by Jose Galvez.

Most Latinos turn to Catholic rituals to mark the moments of their lives, like this family here, during the baptism of their child.

suffering and wounded Christ, crowned with thorns, dressed with a purple cloth, and girded with a rope. Another devotional expression to Christ is that of the Sacred Heart, which represents to Mexican Americans a symbol of his eternal love for all humankind; this image is frequently found on a badge known as a *detente* which is usually carried in a person's wallet and/or displayed in home altars. In New Mexico, Jesus Christ receives the title of Nuestro Padre Jesús Nazareno by the Penitentes who emphasize his saving passion. Also in New Mexico, Jesus is honored as the Black Christ of Esquipulas in the famous shrine of Chimayó.

Devotions to the Virgin Mary concentrate on La Virgen de Guadalupe (discussed earlier). Along with the Sacred Heart, she is also enthroned in the homes of Mexican Americans throughout the American Southwest. Another important representation of the Virgin Mary is Nuestra Señora de San Juan de los Lagos located in San Juan, Texas. Mexican American migrant workers make the shrine the focal point of the beginning and the end of their entry into the seasonal migrant stream; it is a tradition for many migrant families to have their vehicles blessed at the shrine before beginning their northern journey.

Finally, there are devotions to specific saints such as San Antonio de Padua, who is venerated throughout the American Southwest as the intercessor for finding lost things. In Texas and California there are special devotions to San Martín de Porres and San Martín Caballero (St. Martin of Tours). San Martín de Porres was a humble mulatto who is said to have been a hard worker and the friend of humble people and lowly creatures. San Martín de Caballero is a fourth-century pagan Roman solider who converted to Christianity and devoted his life to preaching the gospel to the poor. Mexican American business merchants display his image in their establishments as a reminder to treat the poor with dignity and respect as did San Martín de Caballero.

Protective Constellation

The last constellation identified by the Mexican American Cultural Center focuses on the numerous practices and prayers evoked to obtain divine protection. Practices such as blessings, the use of religious objects, pilgrimages, and vows are examples. Blessings are expressions of one's faith and thanksgiving and are an integral part of Mexican American culture. They have been defined as having either an ascending or descending direction and often include a combination of both. An ascending blessing is a prayer of praise or thanksgiving often found in statements like "Bendito sea Dios" (Blest be God), which is a common phrase among Spanish-speaking peoples. A descending blessing calls upon God to protect or to make holy the person or object that is being blessed. Examples of religious objects are things such as medallitas (religious medals) and veladoras (candles) that are brought to a priest for a religious dedication or blessing. Pilgrimages in the Mexican American culture are an essential part of Mexican American popular piety known as *peregrinaciones*. The pilgrimage is an act of prayer and symbolizes struggle and sacrifice on behalf of the faithful as they seek to journey to a designated sacred location. Pilgrimages are practiced by Mexican American Catholics throughout the Southwest. The most popular are to the Basílica de Nuestra Señora de Guadalupe in Mexico City, and the Santuario de Chimayó in northern New Mexico. During the United Farm Workers movement in northern California in the mid-sixties, pilgrimages became sacred acts within a political context, and they served to empower the participants. Last, we have promesas, which can be either a petition for a favor or a vow (known as a *manda*, which is the fulfillment of the stipulations accompanying the petition). Once a favor is considered granted, the manda must take place and can manifest itself through numerous forms of popular piety. The most popular among Mexican Americans is to go to a designated church or shrine in order to leave an ofrenda (offering). It is customary to leave a milagrito (a charm) in the form of the human body, or a part of the body, that has been cured. It is also popular to place a photograph of the person cured or a testimonial letter on the altar or shrine, witnessing to the help received.

As mentioned previously, popular piety is an indispensable dimension of Mexican and Mexican American Catholicism that originates with Spanish-Indian contact in northern New Spain and that is sustained by the amalgamation of racial, cultural, and religious traditions, known as the *mestizaje* throughout this period, and carried over into the Mexican period of the northern frontier. However, with the U.S. occupation of the American Southwest after 1848, this religious tradition would be redefined by the new "American" Church.

Marginalization of Religiosity

With the establishment of the American Catholic church, Mexican popular piety was to be transformed to a so-called marginal and deviant religious tradition by ecclesiastical authority, which now became controlled and structured by a new European clergy. Traditional Mexican religiosity was to be forgotten or terminated, and replaced first with French, later with Irish, canons of institutional Catholicism. European Catholicism was Counter-Reformational in nature and was characterized by a strong institutional and external identity.

While Mexican religiosity recognized and underscored the sacred as an integral part of everyday life experiences and beliefs of a people, a "good" Roman Catholic in the European tradition was a person who publicly followed the tenets of the institution, such as attending Mass or tithing on a regular basis. As a result, Mexican/Mexican American popular piety was judged deficient because it did not conform to the general norms and practices of the newly established European church. In Texas, for example (once it was designated a prefecture of the New Orleans diocese by Rome in 1840), certain French Oblate priests resisted their new assignment to Brownsville, characterizing the Mexicans as "greasers" and "uncivilized" because they would or could not contribute to the church coffers on a regular basis. Dominic Manucy, a clergyman of Italian and Spanish descent, and apostolic vicar of Brownsville, claimed that you could not ". . . obtain money from these people, not even to bury their parents."

In New Mexico, the most overt conflict between popular and institutional religion was exhibited following the appointment of Jean Baptiste Lamy of France as apostolic vicar of the Santa Fe diocese. On 1 January 1853, Bishop Lamy wrote his first pastoral letter to the laity, introducing new rules for reinstituting tithing, something

that had been banned in Mexico by the Law of San Felipe in 1833. From Bishop Lamy's perspective, a good flock was one that remained ". . . devoted to right order and legitimate authority," and hence the mark of a successful church was that it adopted the official practice of tithing. Such a dictate was met with direct opposition by the famous cleric, Padre José Antonio Martinez from Taos, on the grounds that it placed an unfair burden upon the poor.

Padre Martinez is a major historical figure in New Mexican history. He played the role of scholastic father for native clergy, and he strongly influenced the citizenry of Taos from 1826 to 1857. He is credited with having established schools for children at the Indian Pueblos in the late 1820s and by 1834 had founded a seminary out of which sixteen native priests were ordained. The ideals of liberation offered by Mexico's first revolutionary hero, Padre José Miguel Hidalgo, deeply influenced Padre Martinez and his views toward civil and ecclesiastical authority.

Padre Martinez's action towards Lamy's dictate was interpreted by the bishop as a boycott to force him out of the diocese. In response, the bishop retaliated with a more forceful policy. In a second pastoral letter issued on 14 January 1854, Bishop Lamy incorporated church dogma on the Immaculate Conception to underscore the importance of tithes, as well as the consequences for individuals who failed to comply. Simply stated: "Believers who did not support the church materially did not have the right to receive the holy sacraments." The ongoing conflict between Padre Martinez and Bishop Lamy led to Martinez's being suspended, then formally excommunicated, by the bishop from the Santa Fe diocese in 1857.

An historical examination of

Mexican American Catholicism in relation to the American Catholic church establishes that Mexican American religiosity is a self-reliant tradition that, with the incorporation of the American Southwest, came into conflict with a "legitimate" and ethnically distinct clergy which then transformed indigenous religion expression from a popular to a marginal position. The marginal relationship between Mexican American Catholics and the institutional church remained consistent throughout the history of the American Southwest and did not change until the emergence of the Chicano movement in the 1960s.

Impact of Marginalization

Unfortunately, the impact of marginalization has been destructive to Mexican American Catholics and their issues of community formation. The transition from a popular to a marginal belief system has involved a group of believers with access to few, if any, leadership roles within the American Catholic church. For the most part, Mexican American Catholics have remained inactive within the formal structures of the institution because of the neglect and marginalization of popular piety by the hierarchy. Where other disenfranchised groups, like African Americans, have developed leaders and social movements through their religious structures and traditions, Mexican American Catholics have been discouraged by the formal religious structures from taking an active leadership role in their church or community. In fact, historically, the American Catholic hierarchy has been diametrically opposed to Mexican American collective action for economic or political change.

Need for Change

A U.S. Catholic bishops' pastoral letter for Latinos that does not build on historical knowledge in order to provide fundamental changes within the structures of institutional American Catholicism will remain ineffective. For the institutional church to ignore the important role of Mexican American popular religion in building community and providing a solid foundation for ethnic identity would be a mistake. Unfortunately, the bishops' pastoral letter stresses the need to control popular religiosity by warning that such "unsophisticated practices" must be properly oriented and guided by the official church. Such a perspective has been and remains blind to the popular identity and traditions of the people and how their relationship to the sacred can help breathe new life into an increasingly moribund church. That Mexican American and Latino Catholics by the thousands are rejecting Roman Catholicism for Fundamentalist traditions should come as no surprise. According to the sociologist Andrew Greeley, Latinos are leaving the American Catholic church at a rate of approximately sixty thousand people a year. Since 1975, 8 percent of the total Latino population has abandoned Roman Catholicism. This figure is 15 percent for Mexican Americans, and as high as 24 percent for Puerto Ricans. Mexican American religiosity has clearly not found a respected voice within the institutional canons of American Catholicism. Since 1848, Mexican Ameri-

Courtesy of *Los Angeles Times*, photo by Jose Galvez.

Although Evangelical Protestantism has made inroads among Latinos, the Catholic Church has also found new enthusiasm.

the formal institution and the everyday life experiences of the people.

In contrast, Protestantism grants Mexican Americans and Latinos the ability to find order in their relation to the sacred, what Raoul E. Isáis-A. refers to as a "democratization of the ritual," where believers are personally and emotionally involved in constructing and understanding the sacred. They have ministers and leaders who look like them, speak their language, and live their struggles. Such an approach to the sacred underscores the unique political, economic, and cultural dimensions from which Mexican American religiosity has emerged.

If the Roman Catholic church of the United States is serious about arriving at some consensus with its Mexican American brethren, it will need to transform the canons that define its relationship to the sacred. Such a change will require that the institutional church grant more authority to the laity. For Mexican Americans and other Latinos, this means that their identity and their traditions would be granted recognition and legitimacy by the hierarchy. These religious traditions can be expressed through the Charismatic Catholic Movement or through Basic Christian Communities, both of which have historically empowered thousands of Latinos throughout the Americas. Unfortunately, neither tradition is an integral part of the contemporary Roman Catholic church in the United States. If there is any hope of true acceptance for and by Mexican American Catholics, the institutional church and its structure will have to change.

can popular piety and, hence, Mexican American cultural identity remain outside the American Catholic church. There exists a chaotic void between the demands of

REFERENCES

Abalos, David T. *Latinos in the United States: The Political and the Sacred*. Notre Dame, Ind.: University of Notre Dame Press, 1986.

Elizondo, Virgilio. "Our Lady of Guadalupe as a Cultural Symbol: The Power of the Powerless." In *Concilium,* vol. 102, ed. by David Herman Schmidt. New York: Crossroads, 1977.

Gallup, George, Jr., and Jim Castelli. *The People's Religion: American Faith in the 90s.* New York: Macmillan, 1989.

Greeley, Andrew. *The Catholic Myth: The Behavior and Beliefs of American Catholics.* New York: Charles Scribner's Sons, 1990.

Hendren, Luciano C. "Daily Life on the Frontier." *In Fronteras: A History of the Latin American Church in the USA since 1513,* ed. Moises Sandoval. San Antonio: Mexican American Cultural Center, 1983.

Isaís-A., Raoul E. "The Chicano and the American Catholic Church." In *Grito Del Sol Quarterly Book,* ed. Octavio I. Romano-V. Berkeley, Cal.: Tonatiuh, 1979.

Juarez, Roberto J. "La Iglesia y el Chicano en sud Texas." *Aztlan,* vol. 4, no. 2, 1974 (Fall).

Maduro, Otto. *Religion and Social Conflict.* New York: Orbis Press, 1982.

Mexican American Cultural Center. *Faith Expression of Hispanics in the Southwest.* San Antonio: Mexican American Cultural Center, 1990.

Pulido, Alberto L. "Are You an Emissary of Jesus Christ? Justice, the Catholic Church, and the Chicano Movement." *Explorations in Ethnic Studies,* vol. 14, 1991 (January).

————. "Mexican American Catholicism in the Southwest: The Transformation of a Popular Religion." Unpublished manuscript, 1991.

Romero, Juan. *Reluctant Dawn: Historia del Padre A. J. Martinez, Cura de Taos.* San Antonio: Mexican American Cultural Center, 1976.

Sandoval, Moises. *On the Move: A History of the Hispanic Church in the United States.* New York: Orbis Press, 1990.

Santos, Ricardo. "The Age of Turmoil." In *Fronteras: A History of the Latin American Church in the USA since 1513,* ed. by Moises Sandoval. San Antonio: Mexican American Cultural Center, 1983.

Weber, David J. *The Mexican Frontier 1821–1846: The American Southwest under Mexico.* Albuquerque: University of New Mexico Press, 1982.

Education

As we have stated before, Dr. George I. Sánchez, as early as 1934, was beginning to question the adequacy of testing, in particular the use of intelligence tests, as a means of evaluating the mental capability of lower-class white children and children from minority groups. The tests were based on norms established for white middle-class members of the dominant society and had little relationship to the life style of the members of other groups. Sánchez questioned also the use of such tests for placing youngsters in the educational track systems which would eventually determine, to a large extent, their career possibilities. Since so many of the Mexican-American schoolchildren were either "dropouts" or "push-outs" from the educational system, he questioned the educational curricula that produced so many dropouts and so-called mentally retarded children and so few pupils who finally made it through high school and into colleges and universities.

Noting the language and cultural biases of the I.Q. tests, Sánches suggested that the school system, in areas where there were high concentrations of Spanish-speaking pupils, should provide bilingual and bicultural instruction in order to give the Hispanic pupils an equal opportunity and an equal access to the educational facilities of the nation. Some thirty years later the United States Congress did, in fact, pass a bilingual educational act which was to provide federal funds for bilingual and bicultural education throughout the country. These programs have yet to be evaluated, but it is certainly an effort in the right direction in providing equal opportunity for children whose native language is not English. The 1980s have seen a strong trend towards reversing such goals, however, and a concomitant emphasis (and legal actions) in favor of English-only education.

During the late 1960s, it became generally evident that the nation's colleges and universities were not providing equality of opportunity to students from different cultures or different ethnic groups. Consequently, the schools began to establish

Education provides the skills needed in this automated molybdenum mill in Red River, New Mexico.

ethnic studies and/or black studies, Chicano studies, Indian studies, and Oriental studies. They did so under heavy pressure from students and local communities. These ethnic studies were as legitimate a curriculum as the existing Latin American studies, Russian studies, American studies or Western European studies programs. But the ethnic studies had to be forced upon the colleges and universities by the pressure and active demonstrations of minority groups and their supporters.

Many schools surrendered to the demands to establish ethnic studies without careful consideration and with less concern. One college even assigned students to establish the Chicano Studies Department—that is, to write the curriculum and hire the professors. Would a chemistry department allow its students to

write the curriculum? Would a history department ask students to hire its faculty? Chicano studies are as legitimate as any other program of study. But after the first wave of enthusiasm for their establishment, many such programs have fallen by the wayside, or have been politicized in such a way that blacks, Orientals, Indians, Chicanos, and Puerto Ricans are all fighting for the meager resources that the university administrations offer for ethnic studies. As a result the minority groups began fighting one another rather than confronting the university system which has failed to provide adequate resources for the various minority studies programs.

Chicano studies have yet to be adequately implemented at the high school or at the elementary level. But perhaps with time and enough pressure from students and parents, curriculum changes may in fact be made to the advantage of the minority groups.

To emphasize the critical situation which exists because of this denial of opportunity, Chicanos, with a population base of approximately eight million, have fewer than one hundred who have earned Ph.D.'s. In contrast, the black community with a population base of approximately twenty-five million, has over two thousand persons with a Ph.D.

In order to achieve proportional representation in colleges:

the estimated black enrollment in 1970 would have to be increased by 543,000 (from 470,000 to 1,013,000)—an increase of 116 per cent

the estimated Mexican American enrollment in 1970 would have to be increased by 165,000 (from 50,000 to 215,000)—an increase of 330 per cent

the estimated Puerto Rican enrollment in 1970 would have to be increased by 45,000 (from 20,000 to 65,000)—an increase of 225 per cent the estimated American Indian enrollment in 1970 would have to be increased by 26,000 (from 4,000 to 30,000)—an increase of 650 per cent

The four minority groups, taken together, were under-represented in the 1970–71 academic year by 779,000 students. Instead of the actual 544,000 minority students there should have been 1,323,000 matriculants to achieve statistical parity. (Crossland, 1971: p. 16)

Chicano educators and university students have been quick to join in the "demands" for more adequate education and for more Chicano students and faculty in educational programs. This has occurred in the fields of sociology, medicine, law, social work, as well as other academic fields. A number of professional organizations as well as student organizations have been established in order to attempt to achieve the goal of greater access to college, but it remains to be seen how effective these organizational efforts will be.

Media

The term *media* here is used in a very broad sense to include newspapers, radio, and television, as well as scholarly journals. Over the years there have been any number of Spanish-language radio programs aimed at Mexican Americans with regional or national interests. More recently there have been a number of "grass roots" efforts to establish more relevant Spanish-speaking radio programs related to current issues rather than national issues or Latin American issues and appealing more to the barrio communities.

The same may be said about the Spanish-language newspapers. Many of the older established newspapers, concerned primarily with national or international news coverage, had little to do with Mexican Americans per se but provided a Spanish-language coverage of the news. More recently, local and "self-interest" newspapers have been established as an arm of local or regional organizations. For example, César Chávez's farm workers' organization publishes its own newspaper, *El Malcriado*. And the Crusade for Justice

Local newspaper editor

publishes *El Gallo. The Latin Times* of East Chicago, Indiana, has been published for many years.

In the past decade, special interest periodicals and newspapers, either local or regional in character (and many of them "protest" papers), have flourished. As a matter of fact, up to thirty such newspapers have been printed in the last few years. They have gained such stature that a Chicano Press Association has been established. Most of these papers try to tell the story the way they see it, which is quite often different from the way the establishment media report it. The continuing success of these newspapers varies, in financial terms, but the majority seem able to continue publication. National periodicals such as *Regeneración* and *La Raza* have been published for some time. A national news

magazine, *La Luz*, was established along the lines of the old *Life* magazine and the current *Ebony* magazine. Judging from current circulation, their survival seems assured.

A number of professional journals have also been established; one is called *Aztlán*, another *El Grito*; still others are the *Journal of Chicano Studies* and the *Journal of Mexican American History*.

Several television programs relating to Mexican Americans have been established but not entertainment series. Rather, documentaries and special features are offered. Most of these programs deal with the history of Mexican Americans or are special features about Mexican Americans. We have yet to see more than one full-fledged television series with Chicano actors as we have seen among blacks.

National Organizations

Besides the G.I. Forum and LULAC, two other national organizations were established. One was the Midwest Council of La Raza, an organization begun during a meeting of Mexican Americans at the University of Notre Dame in the early 1970s. This organization, with limited funding, attempted to serve a ten-state area. Its board of directors was elected from residents of the ten different states and it attempted to address itself to the problems of Mexican Americans in a variety of fields over this large geographical area. Lack of funding hampered its endeavors. The Midwest Council of La Raza no longer exists.

An earlier organization was the Southwest Council of La Raza, which is now the National Council of La Raza with offices in Washington, D.C. and Phoenix, Arizona. It was established in 1968 with funding from the Ford Foundation. The original intent

was to help establish barrio organizations in various parts of the Southwest, with programs in voter registration, community organization, and the funding of local projects at the grass roots level. The Tax Reform Act of 1969, however, made it impossible for foundations to make grants to organizations involved in important organizing efforts. Foundations, then, had to go into so-called "hard programs" such as education, housing, and economic development. Apparently the United States Congress was not anxious to have organizations, supported from tax-exempt funds from foundations, organize minority groups. Therefore, many of the activities of the tax-exempt organizations had to change from what one may call realistic "grass roots" organizing activities into more sophisticated and "safe" programs of limited importance and with the

Whether in politics or business, success for a minority depends on grass-roots efforts.

probability of limited success.

Despite the constraints, the National Council of La Raza has been effective in helping local southwestern organizations establish programs and procure either private or public funds for their particular projects. How successful these programs will be in the long run depends both on the national mood as well as the stamina of the local organizations to continue their fight for self-determination.

The Mexican American Legal Defense and Educational Fund (MALDEF) was established in 1968, with a grant from the Ford Foundation. Its purpose was to attack problems of discrimination and segregation among Mexican Americans and to provide law school scholarships for Mexican-American students. Since 1969

MALDEF has assisted over three hundred Chicano law students at a cost of over half a million dollars (MALDEF 1975 Report, p. 12). MALDEF's litigation program is in the broad fields of equal educational opportunity; political access; land and water rights; equal employment opportunity; rights of political association and expression; and abuses of authority, a field which includes prison reform, and the policies and practices of agencies such as the police, Immigration and Naturalization Service, and health and social welfare.

L.A.R.A.S.A., the Latin American Research and Service Agency, does a great deal of research and disseminates it through the organization's quarterly newsletter. L.A.R.A.S.A. was founded in the early 1980s in Denver, Colorado.

The Christian Churches

The Christian churches, except for local   community efforts, have seldom been at the forefront of helping to resolve some of the problems of Mexican Americans. In the late 1940s many of the Protestant organizations did attempt to help the migrant workers or seasonal farm workers with a type of welfare aid and limited health programs. Many of their efforts were also aimed at proselytizing, as distinguished from humanitarian efforts.

The Catholic Church, which claims most Spanish-speaking Americans as its members, has been quite negligent in its efforts to help Mexican Americans or the Spanish-speaking generally. Many people suggest that the Catholic Church responded not to the problems of Mexican Americans but rather to the proselytizing being done by the Protestant churches. In the early 1950s, the Bishop's Committee for the Spanish-speaking was established. In a sense, it was a counter-part to the efforts of the Protestant churches with regard to the problems of migrant workers. It was not until the late 1960s that the Catholic Church actually responded with an establishment of a Division of the Spanish-speaking, which attempted to provide services for Mexican Americans on a national level. The Division of the Spanish-speaking established several regional centers. But at this writing it would appear that the work among Mexican Americans on the part of the Catholic Church is not of the highest priority.

In the early 1970s, Spanish-speaking priests, and Spanish-speaking nuns formed their own organizations (Padres and Hermanas) within the Catholic hierarchy to help provide services for the Mexican American and place in dialogue the important issue of the Catholic Church and its Spanish-speaking constituency. It was also at the time that the first Mexican-American Catholic bishop, P. F. Flores, was appointed. Through his efforts a Mexican-American Cultural Center has been established in San Antonio offering a wide variety of services to Mexican Americans. A second auxiliary bishop, Gilbert Espinosa Chávez, was ordained in San Diego, and in July, 1974 Roberto F. Sánchez was ordained archbishop of Sante Fe. These bishops are making a significant impact on the relationship between the Catholic hierarchy and its Spanish-surname constituents. Today the number of Hispanic bishops has increased but is not truly proportionate.

Foundations

Foundations have been established in this country as non-profit institutions for the purpose of serving the public welfare. This, or course, means identifying subjects and problems of national, regional, or local importance and seeking individuals and institutions who will address themselves to these topics, and granting funds for either investigation of such topics or for the development of programs designed to achieve the resolution of problems. Foundations, then, are the trustees of private monies which have escaped the tax collector, but which in turn should be used in the public arena. Those entrusted with private funds for the public welfare have often been blind and if not blind certainly myopic regarding the concerns of certain segments of the society. The same, of course, can be said for those in charge of public agencies, whether local, state or federal. The record is clear if, indeed, disappointing.

There are over twenty-five thousand

foundations in the United States. In 1972 and 1973 only fifty-two grants were made by all foundations on programs concerning Mexican Americans. Nor are foundations known as equal opportunity employers, nor do they have affirmative action programs in their hiring practices with regard to Chicanos. Although data is hard to come by, so far as we know there is only one Chicano who serves on the board of directors of one foundation. We know of no senior officers (Chicanos) on any of the staffs and we have been able to identify only a handful of Chicano employees beyond the clerical and custodial employment categories.

In the 1950s, the Rockefeller Foundation awarded a grant to Dr. George I. Sánchez to establish the Southwest Council on the Education of the Spanish-speaking. The money was devoted to research, publications and conferences on several issues affecting Chicanos.

In the same period, the John Hay Whitney Foundation established its Opportunity Fellowships. Over one hundred Chicanos were helped to complete educational careers through these grants. Later, the foundation discontinued these fellowships and adopted another approach. Funds were designated for use by a team of persons who would investigate a perceived problem within the community or society and, based on their research, make recommendations to bring about changes within the system. This novel approach helped change structures rather than help individuals improve themselves. Unfortunately, the John Hay Whitney Foundation no longer exists.

The Rosenberg Foundation, a small foundation limited to small grants within the state of California, has made a number of imaginative grants to institutions with creative approaches to problems.

The Ford Foundation, beginning in 1964, has been the most involved in Mexican-American affairs. Among the first grants was one to the University of California at Los Angeles for a research project. Eleven advanced reports and one book were produced. Interestingly enough, the Foundation came under heavy criticism relating to the choice of institution and personnel as not representing the Chicano community. Other grants made by the Ford Foundation include the establishment of HELP (Home, Education, Livelihood Project), The National Council of La Raza and the Mexican-American Legal Defense and Educational Fund. In the field of education, their more recent grants are supporting a few hundred Chicano students in graduate schools. Other foundations could well follow this example.

Several years ago, a group of Chicanos founded Hispanics in Philanthropy (HIP), based in San Francisco, California. This organization will help Hispanics primarily in the United States.

Published Materials

Minorities in general and Chicanos in particular have been neglected in American literature and even in the ordinary textbooks used by elementary, high school, and college students. When Chicanos have been mentioned in the writings of the past, their characterization has most often been less than favorable. An abundance of stereotyped views and derogatory terms have been perpetrated. The Chicano has often been viewed as cowardly, savage, violent, cruel, mean, swarthy, shiftless, a bandit,

Mexican Americans in the Armed Forces

In time of war, Mexican Americans have always contributed more than their share of members to the armed forces of the United States. Those who served did so with great valor and dedication. In fact, Mexican American soldiers earned more Medals of Honor (the highest award given to members of the armed forces for distinguished service) and other citations in World War II in proportion to their numbers than any other minority group.

José P. Martínez, born in New Mexico, and raised in Colorado, was the first draftee in the Pacific Theatre in World War II to win the Congressional Medal of Honor. He distinguished himself in battle with the Japanese on the Aleutian island of Attu near Alaska. On May 27, 1943, he twice lead his pinned-down platoon through heavy Japanese rifle and machine gun fire to capture a strategic pass overlooking the harbor. His citation reads, "he was mortally wounded with his rifle still at his shoulder, absorbing all enemy fire and permitting all units to move up behind him and successfully take the pass."

Other Congressional Medal of Honor winners in the war in the Pacific were Pvt. Cleto Rodríguez of Texas; Pvt. Manuel Pérez, Jr. (posthumously) of Chicago; Staff Sergeant Ysmael Villegas (posthumously) of California; PFC David Gonzales (posthumously) of California and Sgt. Alejandro Ruiz (posthumously) of New Mexico.

Another Mexican American to win the Congressional Medal of Honor was Staff Sergeant Luciano Adams of Port Arthur, Texas. On October 28, 1944, while bullets clipped the branches off the trees around him and hand grenades showered him with broken twigs, he dashed from tree to tree in the Montagne Forest in France and single-handedly knocked out three German machine guns.

Also receiving the Congressional Medal of Honor in the European Theatre were Staff Sergeant Macario García, a Mexican-born farm laborer from Texas who, while wounded, crawled forward to silence two German gun emplacements; Sergeant José M. López of Brownsville, Texas, a machine gunner who killed more enemy soldiers than any other American in World War I or II—over 100—while protecting his company during a withdrawal; nineteen-year-old Pvt. José F. Valdez who bled to death while fighting off an attack from more than 200 of the enemy and directing artillery fire on their position; and PFC Silvestre S.

Herrera who, after his feet were blown off in a minefield, pinned down an enemy position until his comrades silenced it.

During the Korean War the quality and fibre of Mexican American soldiers was again shown to be of the finest calibre. Sgt. Joseph C. Rodríguez, of San Bernadino, California, dashed sixty yards through enemy fire to destroy five well-fortified enemy foxholes that were decimating his platoon. Nineteen-year-old PFC Edward Gómez of Omaha smothered a live grenade with his body. Others whose heroic conduct merited the Medal of Honor were PFC Eugene Obregón (posthumously) of Los Angeles; Cpl. Rodolfo Hernández of California; Cpl. Benito Martínez (posthumously) of Texas; and Sgt. Ambrosio Guillen (posthumously) of Colorado.

---

or a thief (Robinson, 1963: passim; Webb, 1935: passim). Even specialized books on race and minorities, for example in sociology, did not mention Mexican Americans until recent years. Some studies of Chicanos have been published, but many have come under serious attack by some Mexican-American scholars, as being ahistorical and perpetuating myths and stereotypes (Romano, 1968: passim; Hernández, 1970: passim).

Book companies have long neglected materials concerning Mexican Americans. It was not until the publishing of such materials became profitable that the book companies jumped into the stream and are more than eager to publish materials about Mexican Americans. Many book companies are revising their old texts and including materials on minorities.

In many instances commercial publishers were reluctant to publish Chicano authors and this has led to the establishment of a few Chicano publishing houses and distributing centers—for example: El Dorado Distributors, Cultural Distribution Center, Quinto Sol, and La Causa Publications.

Dr. Gary Keller, a Chicano from El Paso, Texas, was provost and dean of the graduate school at such institutions as Eastern Michigan University and the New York state university system (SUNY at Binghamton, New York). Currently he is with Arizona State University in Tempe. In addition, he founded the Bilingual Press, which publishes books on Chicanos and others as well as sells books on Chicanos published by other Presses.

Government Agencies

Among the most notorious in their neglect of certain segments of the population, in this instance Mexican Americans, have been the state and federal governmental agencies.

In 1962, the Civil Rights Commission became interested in Mexican Americans by funding a small study on the status of Spanish-speaking people in the United States. It was not until the late 1960s that

Graciela Olivarez
(9 March 1928 – 19 Sept. 1987)

The daughter of a Spanish father and a Mexican mother, Graciela Olivarez was raised in Sonora, Arizona, and quit school at the age of 15 to go to work. While working as a bilingual secretary in a Phoenix advertising agency she had the chance to substitute for a radio announcer and became an instant hit with the Chicano audience. After moving up to hostess of an "action line" program she became involved in civil rights work. She was later appointed to head the Arizona branch of the federal government's Office of Economic Opportunity.

When Olivarez told University of Notre Dame president Father Hesburgh of her frustration and lack of effectiveness as director of the Arizona OEO, he offered her a scholarship to the Notre Dame law school, even though she lacked a high school diploma. In May of 1970 she became the first woman graduate of the Notre Dame law school. Since then, she received numerous honorary degrees.

Back in Phoenix, she worked as a consultant to the Urban Coalition, then as the director of Food for All, a food stamp program. She continued working for Mexican-American civil rights movements and became an advocate for women's rights in Arizona. She then served as director of the University of New Mexico's Institute for Social Research and Development before accepting an offer from Governor Jerry Apodaca to head the New Mexico state planning office.

Graciela Olivarez was the highest ranking woman government official in New Mexico and perhaps the entire Southwest. She and her staff of 62 were responsible for reviewing long-range and short-range planning for all New Mexico state agencies. Her job required her to work twelve-hour days, yet she still did volunteer work with the Mexican American Legal Defense and Education Fund and other organizations. Although she has turned down offers to go into politics, *Redbook* magazine suggested that she would make an ideal secretary of health, education and welfare. During the Carter administration she did serve as director of the federal government's Community Service Administration.

In 1980 she started Olivarez Television Company, Inc., the only Spanish-language television network in the country. She continued her work in broadcasting and philanthropy until her death in 1987.

the Civil Rights Commission actually came through with serious studies of the education of Mexican Americans and the administration of justice with respect to Mexican Americans.

Under the administration of President Lyndon B. Johnson, the Cabinet Committee on Mexican-American Affairs was established. It was founded under pressure from Mexican Americans and in an effort to ward off demonstrations and riots which were in the offing. The Cabinet Committee on Mexican-American Affairs represented an attempt to bring together the cabinet officers under the direction of Vicente Ximenes and have each cabinet department seriously concern itself with the plight of Spanish-speaking people in employment, in the services offered by their agency, and in the funding of programs relevant to them. This Cabinet Committee was well on its way to significant work at the end of Johnson's administration. Under the Nixon administration the committee became the Cabinet Committee on Opportunities for Spanish-Speaking People, including Puerto Ricans, Cubans, and others.

Unfortunately the Cabinet Committee under the direction of Mr. Henry Ramirez became less an advocate for the Spanish-speaking people and more an apologist for the federal government. Many of the efforts of the Cabinet Committee were not to produce programs for the Spanish-speaking people of the country but rather to promote the administration and the reelection of the president. The Nixon administration did hire more Chicanos at top level jobs than any previous administration, but it also fired them. It is clear that it was more interested in vote-getting than in the resolution of problems.

It is unfortunate that a minority in this society which has contributed so much to the making of the country can be so neglected by its institutions such as the school system, the government agencies, the churches, and the foundations, while these same institutions are promoting the general welfare of the dominant society. Is it any wonder that the minorities soon learned that in order to gain some benefits and to attract attention to their plight, they must remember that the society has taught them that the wheel that squeaks the loudest gets the most grease? Unfortunately this often leads to violence, demonstrations, and rioting in order that they may claim for themselves·even a small share in their own society.

REFERENCES

Crossland, Fred E. *Minority Access to College.* New York: Schocken Books, 1971.

Hernández, Deluvina. *A Mexican American Challenge to a Sacred Cow.* Los Angeles: University of California, 1970.

Mexican American Legal Defense and Educational Fund. 1975 Annual Report.

Robinson, Cecil. *With the Ears of Strangers.* Tucson: University of Arizona Press, 1963.

Romano, Octavio. "The Anthropology and Sociology of the Mexican Americans," *El Grito,* vol. 2, no. 1 (Fall 1968).

Webb, W. P. *The Texas Rangers.* Boston and New York: Houghton Mifflin Co., 1935.

Appendix I

Court Record of Superior Court of California,
San Jose, California. Gerald S. Chargin Presiding.

The following statements of the Court were recorded by the official court reporter, Susan K. Straim, C.S.R.

September 2, 1969　　　　10:25 a.m.

STATEMENTS OF THE COURT

The Court: There is some indication that you more or less didn't think that it was against the law or was improper. Haven't you had any moral training? Have you and your family gone to church?

The minor: Yes, sir.

The Court: Don't you know that things like this are terribly wrong? This is one of the worst crimes that a person can commit. I just get so disgusted that I just figure what is the use? You are just an animal. You are lower than an animal. Even animals don't do that. You are pretty low.

I don't know why your parents haven't been able to teach you anything or train you. Mexican people, after 13 years of age, it's perfectly all right to go out and act like an animal. It's not even right to do that to a stranger, let alone a member of your own family. I don't have much hope for you. You will probably end up in State's Prison before you are 25, and that's where you belong anyhow. There is nothing much you can do.

I think you haven't got any moral principles. You won't acquire anything. Your parents won't teach you what is right or wrong and won't watch out. Apparently, your sister is pregnant, is that right?

The minor's father: Yes.

The Court: It's a fine situation. How old is she?

The minor's mother: Fifteen.

The Court: Well, probably she will have a half a dozen children and three or four marriages before she is 18.

The county will have to take care of you. You are no particular good to anybody. We ought to send you out of the country—send you back to Mexico. You belong in prison for the rest of your life for doing things of this kind. You ought to commit suicide. That's what I think of people of this kind. You are lower than animals and haven't the right to live in organized society—just miserable, lousy, rotten people.

There is nothing we can do with you. You expect the County to take care of

247

you. Maybe Hitler was right. The animals in our society probably ought to be destroyed because they have no right to live among human beings. If you refuse to act like a human being, then, you don't belong among the society of human beings.

Mr. Lucero: Your Honor, I don't think I can sit here and listen to that sort of thing.

The Court: You are going to have to listen to it because I consider this a very vulgar, rotten human being.

Mr. Lucero: The Court is indicting the whole Mexican group.

The Court: When they are 10 or 12 years of age, going out and having intercourse with anybody without any moral training—they don't even understand the Ten Commandments. That's all. Apparently, they don't want to.

So if you want to act like that, the County has a system of taking care of them. They don't care about that. They have no personal self-respect.

Mr. Lucero: The Court ought to look at this youngster and deal with this youngster's case.

The Court: All right. That's what I am going to do. The family should be able to control this boy and the young girl.

Mr. Lucero: What appalls me is that the Court is saying that Hitler was right in genocide.

The Court: What are we going to do with the mad dogs of our society? Either we have to kill them or send them to an institution or place them out of the hands of good people, because that's the theory—one of the theories of punishment is if they get to the position that they want to act like mad dogs, then, we have to separate them from our society.

Appendix II
Inquest on Salazar's Death*

A coroner's inquest was held to determine the cause of death of noted Chicano writer Ruben Salazar, news director of KMEX and Los Angeles Times columnist. Salazar was killed when struck in the head by a projectile fired from a deputy sheriff's tear-gas gun.

The coroner's inquest is not legally binding which means that no legal action can be determined by its seven member jury. The inquest serves as a fact finding body which is nothing more than a catharsis to alleviate the tensions brought on by Ruben Salazar's death.

The sheriffs Department opened up testimony the first few days introducing a video tape which supposedly showed Chicanos throwing rocks and bottles at them at Laguna Park. In their two days of testimony, the did not show any Chicanos being attacked and beaten by sheriff deputies. Their testimony was contradicted by two members on the editorial staff of LA RAZA and numerous other Chicano witnesses.

*Reprinted as it appears in *La Raza,* Vol. no. 3, Special Issue (no date given). We are indebted to Mr. Raul Ruiz for permission to use the article.

Hearing officer Norman Pittluck did not cross-examine the deputies or question the validity of their pictures, but cross-examined Chicano witnesses at length. At times, Deputy District Attorney Ralph Mayer, who was submitting questions to Pittluck to ask Chicano witnesses, appeared to be questioning their integrity. It's the same in the court system as it is elsewhere, two sets of rules. One for the people in power and the other set for Chicanos and other oppressed minorities.

Eventually, the inquest got to the matter of Ruben Salazar's death which occurred at the Silver Dollar Bar.

Manuel Lopez testified that:
"I saw two men, one had a rifle and the other a revolver, enter the tavern." Lopez testified that he was the individual responsible for notifying the deputies that there were "armed Chicanos inside the bar."

The deputies unholstered their guns, obtained shotguns and tear-gas weapons from their cars and proceeded to clear the sidewalk area around the Silver Dollar. ***They ordered people on the sidewalk into the bar, threatening them

249

with their weapons. The testimony from the deputies:

Deputy sheriff Louis Brown: I cannot recall my partner ordering persons into the Silver Dollar Bar moments before the projectile was fired."

*Deputy sheriff Charles Brown said basically the same. It became obvious that the sheriff deputies had carefully released their stories before hand. How can two individuals who are shown in photographs taken by LA RAZA "claim" that THEY CAN'T REMEMBER forcing people in? They clearly remembered events that favor the sheriff's position but were hazy whenever photographs depicted them in an unfavorable situation. Both deputies claim that they do not remember seeing the people who are shown in photograph number_____. The photo shows Deputy Brown pointing his shotgun at the four men, one of whom has his hands up. The four testified that Brown ordered them into the bar before the tear gas was fired.

Jose Naranjo, another witness, testified that the deputy held his shotgun close to the face of a women and told her: "Get inside. This gun is loaded. I mean it."

Gustario Garcia, who works for KMEX, stated that he was told by deputies:

"Get in the bar, otherwise you're going to get killed."

Nicholas Kleminko, Angel Tony Garcia and Jimmy Flores testified that a deputy aimed his shotgun at Jimmy and warned, "If you're reaching for a gun, that's it for you. Get inside the bar or we'll shoot."

Moments after the small group of people were forced into the bar, Deputy Thomas Wilson fired a first and then a second shot of tear gas into the bar. The projectile from the first shot killed Salazar. Wilson fired a Federal Flite-Rite missle through the open doorway of the bar. The entrance to the bar was gained by parting two hanging curtains.

The Federal Flite-Rite is a wallpiercing projectile that can penetrate inch thick pine board. ***It's maximum range is 300 yards, yet Wilson fired it at a range of no more than 15 feet. The muzzle volicity of the Flite-Rite is 300–325 feet per second; it is 9 ½ inches long and 1 ½ inches in diameter. It can justifiably be called "a small cannon."

***Wilson testified that he:

". . . did not know what type of tear gas he had and that under the circumstances it didn't make that much difference to me."

*It was the first time in his eight years as a deputy sheriff that he had ever fired that type of projectile or even the tear gas gun that killed Salazar. Under the current training procedures, they do not actually obtain experience in firing tear-gas but still are allowed to fire, without experience, in actual crowd control situations and this time it cost the life of Ruben Salazar.

The manufacturer's warning on the Flite-Rite reads:

"Not to be used against crowds. For driving out barricaded persons."

What the sheriffs did is more than negligence or manslaughter. It is plain MURDER! First, they did not check out Manuel Lopez's report that armed men were inside the Silver Dollar Bar. All the men and women inside the bar testified that no "armed Chicano" came in.

Secondly, they shoved the people into the bar, threatening them with weapons instead of searching them outside on the sidewalk. By forcing them into the bar, the deputies were endangering the people's lives but that doesn't carry much weight with the Sheriff Department.

Thirdly, Wilson fired a Federal Flite-Rite missle into a crowed bar in which people had moments before been forced into. Wilson further testified that he was familiar with the Silver Dollar's interior and that:

"I tried to ricochet the missle off the ceiling and hit the rear of the bar."

How in the hell could Wilson have aimed at the ceiling and hit Ruben Salazar in the head, not on the richochet, but directly in the temple area? Wilson fired from the right side of the Silver Dollar entrance, no more than 3 feet from the curtain. Salazar sat about 10 feet from the doorway. The projectile passed through Salazar's head. Yet, this "perro" still has the audacity to say that he aimed for the ceiling. One must really question at what Wilson was really aiming at!

Twelve persons inside the bar have testified that they heard no warnings of any kind given before the shots by Wilson were fired. Wilson and the other deputies claim that they gave repeated warnings.

Mrs. Katherine Castello and others who viewed the action from across the street, testified that they heard no warnings before the shots were fired.

George Garcia Muñoz testified that:

"I saw a minature cannon (the Federal Flite-Rite) pointed through a part in the center of the curtain. The curtain was parted by some other deputy standing next to the deputy holding the cannon."

Guillermo Restrepo, a reporter from KMEX who accompained Salazar during the riot, testified that Salazar often looked behind him as he walked down Whittier Blvd., and at one point, he (Restrepo) asked Salazar what was wrong, and Salazar answered "I think I'm stupid" but did not elaborate. Later Salazar told him:

"Guillermo, I'm getting scared." Again Salazar did not explain.

Restrepo also testified that after the shooting at the Silver Dollar Bar, that he approached three different groups of sheriff deputies and showed them his press card and told them Salazar had been shot in the bar. All three times, deputies pointed their guns at him, disregarding his press credentials and said "Get out of here. Move on."

Sargeant Robert Laughlin proceeded to arrive in his squad car, after receiving a report about "armed men in the cafe." Sargeant Laughlin parked across the Silver Dollar Bar and fired three more rounds of tear-gas. The Sheriffs are amazing. Without consulting other deputies as to what previous action had been taken, Laughlin shoots three more rounds of tear gas!

Under testimony, Deputy James Lambert, Wilson's partner, testified that about 7:30 p.m., he was notified by a man that a body was inside the bar. Lambert "suggested that the man go inside and bring the body out." Incredible training that the sheriffs receive . . . they send civilians to do their jobs.

Attorney Dalton twice attempted to subpoena the Sheriff Department to produce a training manual, "Crowd and Riot Control Enforcement," that covers the use of tear gas. Twice, Inquest hearing officer Pittluck refused to sign the subpoena! Was it because the testimony given by the sheriffs conflicted with the training manual and manufacturer's instructions?

The Inquest jury vote was split. Four voted "at the hands of another while three "accidental." These are very vague terms and have no legal bearing. The coroner's inquest is a purely political tactic to quiet the Chicano community.

Two weeks later District Attorney Evelle Younger announced that he would not file charges against Deputy Wilson because "no criminal charge is justified, and this case is considered closed."

Sheriff Pitchess stated "our investigation indicates that the actions of our personnel on August 29th were proper and that he was satisified that deputies had not forced persons into the Silver Dollar Bar." Sheriff Pitchess also stated that the "use of the Flite-Rite Missle was proper."

The news has not been quietly greeted in E.L.A. More community organizations now clearly read the message and have chosen to go "underground." THEY WILL BE HEARD FROM.

Index